Mr Gary Noble.

LA TANTE CLAIRE

Amitié

LA TANTE CLAIRE

PIERRE KOFFMANN
AND TIMOTHY SHAW / PHOTOGRAPHS BY ANTHONY BLAKE

HEADLINE

First published in 1992
by HEADLINE BOOK PUBLISHING PLC

10 9 8 7 6 5 4 3 2 1

This book produced for Headline Book Publishing PLC
by Amazon Publishing Ltd, 57 Beaconsfield Road,
St. Margarets, Middlesex TW1 3HX

Editor: Kate Whiteman
Design: Cooper·Wilson Design
Proofreading: David Crane and Gill Edmonds, Carole Fahy
Typesetting: Litho Link Ltd, Welshpool, Powys.

British Library Cataloguing in Publication Data
Koffman, Pierre
Tante Claire
I. Title II. Shaw, Timothy
641.594477

ISBN 0-7472-0616-3

Printed and bound in Great Britain by
Clays Ltd, St Ives PLC

HEADLINE BOOK PUBLISHING PLC
Headline House
79 Great Titchfield Street
London W1P 7FN

CONTENTS

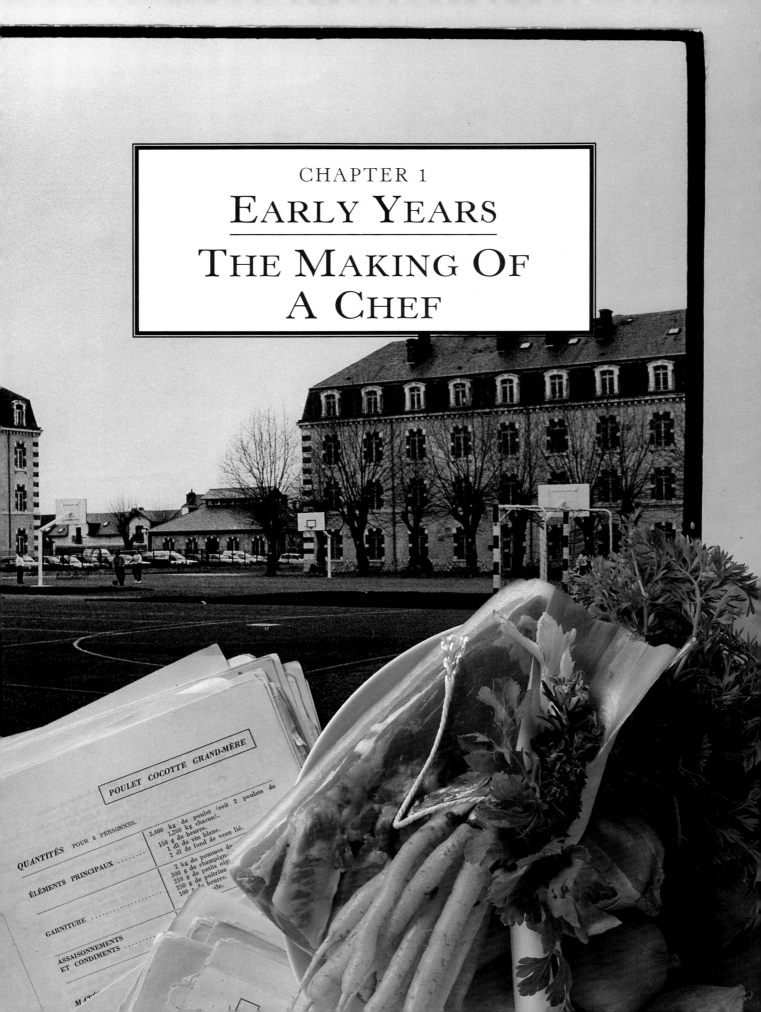

CHAPTER 1
EARLY YEARS
THE MAKING OF A CHEF

It was almost by chance that I became a cook. Had I been free to choose any job I wanted, and to fulfil my deepest boyhood ambitions, there is no doubt at all that I would have been a peasant farmer. Today I would have had my own smallholding, probably somewhere in south-west France, and I would be spending my time looking after ducks, cows, crops, and a few fields of vines, driving a combine harvester, and working on the land. I would never have seen the inside of a professional kitchen. A farmer's life would not have been a bad one, and I think it would have made me happy, but it was not to be. My destiny and my luck lay elsewhere. At the age of fifteen I had no way of foreseeing the road my life was going to take, and indeed, if anyone could have told me what that road would be, I would have found it impossible to believe them.

I started my course at catering college with a good deal of regret at the loss of a countryman's existence. Though food and cooking were important to me in my everyday life, I cannot say that I put on my white jacket joyfully, nor did I feel unbounded enthusiasm for the trade of a cook. It was far from being a case of love at first sight. Only very gradually did the *métier* start to attract me, but by the end of the first year of my course, I knew passionately that cooking was the most exciting thing I had ever encountered.

The peasant's life had appealed to me because I had got to know it well during the months and weeks I spent at my grandparents' farm, watching my grandfather while he worked, and helping him in the fields. It was a life about which I harboured few illusions. I knew all about its hardship and its long hours of relentless, physical labour; but I was also aware of its virtues and its rewards, and my appreciation of these has never left me, and has even been important to me as a cook. I value things like the peasant's simple, unadorned power of endurance; his dogged, inner determination; his pride in hard work brought to a good conclusion; his sense of partnership with the land, a respect for it; and a sort of wise patience with the unalterable ways of nature. In the kitchen I have always had the same kind of admiration for a job well done, because the fatal consequences of bad workmanship are as evident in cooking as they are on the land. I have the same natural respect for my ingredients as the farmer has for his earth and his wheat; and I have the same patience with things like tastes and cooking times as he would have with the basic course of nature. In ways like these, I often think that the peasant I once wanted to be is still very much part of me, even though I am a *chef de cuisine* and not a farmer, and that in the course of my lifetime I have managed to bring the two characters very happily together.

I was born on 21 August 1948 at Tarbes, a town which is usually best remembered for its horses, its haricot beans and Maréchal Foch, who was born there. It is built between two rivers, the Adour and the Echez, not far from the Spanish frontier, at the very edge of a long plain which runs parallel to the foothills of the Pyrenees. The equivalent of an English county town, Tarbes has a distinguished Roman and mediaeval past, and suffered no less than three dramatic sieges during the Wars of Religion. Its prosperity today is due to its having become an important nineteenth-century garrison town with its own arsenal and a Napoleonic stud farm for the breeding of cavalry horses. Everywhere there are squares, streets and statues which commemorate the battles and generals of France's military past. Our flat was in an old building, long since demolished, in the Cours Gambetta; from our balcony you looked in one direction towards the Place Verdun, the main square, and, in the other, down a wide boulevard with trees and fountains, until you came to the equestrian statue of Maréchal Foch and the long, neo-classical facade of the main barracks. In the distance you could see another powerful horizontal line, that of the peaks of the Pyrenees. They were like a row of jagged, incoherent teeth, mysterious and bluish sometimes, when hidden by mist, or else bright and white with snow, and sharper than ever in the winter sunlight, like chunks of ice cream, I used to think.

I was the second of four children. Of my two sisters, Nicole, the eldest, was born a year before me, in 1947, and Martine was born in 1950. My brother Daniel was born in 1952. It was about 1953, when I was five, that I can remember my first family lunch at Tarbes. All six of us were sitting round the table, and it must have been summer because the windows were open and I remember the sound of a bugle coming from the barracks at the far end of the boulevard. We were eating a stew, which had a delicious smell, and I recall my father smiling when I asked for another helping. It was my mother's traditional *boeuf en daube*, made just with ox cheeks, which have an excellent flavour, and are the best parts to use for this sort of stew. I still do a *daube* at La Tante Claire, but whereas at home it was often the only dish of the meal, at the restaurant it is generally followed by a light dessert.

JOUE DE BOEUF EN DAUBE

·

OX CHEEK BRAISED IN RED WINE

·

700 g / 1½ lb ox cheek, cut into 12 large pieces
100 g / 3½ oz seasoned flour
50 ml / 2 fl oz vegetable oil
150 g / 5 oz carrots, roughly diced
150 g / 5 oz onions, roughly diced
1.1L / 2 pt good red wine
4 garlic cloves, chopped
1 Bouquet garni (page 11)
120 g / 4 oz button onions, peeled
30 g / 1 oz butter
½ teaspoon sugar
200 g / 7 oz carrots
200 g / 7 oz Home-made noodles, (page 196)
1 tablespoon finely chopped parsley
salt and freshly ground pepper

·

Preheat the oven to 200°C / 400°F / gas 6.

Roll the pieces of meat lightly in the seasoned flour. Heat the vegetable oil in a large, heavy heatproof casserole until very hot, then brown the meat quickly and evenly. Add the diced carrots and onions, cover and sweat gently for 10 minutes.

Holding the lid over the pan, pour away all the cooking fat. Deglaze with the red wine and bring to the boil. Add the garlic and bouquet garni and season. Replace the lid and cook in the oven for about 2½ hours, until the meat is very tender. Stir regularly during cooking, adding a little water if there is too much evaporation.

Meanwhile, put the button onions into a pan large enough to hold them all in a single layer. Pour over just enough water to cover and add the butter, salt and sugar. Cover with a piece of greaseproof paper and press it down onto the onions. Bring to the boil and simmer over very low heat, tossing the onions very gently from time to time, until they are brown and shiny.

Keep warm and covered until ready to use.

Take the daube out of the oven. Lift out the pieces of meat with a slotted spoon, and place in another pan. Pass the sauce through a fine sieve over the meat. Discard the vegetables and bouquet garni. Add the button onions to the daube and simmer for 10 more minutes.

Meanwhile, cook the carrots and noodles separately in salted boiling water, drain and add a knob of butter. Serve the daube in warm plates and arrange the onions and carrots around the meat. Pile a small bundle of noodles on each plate, sprinkle with a little chopped parsley and serve immediately. (Photograph p. 10)

Joue du Boeuf en Daube (recipe p. 9)

BOUQUET GARNI

———— • ————

*A good bouquet garni is of great importance in cooking,
and will give recipes a better flavour.*

1 celery stalk with leaves, washed
4 parsley stalks, washed
1 bay leaf
2 sprigs of thyme
3 green leek leaves, washed

———— • ————

*Wrap the celery, parsley, bay leaf and thyme in the
leek leaves. Fasten the bouquet garni with string at
both ends and in the middle.*

SUPRÊMES D'ORANGE AU VIN EPICÉ

———— • ————

ORANGE SEGMENTS IN SPICED RED WINE SAUCE

———— • ————

5 large oranges
250 ml / 9 fl oz good fruity red wine
4 tablespoons caster sugar
½ cinnamon stick
1 cardamom pod
30 g / 1 oz currants
50 ml / 2 fl oz port
1 tablespoon Grand Marnier
3 tablespoons desiccated coconut shavings, toasted

———— • ————

*Using a sharp knife, peel and segment the oranges,
removing all the pith and seeds.*

*Put the wine, sugar, cinnamon stick, cardamom pod
and currants in a saucepan and bring to the boil.
Reduce the liquid to 150 ml / 5 fl oz. Take the pan off
the heat and mix in the port and Grand Marnier.
Allow to cool then discard the cardamom pod and
cinnamon stick.*

*Arrange the prepared orange segments in a glass bowl,
pour over the sauce, cover and refrigerate until
thoroughly chilled. From time to time, spoon some of
the sauce gently over the orange segments so that they
absorb the flavour of the sauce.*

*Serve in chilled glass dessert bowls, taking care not to
break the orange segments. Sprinkle with the golden
coconut shavings.*

════════════════

My mother, Germaine, is a descendant of generations of Gascon peasant farmers, and she was born in a little village called Saint Puy, about fifty miles to the north of Tarbes. This was the village I knew so well; and it was my maternal grandparents, Marcel and Camille Cadeillan, who had always lived there, whom I came to love so deeply. For me the Oratoire, as their farm was called, never ceased to be a place imbued with happiness and delight; but my mother has very different feelings about it. Her childhood had not been very happy, and even after she was married, she never liked to go back to the farm except for very short visits. 'Too many memories,' she often says, 'Too many memories.' Brought up there in the 1920s and 1930s, she knew too well the darker and harsher side of a peasant's life. She can remember when candles and oil-lamps made way for the first electric light, how food was lowered down the farm well to keep it cool because there was no refrigerator, and how the baker travelled round the village in a horse-drawn van, delivering his big round loaves of country bread. But she also remembers how hard the physical work on the farm could be, not only for the men but also for the women and girls, especially at the time of the summer harvest when they spent days cooking food for about forty harvesters and serving them at long trestle tables in the field behind the farm. My mother remembers pulling little bits off the chickens she was serving and pushing them quickly into her mouth because there would be no time to eat anything else before the evening; and she remembers trying helplessly to shield herself from the heat of the fire as she crouched down beside it on a torrid July day, turning the spit to roast the countless chickens and ducks. She remembers how bony the little fish were which my grandfather used to catch in the local ponds; but, on the other hand, the roast ortolans, which he trapped and drowned in armagnac, were delicious, as were the snails grilled above the wood embers. The day started early, even for children, and my mother and her younger sister always had to be down for breakfast sharply at seven, properly and neatly dressed, brushed and clean after washing in cold water. The breakfast, like many other meals at the farm, consisted of soup, usually made from beans or lentils or cabbage, some smoked ham and a few slices of one of my grandmother's terrines or pâtés eaten with local bread toasted at the fire.

At mealtimes everybody drank a glass or two of rough red wine, so rough, in fact, that it left a strong red stain on the inside of your glass when you had finished it. The wine came from the vines on my grandfather's farm; and the grape-picking and wine-pressing which took place there in late September or early October was another of the great annual events of the countryside. For my mother it meant more hard work as she cooked the lunches for the hungry *vendangeurs* and helped her sister to carry plates and dishes. Many of the workers were Spaniards who came regularly each year to France to earn money at the time of the grape-picking; some, however, were French, and they came from all over the country.

In the autumn of 1946, when the memories of the war years and the Occupation were still fresh, one of the temporary *vendangeurs* was a northerner called Albert Koffmann. He had come all the way down to the Gers from Paris, and planned to work for a few weeks in the vines and then return home. But fate had other plans for him. He arrived at Saint Puy and was duly hired at my grandparents' farm but, instead of returning to Paris at the end of the grape-harvest, he fell in love with their eldest daughter and stayed behind to marry her. It was a quick courtship, and I sometimes wonder

if my mother's cooking did not have something to do with it. My father never forgot a certain dish of stuffed quails which was one of the first things my mother ever cooked for him. I can well imagine how good they must have been, braised in the old iron cooking-pot, as it rested on a bed of embers in the open fireplace, and with more embers glowing in the hollow of its concave lid.

CAILLES FARCIES BRAISÉES

BRAISED STUFFED QUAILS

8 quails, boned and seasoned
2 tablespoons vegetable oil
150 g / 5 oz boneless hand and belly of pork, diced
75 g / 3 oz chicken livers, trimmed and diced
50 ml / 2 fl oz brandy
4 juniper berries, crushed
75 ml / 3 fl oz double cream
1 egg yolk
150 g / 5 oz foie gras, diced

Braising stock
50 g / 2 oz butter
120 g / 4 oz carrots, thinly sliced
120 g / 4 oz onions, thinly sliced
250 ml / 9 fl oz Chicken stock (page 49)
100 ml / 4 fl oz madeira
1 bay leaf
1 sprig of thyme
2 tablespoons vegetable oil or duck fat
salt and freshly ground pepper

Preheat the oven to 200°C / 400°F / gas 6.

Heat the oil in a frying pan until very hot, then add the pork and chicken livers and cook until just golden brown. Deglaze with the brandy. Add the juniper berries and salt and pepper to taste. Purée in a food processor and rub through a fine sieve. Refrigerate until well chilled. Mix in the double cream, egg yolk and the diced foie gras. Stuff the quails with this mixture and pull the skin tightly to enclose the stuffing. Tie the stuffed quails with string and refrigerate while you prepare the braising stock.

In a heatproof casserole, melt the butter over medium heat. Add the carrots, cook for 5 minutes then add the onion and sweat gently until soft. Add the chicken stock and madeira and bring to the boil.

Heat the oil or duck fat in a frying pan. When very hot, brown the quails quickly all over. Put them in the braising stock and cover the casserole with foil. Cook in oven for 20 minutes, until tender.

Put the quails on a warm serving plate. Pass the braising stock through a fine conical sieve and pour it over the quails.

———————————

For my mother the marriage was certainly a way of escaping from her parents' farm where she had never been very happy. She adored her father but did not get on well with my grandmother, and this led to much conflict. My mother had always told me that before she met my father she was very much in love with a young farmer who lived in another village, but he was in love with another girl as well as with her. He could not make up his mind which of them he should marry, so he decided to leave the choice to destiny. There was a fork in the road near his farm where the left hand branch led to Saint Puy, Germaine's village, and the other to the village of the second girl. One day the farmer rode out on his horse, and, when he came to the fork, he dropped the reins and allowed the horse to take whichever road it wanted, vowing that he would marry the girl who lived at the end of it. The horse turned to the right and the farmer kept his promise.

Destiny's decision was very probably the right one. My mother would never have been happy as a farmer's wife. She never really liked

the country or the hardships of village life in those days; and even though she is proud of coming from peasant stock, she has always felt far more at ease with the streets and shops of a town than with ploughed fields and cowsheds and pigs. My mother was always good-natured and *agréable*; even now she is never without an enticing, sparkling twinkle of fun about her eyes and smile, and she still has a teasing, rather jaunty way of appearing always to be on the point of giving you a little nudge with her elbow, to make quite sure you are taking part in the general enjoyment. For she loves to enjoy herself. She has always appreciated good food and loves to cook well, especially for other people. When we were children, she was always comforting in moments of frustration or despair, and her rages, even when justified, were never long-lasting. My father sometimes complained that the food we ate was costing too much, and that my mother had 'holes in her pocket' when she went to the market or the butcher's, whereupon she would reply that he was mean and calculating. In reality I think that my father was just trying to be sensibly economical and my mother, for her part, was always a very good food buyer. If she spent more money than usual one day, it was always for a very good reason. A guinea fowl might go further than a chicken, for example, or a particular fish might be of exceptional quality. But whatever worries my parents might have had about money at that time, my mother never discussed them. She always had the cheerful self-confidence of someone who is at ease with her surroundings and who enjoys being in other people's company. The one thing she hated was to be alone.

PINTADE DE BRESSE AU GRAND MARNIER

GUINEA FOWL WITH GRAND MARNIER

1 × 1.25 kg / 2¾ lb guinea fowl
40 g / 1½ oz plain flour
2 tablespoons vegetable oil
50 ml / 2 fl oz Grand Marnier
2 onions, finely chopped
1 shallot, finely chopped
1 leek, white part only, washed and chopped
12 soft prunes, stoned
zest of ½ lemon, blanched 3 times and cut into thin shreds
40 g / 1½ oz butter, at room temperature
salt and freshly ground pepper

Stock:

carcass of the guinea fowl
3 tablespoons vegetable oil or duck fat
2 carrots, finely chopped
2 onions, finely chopped
2 shallots, finely chopped
1 garlic cloved, peeled, crushed and chopped
50 ml / 2 fl oz Grand Marnier
100 ml / 4 fl oz dry white wine
3 tomatoes, quartered
1 Bouquet garni (page 11)

Cut the guinea fowl into pieces; wings, drumsticks, thighs, and cut the breasts into 2 chunks. Chop the carcass and use it to prepare the stock.

To make the stock: Heat the oil in a large saucepan. When very hot, add the chopped carcass and brown. Add the carrots and cook until they start to brown, stirring constantly. Add the onion and shallots, cook until brown, then add the garlic. Flame with the Grand Marnier, deglaze with the white wine and add the tomatoes. Season and bring to the boil, adding the bouquet garni. Simmer for 30 minutes.

Roll the pieces of guinea fowl in flour and sprinkle with salt and pepper. Heat the oil in a large frying pan until very hot. Brown the meat in it for no more than 5 minutes. Add the onions, shallot, and leek and cook for 10 minutes. Pour off all the fat from the pan, flame with Grand Marnier and pour in the stock. Bring to the boil, then simmer for 20 minutes. Lift out the guinea fowl pieces with a slotted spoon and place on a warm serving plate. Keep warm.

Pass the sauce through a fine conical sieve into a pan. Add the prunes and lemon zest. Whisk in the butter over low heat and check the seasoning. Spoon the sauce over the meat and serve immediately.

My father, on the other hand, was by nature a solitary person. He was something of an outsider. It was as a mysterious stranger that he first arrived at my grandparents' farm in the autumn of 1946; and even now there is always an important part of him which remains secret, private and inaccessible to others. As a boy I remember him as a strongly-built, thick-set man, slightly shorter than my mother, with sharp dark eyes, black hair and a narrow, very determined mouth. Though he used to laugh and play with us when we were children, we had to be wary of his moods and sudden tempers. He had all the unpredictability of the loner which was very different from the steady, good-humoured affection which we knew we could always be sure to find in my mother. The Koffmanns were a Russian Jewish family from Odessa and I have always felt that it was my father's Jewishness which created the barrier between him and my grandparents. It was not that they were consciously prejudiced against Jews; they were peasants, rooted in their village, who had never seen the streets of either Bordeaux or Toulouse, and, though they were quite familar with Spaniards or Italians, they could only see my father as a peculiar sort of northerner, strange and extraneous, the precise nature of whose origins they could not fathom or understand. My father did his best to bridge the gap between them, but he never succeeded.

On one occasion he bought my grandparents a pair of cows – a precious gift for a peasant of those days, and he tried to help them in other ways as well. The narrowness of their outlook remained unchanged, however, and in the end my father gave up the struggle and did indeed become the irritable, solitary outsider they supposed he was. Perhaps this had some bearing on my parents' decision, many years later, to live separately, though they are both in Tarbes and still see each other from time to time.

Albert Koffmann was born in Paris in 1915. His parents had come to France from Odessa in the period between the revolutionary events of 1905 and the start of the First World War. It seems typical of my father's solitariness that he has never taken any interest at all in the story of his parents' lives, and has no knowledge of their adventures or their journey or their memories of Tsarist Russia. It is almost as though he had never had anything to do with them. Perhaps his childhood was not a very happy one, and he has never taken much pleasure in remembering it. His father deserted his mother when Albert was quite small, leaving her with four children to bring up on her own in a bleak railway suburb not far from the Gare du Nord, where life cannot have been very easy.

My father's first job was with a furrier. He hated it because the hairs and the dust irritated his lungs, but he was still doing the work in 1939. When war was declared he joined an infantry regiment, and from that he was drafted to the medical corps as a stretcher-bearer. A photograph of my father at this time shows him in his best uniform, sitting pensively in front of the camera, with his straight, dark hair brushed neatly back from his forehead and a wistful, rather lonely look about his eyes. In 1940 his unit was captured near Epinal, in north-east France, and he was imprisoned, along with about fifty thousand other French soldiers, in the buildings of the great glass-works at Baccarat. Six weeks later the Germans released him. Luckily for my father, they needed more medical orderlies for Paris, so he was given special papers and sent to work in one of the big hospitals there. After a year or so he was again released by the Germans and again given special papers, so that his luck took yet another favourable turn. He was probably safe now from arrest as a Jew because he could claim the status of *ancien combattant*, but he was not safe from being drafted to Germany to do forced labour. In 1942 his luck seemed to continue, and he got a job as private chauffeur to the directors of a timber firm which made pre-fabricated wooden huts and which had been officially incorporated into the German industrial system. The company was therefore privileged and none of its employees was liable for forced labour. This meant that my father was now doubly protected, and he could drive his employers all over France without any danger. My father's life and adventures during the Occupation are another of his private secrets. There are many little things I would like to know about him at this time, but whenever I ask him questions, he looks at me oddly and just says: 'I survived. I am here. That's the important thing, isn't it?'

When I was born, my father was still working as a private chauffeur, which meant that he was not often at home. It was only after several years that he got a local job at Tarbes, as mechanic at the main Citroën garage, and I began to be much more aware of his presence in the flat and of his rather volatile personality. I think my father has always been a man who finds it difficult to express affection or gratitude though often he would have liked to do so. It was only much later, for example, that I discovered how much he had really loved us when we were small, how proud he was that I had been able to start La Tante Claire, and how he had approved of me when I was a boy. Once, when I was about sixteen, he got me a temporary job at a small *charcuterie* factory at Tarbes which produced sausages and pâtés and smoked hams. It only lasted for a short time, and I remember I quite enjoyed it; but it seems that the owner of the firm came to see my father to compliment him on my performance. 'How he works! How he works, that boy!' he said, 'Why, he's better at it than all my other workmen!' My father was overjoyed, of course, but at the time he never said a word about it to me.

Nevertheless, in spite of my father's tendency to be reserved and inaccessible at certain times, there were moments when he gave us great happiness and pleasure. It was he who drove us in his car at weekends to my grandparents' farm at Saint Puy. For me the journey was a momentous one. At first the whole family would go in the car together, but, gradually, my sisters and my brother went less and less until I was the only one to go. I loved the farm and I loved my grandparents. The holidays I spent at the farm were like a glimpse of paradise, and I have described them in my earlier book *Memories of Gascony*. I often feel as if I had two childhoods instead of one, each totally different from the other though both were experienced simultaneously. One childhood I spent with my parents in our flat in Tarbes, and another, a real country childhood, I spent with my grandparents at Saint Puy. Everything about the farm which my mother remembered with the bitterness of her early years was to me, a generation later, a source of continual, unforgettable joy. The harvest, for example, with its excitement and turmoil, and the ox-drawn reapers and the clatter and dust of the threshing machine and the big outdoor lunches of the harvesters, which meant so much heat and hard work for my mother, was the crowning delight of my summer holiday. Each season had its memories; of springtime blossom in the orchards; of wild mushrooms in the autumn; of the excitement with which we awaited my grandfather's return from a winter afternoon's shooting with some woodcock or a wild duck in his bag; or, in January, of the ceremonial killing of the two farm pigs.

SARCELLE À L'ORANGE

———— • ————

TEAL WITH ORANGE SAUCE

———— • ————

8 teal
3 Seville oranges, well scrubbed under warm running water
200 ml / 7 fl oz vegetable oil
50 ml / 2 fl oz cointreau
200 ml / 7 fl oz good quality dry white wine
segments of 2 Seville oranges, for garnish
30 g / 1 oz butter
salt and freshly ground pepper

———— • ————

Preheat the oven to 230°C / 450°F / gas 8.

Squeeze the 3 oranges, reserve the juice and stuff the teal with the coarsely chopped skins. Truss and season. Heat the vegetable oil in a large pan. When very hot, brown the teal quickly on both sides, then transfer to the oven and cook for 15-20 minutes. They should remain slightly underdone.

Pour off the fat from the roasting pan and flame the teal with the cointreau. Transfer them to a warm serving dish, breast-side down, cover with foil and keep warm.

Drain any remaining fat from the roasting pan, deglaze with the wine and reduce completely. Add the orange juice, reduce by half, then whisk in the butter and check the seasoning. Pour the sauce over the teal, arrange the orange segments on the dish and serve immediately. (Photograph p. 18)

JAMBON SALÉ

—•—

SALT-CURED LEG OF PORK

—•—

1 × 10 kg / 22 lb leg of free-range pork, from a
reputable supplier
10 kg / 22 lb coarse sea salt
wine vinegar
coarsely ground pepper

—•—

*Sprinkle a 5 cm / 2 in layer of sea salt in a large
wooden box. Lay the leg of pork on top, rind-side
upwards. Cover with the rest of the salt, making sure
the pork is completely covered. Lay a wooden plank
over the meat and weight with a 10 kg / 22 lb weight
(a dozen tins of tomatoes will do) to extract as much
moisture as possible from the meat.*

*Leave the pork in the salt for 1 day per 500 g / 18 oz
meat. (Thus a 10 kg / 22 lb leg of pork will need 20
days' curing.)*

*Remove all salt with a brush. Rub the ham
energetically all over with wine vinegar, then dry
thoroughly with a tea towel. Spread the coarsely
ground pepper all over the cut, fleshy side of the meat,
making sure that it penetrates the flesh around the
bone.*

*Wrap in a muslin cloth and hang in a well-ventilated
cold larder for 6 months.*

PAPILLOTES DE CÔTES DE PORC AUX CHANTERELLES

—•—

BONED PORK CHOPS WITH CHANTERELLES EN
PAPILLOTE

—•—

4 pork chops 4 cm / 1 ½ in thick, boned and
seasoned
1 tablespoon butter
300 g / 11 oz chanterelles, wiped with a damp cloth
and chopped
50 ml / 2 fl oz port
2 tablespoons vegetable oil
4 slices of Parma ham, thinly sliced
4 teaspoons clotted cream
1 tablespoon parsley, finely chopped
salt and freshly ground pepper
four 25 × 10 cm / 10 × 4 in squares of greaseproof
paper, lightly buttered

—•—

*Preheat the oven to 220°C / 425°F / gas 7. Melt the
butter in a shallow pan. Add the chanterelles and port;
season and cook for about 12 minutes. Set aside.*

*Heat the oil in a frying pan. When very hot, add the
seasoned pork chops and brown them on both sides.
Leave to cool. Cut each chop horizontally into 2 equal
slices. Lay the 4 squares of greaseproof paper on the
work surface and place half a chop on each,
browned-side down. Sprinkle with some of the cooked
chanterelles, lay a slice of Parma ham on top and
sprinkle over the rest of the chanterelles. Cover with
the other half of the pork chop, cut-side downwards.
Spoon a small dollop of clotted cream on each stuffed
chop without spreading it and top with chopped
parsley. Wrap well but loosely, twisting the ends of the
paper to seal the package.*

*Arrange in an ovenproof dish and cook in the
preheated oven for 20 minutes. Serve the chops in their
paper parcels, leaving each person to open his or her
own papillote.*

Sarcelle à l'Orange (recipe p. 16)

Gâteau aux Noisettes (recipe p. 21)

My Tarbes childhood was very different. In a town there was not the rolling space of the Gascon countryside or the natural cycle of the life of a farm or the long, lazy days spent fishing in the river Gèle or the journeys to Fleurance market, with my grandmother, in the local bus packed with crates of ducks and geese and poultry and rabbits. Instead there was just school and homework and dull, regular routine. When I pick out my face in the long rows of staring, immobile children which stretch from right to left across the annual pictures of school groups; or when I look at photographs of myself and my sisters and brother, sitting together at a school desk in our black smocks and white collars, a slight look of alarm on our wondering faces, I am reminded of the tedious monotony I felt as I endured day after day in a local classroom. Mathematics I enjoyed, but the subtleties of grammar or history were usually pushed aside in my mind to make way for daydreams about the farm, the village and food; about how, that very weekend perhaps, my grandmother might give us a couple of pigeons to take home, or what my mother was cooking for supper – perhaps another of her rich soups made from oxtail and silverside and some of the fresh vegetables she had bought that morning at the market in Tarbes.

PETITE MARMITE

CLEAR SAVOURY BROTH

Makes 2.5 L / 4½ pt
1.25 kg / 2¾ lb silverside, cut into large chunks
1.75 kg / 3¾ lb oxtail, jointed
200 g / 7 oz carrots, peeled and left whole
1 onion, halved and stuck with a clove
250 g / 9 oz green part of leeks, cleaned
1 celery stalk, washed
4 garlic cloves, unpeeled and left whole
30 g / 1 oz coarse sea salt

Heat a cast iron frying pan until very hot, then put in the onion, cut-side down, and dry-roast until browned. Put all the meat in a very large saucepan and cover with cold water. Add the salt and bring to the boil. Reduce the heat, add the carrots, the clove-stuck onion, leeks, celery and garlic. Simmer the broth for 4 hours. Pass through a fine conical sieve and skim away any fat that rises to the surface.

The meat can be kept for another use.

PIGEONNEAU ROTI À LA CIBOULETTE

ROAST PIGEON WITH CHIVE SAUCE

4 young pigeons
300 ml / 11 fl oz vegetable oil
20 g / ¾ oz shallots, sliced
500 ml / 18 fl oz dry white wine
200 ml / 7 fl oz Chicken stock (page 49)
50 g / 2 oz chives, snipped
100 ml / 4 fl oz double cream
salt and freshly ground pepper

Preheat the oven to 230°C / 450°F / gas 8.

Heat the oil in a roasting pan, season the pigeons and seal them on both sides. Roast in the oven for 15 minutes of you like them pink or 18 minutes if you prefer them more cooked. Take the pigeons out of the pan and keep warm.

Sweat the shallots in the roasting pan for 2 minutes. Discard the fat from the pan, add the white wine and reduce completely. Add the stock and reduce by half.

Meanwhile bone out the pigeons and keep warm. Chop the bones of one of the pigeons, add it to the stock and cook until the stock is reduced. Add the chives and cream and bring to the boil. Put the sauce into a

blender and blend for 1 minute, until completely liquid.
Pas through a sieve, check the seasoning and keep hot.
Place the pigeons on a plate and pour over the sauce.

I really remember very little of my town childhood, and I can only try to feel my way back to it by turning over the pages of our old photograph album. Some snapshots show outings or picnics in the Pyrenees about 1950, the time when my father started to work at the local garage. Very often he is in the pictures, standing beside his Citroën, smiling and happy, holding up my baby sister Martine, while I and my elder sister, Nicole, are sitting rigidly or ignoring the camera altogether. Other pictures were taken in the public gardens at Tarbes. Here too we are happy and playing games and my father is smiling, or else we are posing dutifully in front of the tall, domed, elegantly ornate conservatory. Town and country are as far apart from each other as two different planets. The statues and the neat, curving lakes and the orderly groups of trees and the polite, exotic birds of the public park were like embalmed, artificial things if you compared their placid existence to the noisy life of the ducks, cocks and guinea fowl of the farmyard at Saint Puy or the stamping and lowing of the oxen as they drew a cart or a plough, urged on by my grandfather's strange, inarticulate cries of encouragement.

There was not much social life at Tarbes. Our most frequent guests were an aunt, a sister of my father's, and her husband. They were a curiously single-minded couple whose sole reason for visiting Tarbes was to spend as much time as possible at the town's best and most expensive *pâtisserie*, where they sat for hours at their favourite table consuming cake after cake, and drinking cup after cup of hot chocolate or tea. Sleeping and eating at our flat was no more than a convenient, economical means to this particular end. Their daily routine was unchanging. As soon as breakfast was over, they set off in the direction of the *pâtisserie*; they returned briefly for lunch, then disappeared again until it was time for supper, after which they went to bed. They never invited us to the *pâtisserie*, and after a while this began to irritate my father considerably. My mother tried to soothe him by saying that one day they would bring us back a superb cake as a present, and we would all wait expectantly for that big, square parcel, splendidly gift-wrapped and looked forward to the excitement of opening it. Needless to say, it never appeared.

GÂTEAU AUX NOISETTES

•

HAZELNUT CAKE

•

(Serves 6)
150 g / 5 oz light brown sugar
120 g / 4 oz plain flour
65 g / 2½ oz butter
120 ml / 4 ½ fl oz sour cream
½ teaspoon baking powder
1 egg, size 4
100 g / 3½ oz hazelnuts, lightly toasted and skinned

•

Preheat the oven to 180°C / 350°F / gas 4.

Roughly chop the hazelnuts into halves. Generously butter a 19 × 19 × 3 cm / 7½ × 7½ × 1½ in cake tin. In a bowl, mix together the brown sugar and flour and rub in the butter to a sandy texture. Spread half this mixture into the prepared cake tin. Whisk together the sour cream, baking powder and egg and add to the bowl containing the remaining pastry mixture, mixing well. Pour into the cake tin and spread evenly. Sprinkle with the chopped hazelnuts and bake in the oven for 40 minutes.

Leave the cake in the tin to cool, then invert it onto a plate so that the pretty hazelnut topping shows. Serve with hazelnut Crème anglaise (page 41).
(Photograph p. 19)

BAVAROIS À LA VANILLE AUX FRAISES

•

VANILLA BAVAROIS WITH STRAWBERRIES

•

(Serves 6)

The sponge
4 eggs
120 g / 4 oz caster sugar
120 g / 4 oz plain flour
butter, for greasing

The bavarois cream
250 ml / 9 fl oz milk
4 egg yolks
60 g / 2 oz caster sugar
1 vanilla pod, split lengthways
2 gelatine leaves, soaked in cold water and drained
250 ml / 9 fl oz whipping cream, lightly whipped

The strawberry garnish and coulis
1.5 kg / 3¼ lb ripe strawberries
sugar to taste

•

First make the sponge: Preheat the oven to 180°C / 350°F / gas 4. Lightly butter a shallow baking tray (33 × 23 × 2cm / 13 × 9 × ¾ in) and line it with a sheet of greaseproof paper. Butter and flour lightly, shaking off the excess flour.

Over a double boiler whisk the eggs and sugar until thick and fluffy and just hot to the touch. Take off the heat and carry on whisking until cool. Gradually sift in the flour, folding it in with a metal serving spoon. Make sure the mixture is homogeneous but do not overmix. Spread the mixture quickly and evenly over the prepared baking tray and bake for 15-17 minutes, until golden and springy.

Turn out onto a clean tea towel, remove the paper and fold the tea towel over the sponge. When cool, use a bread knife to split the sponge horizontally into two layers. Cut out two 14 cm / 5½ in circles from one of the sponge layers. Cover with a tea towel and set aside. Cut the other layer into about twenty 3.5 × 8 cm / 1½ × 3¼ in pieces. Cover with a tea towel.

Now make the bavarois cream: Scrape all the seeds from the vanilla pod into the milk and bring to the boil. Whisk together the egg yolks and the sugar, then pour on the boiling milk, whisking well. Pour back into the pan and heat gently, stirring continuously with a wooden spoon. As soon as the custard thickens enough to coat the back of the spoon, it is ready. Remove from the heat and whisk in the softened gelatine leaves until dissolved. Pass through a fine conical strainer into a small bowl and leave to cool.

Line a 1.8 L / 3 pt charlotte mould with clingfilm. First, lay the small pieces of sponge overlapping around the sides. Then, pressing down firmly, put a circle of sponge at the bottom. Everything should now hold together well. When the jellified custard is cool, pour it little by little into the lightly-whipped cream, whisking gently until homogeneous. Pour into the sponge-lined charlotte mould, cover with the second circle of sponge and fold over the overhanging clingfilm. Leave in the fridge to set for at least 3 hours.

To make the varnish and coulis: Wash the strawberries; purée 1 kg / 2¼ lb in a blender and pass through a fine conical sieve. Add sugar to taste and whisk well to dissolve. Chill in the fridge. Just before serving, halve the rest of the strawberries. Pour some coulis on to the plates and place a slice of bavarois in the middle. Garnish with the halved strawberries.

FEUILLANTINES AU PAMPLEMOUSSE ROSE

•

PINK GRAPEFRUIT SNAPS

•

4 pink grapefruit, peeled and segmented, for garnish
100 g / 3½ oz butter, softened
120 g / 4 oz caster sugar
a pinch of grated grapefruit zest
strained juice of 3 grapefruit; about 600 ml / 1 pt
40 g / 1½ oz flour, sifted
1 heaped tablespoon cornflour
40 g / 1½ oz sugar

•

Preheat the oven to 200°C / 400°F / gas 6. Put the softened butter in a bowl, with 50 ml / 2 fl oz grapefruit juice, the zest and the flour, and mix thoroughly. Spread thinly and evenly on a large buttered baking tray and bake for about 18-20 minutes until nicely browned.

As soon the mixture comes out of the oven, cut out twelve circles using a coffee cup and a sharp knife (this pastry will remain soft until it cools down.) When cool and hard, pull out the crisp circles and let them rest on a sheet of greaseproof paper.

Meanwhile, prepare the sauce. Put the cornflour, sugar and 100 ml / 4 fl oz of the strained grapefruit juice into a small saucepan. Whisk until no lumps are left, then refrigerate until well chilled.

Pour the sauce onto 4 chilled serving plates and place one feuillantine on each plate. On top of each, arrange 4 grapefruit segments, then another feuillantine *on the top of the grapefruit. Finish with 4 more grapefruit segments and a last feuillantine.*

Once Tonton Henri and my aunt had departed, full of expressions of gratitude for the success of their holiday and of reassurances that it would not be long before we saw them again, life at Tarbes soon returned to its ordinary routine character. It was hard to get away from it except, of course, to Saint Puy in the holidays.

When my father drove us back to Tarbes after a weekend or a holiday at the farm, my grandmother always gave us presents. Sometimes these were cuttings or flowers or plants which always died at once at Tarbes because my mother had no skill with them; but often they were something to eat, like rabbits or a plump chicken.

Sometimes we would bring back a sackful of snails which my grand-father and I had captured on one of our nocturnal snail hunts as we prowled about the hedgerows, seeking our prey with the aid of electric torches. After the snails had been starved, purged and washed, my mother would cook them with white wine, Bayonne ham, lots of garlic, tomatoes, parsley and sausage meat or serve them with delicious savoury butter. They were *petits gris*, the local indigenous snails of south-west France, and they were always delicious – so delicious, in fact, that I put them on the menu at La Tante Claire. At the restaurant, of course, the recipes are rather more elaborate. I wrap the snails in filo pastry, or cook them and serve them in puff pastry cases with wild mushrooms, but their taste still reminds me so much of my mother's kitchen at Tarbes.

CROQUETTES D'ESCARGOTS BOURGUIGNONNES

DEEP-FRIED SNAILS IN PASTRY

24 cooked snails
250 g / 9 oz Savoury butter for snails, softened (see next column)
30 g / 11 oz filo pastry
2 egg yolks lightly beaten with 1 tablespoon water, for eggwash
2 L / 3½ pint vegetable oil, for deep-frying

Coat each snail with a generous teaspoon of butter and roll quickly between the palms of your hand. Refrigerate to harden.

Using a small bowl and a sharp knife, cut forty-eight 10 cm / 4 in circles out of the filo pastry. Keep them covered with clingfilm to prevent them from drying out. Prepare 1 croquette at a time by brushing eggwash onto 2 pastry circles. Put a butter-coated snail on the eggwashed side of 1 pastry circle and gather the pastry at the top, to enclose the snail completely.

Cover this side of the croquette with the other eggwashed brushed pastry circle, gathering the folds on the other side, pressing well with the tips of your fingers to seal the package completely. Keep cold while you prepare the rest of the snails.

Deep-fry in hot oil until golden brown. Serve immediately. (Photograph p. 26)

BEURRE D'ESCARGOTS

SAVOURY BUTTER FOR SNAILS

500 g / 1 lb 2 oz butter, at room temperature
75 g / 3 oz parsley, finely chopped
75 g / 3 oz shallots, finely chopped
30 g / 1 oz garlic, crushed and finely chopped
6 anchovy fillets, finely chopped
1 tablespoon Pernod or pastis
50 g / 2 oz nibbed almonds
salt and freshly ground pepper

Mash all the ingredients together and check the seasoning. This butter keeps very well in the freezer.

FEUILLETÉ D'ESCARGOTS AUX CÈPES

PASTRY CASES FILLED WITH SNAILS IN A SAUCE

40 cooked snails
4 tablespoons vegetable oil
75 g / 3 oz lean smoked bacon, very finely chopped
40 g / 1½ oz shallots, finely chopped
2 garlic cloves, crushed and finely chopped
1 tablespoon tomato purée
2 tablespoons brandy
350 ml / 12 fl oz red wine
1 small Bouquet garni (page 11)
300 g / 11 oz ceps, wiped with a damp tea towel
30 g / 1 oz butter
1 tablespoon finely chopped parsley
4 warm cooked vol-au-vent cases
salt and freshly ground pepper

In a shallow pan, heat 2 tablespoons oil. When very hot, add the snails and sauté for 5 minutes. Add the bacon, shallots and garlic and sweat for 1 minute. Stir in the tomato purée and cook for 1 minute, stirring all the time. Flame the mixture with the brandy. Add the red wine and the bouquet garni and season well. Cook over a gentle heat for 20 minutes.

Meanwhile, sauté the ceps over medium heat in the remaining oil for 10 minutes, then season. When the snail sauce becomes thick, whisk in the butter and add the parsley. Spoon the ceps into the hot vol-au-vent cases and divide the snails and their sauce between them. Serve immediately.

Both my mother and grandmother were excellent cooks, and both had a deep and natural understanding of food. If they had entered a cookery competition, however, I think that my mother would have won it. My grandmother's cooking was completely traditional and comparatively straightforward, but it was special because she put her whole heart into it. My mother was really the better cook because she was far more daring and adventurous. She could prepare crayfish and duck in ways that would compare favourably with any dish in a first-class restaurant; and I often think of her skill when I create my own recipes at La Tante Claire.

SALADE DE LANGOUSTINES, HARICOTS, MAGRET ET TRUFFES

•

SALAD OF LANGOUSTINES, HARICOT BEANS, SMOKED DUCK BREAST AND TRUFFLES

•

12 langoustine tails, cooked
12 thin slices of smoked duck breast
20 g / ¾ oz sliced truffle
1 head curly endive, trimmed and washed
50 ml / 2 fl oz Vinaigrette (see below)
100 g / 3½ oz haricot beans, cooked
1 teaspoon snipped chives
1 large tomato, skinned, deseeded and diced
salt and freshly ground pepper

•

Season and dress the curly endive and haricot beans separately. Arrange a little bunch of endive on each plate, encircle with beans and arrange the langoustines and duck breast on the plate. Add a few slices of truffle, sprinkle over the chives and add the diced tomato.

SAUCE VINAIGRETTE

•

2 teaspoons Dijon mustard
½ teaspoon salt
1 tablespoon wine vinegar
100 ml / 4 fl oz extra virgin olive oil or sunflower oil
freshly ground pepper

•

Mix together the mustard, salt and vinegar. Pour in the oil in a thin trickle, whisking continously until the vinaigrette becomes thick and homogeneous. It keeps well in a screw-top jar in a cool place.

Croquettes d'Escargots Bourguignonnes (recipe p. 24)

CONSOMMÉ DE CANARD AUX BETTERAVES

•

DUCK CONSOMMÉ WITH BEETROOT

•

1 × 1.5 kg / 3 lb 5 oz oven-ready duck

To clarify the broth:
500 g / 1 lb lean beef, finely minced
100 g / 3½ oz raw beetroot, scrubbed and halved
50 g / 2 oz carrot, finely grated
75 g / 3 oz leek, green part only, very finely chopped
250 g / 9 oz tomatoes, very finely chopped
2 celery stalks, very finely chopped
2 egg whites

Ravioli:
30 g / 1 oz butter
50 g / 2 oz spinach, cooked
30 g / 1 oz onion, very finely chopped
meat from the duck thighs cooked in the broth, finely diced
30 g / 1 oz gruyère, finely grated
1 egg yolk
75 g / 3 oz Home-made pasta dough (page 196)
2 tablespoons vegetable oil
salt and freshly ground pepper

Garnish:
40 g / 1½ oz cooked beetroot, finely diced and kept warm
4 tablespoons double cream
30 g / 1 oz caviar

•

The broth: *Prepare a* Petite Marmite *following the recipe (page 20) using the duck, instead of silverside. Add all the vegetables except the beetroot. Skim well during and after cooking, making sure no fat is left. Pass the broth through a fine sieve into a clean pan, leave to cool and remove any fat floating on the surface.*

Clarification: *In a bowl, mix together the clarifying ingredients. Whisk them into the broth and bring to the boil. As soon as the broth starts to simmer, stop whisking and simmer gently for 1 hour. Pass the consommé very delicately through a fine conical sieve, lined with a piece of muslin. Discard the clarification ingredients, but keep the duck. Check the seasoning and keep the consommé hot. Cut one of the duck breasts into fine julienne and reserve it for the garnish.*

The ravioli: *Sweat the onion in the butter. When transparent, add the spinach and the meat from the duck thighs. Season and cook for no longer than 3 minutes. Allow to cool completely before mixing in the gruyère and egg yolk. Season with a pinch of salt and pepper.*

Following the instructions on page 196, roll out the pasta dough on the thinnest setting and cut the sheet of pasta into 16 squares. Put a teaspoon of the ravioli stuffing on 8 of the squares and cover with the remaining squares. Moisten the edges and press with your fingers to seal the filled ravioli. Cook for 2 minutes in boiling salted water with the oil added.

Ladle the consommé into 4 warm bowls. Put 2 ravioli in each bowl and divide the finely diced beetroot and the reserved julienne of duck between the bowls. Trickle 1 tablespoon double cream over each bowl, sprinkle with caviar and serve piping hot. (Photograph pp. 30-31)

Generally speaking, my mother had a far wider range of recipes than my grandmother. Hers was already town cooking rather than country cooking. At the farm a ham or a sausage was always hanging from the beam, and you could just take one down and cut off a piece. My grandparents lived off their own produce, and only very rarely bought food from a shop. My mother in Tarbes, on the other hand, would buy a whole variety of different ingredients, which meant that although her cooking was based on that of her own mother, and had its important peasant roots, she could develop it further into a real *cuisine bourgeoise*. Her approach was more subtle and elaborate in its way, a small, modern example of how French cooking in general managed to improve itself technically during the seventeenth and eighteenth centuries as it worked its way up the social hierarchy from the level of the regional peasants to the wealthy middle classes and thence to the great establishments of royalty and the aristocracy, finally becoming the *haute cuisine* of the big restaurants. I would not want to give the impression, however, that the quality of my mother's cooking came merely from her being able to buy costly ingredients. *La bonne cuisine* depends on taste and skill long before it comes to depend on money, and it is a great mistake to think otherwise. My mother could cook an expensive dish well, but she could also cook an ordinary, inexpensive dish and make it taste equally delicious.

COU DE CANARD FARCI

STUFFED DUCK'S NECK

the skin of a duck's neck
25 ml / 1 fl oz vegetable oil
15 g / ½ oz shallot, very finely chopped
1 clove garlic, peeled, crushed and very finely chopped
1 small sprig of thyme
½ bay leaf
75 g / 3 oz chicken livers, trimmed, sinews and yellow gall stains removed
150 g / 5 oz lean pork, finely minced
65 g / 2½ oz pork fat, finely minced
30 g / 1 oz raw foie gras, finely minced
1 egg
4 teaspoons armagnac
2 tablespoons madeira
700 g / 1½ lb duck fat
salt and freshly ground pepper

First, make the stuffing: Heat the oil in a small saucepan, add the chopped shallot and sweat gently until transparent. Add the garlic, thyme and bay leaf. Increase the heat to the highest possible, put in the chicken livers, season with salt and pepper and cook quickly until just brown. Drain and set aside to cool.

Melt the duck fat over a very low heat until it reaches 90°C / 194°F. When the chicken livers are cool, mince finely and mix them well, using your hands, with the minced lean pork, pork fat, foie gras, egg, armagnac and madeira. Sprinkle on salt and pepper and check the seasoning at this stage, as it is difficult to adjust after cooking.

Tie one end of the duck's neck skin very tightly with a piece of string, to make a sort of bag. Fill with the stuffing, pushing it down well with a soup spoon. Sew the opening tightly with small stitches, using an ordinary needle and white cotton thread. Immerse the stuffed neck in the heated duck fat. Under no circumstances should the fat boil or bubble.

Cook the stuffed neck for about 1 hour; to check if it is cooked, insert a larding needle into the centre and touch it with your lips. If it feels hot, the neck is ready. Leave to cool in the fat, then take out the stuffed neck, wrap well in clingfilm and refrigerate. It can be eaten cold with bread and salad, like a pâté, or hot as a main dish.

Strain the hot fat through a fine conical sieve, cover, cool and refrigerate. The fat keeps almost indefinitely and can be used to make Confit de canard (page 181). It makes an excellent substitute for vegetable oil in Chou frisé au lard (page 85), and many other recipes.

It was a family tradition to have a good, large roast chicken every Sunday lunch; this was quite an expensive item because it was a real corn-fed farm bird, utterly unlike the supermarket chickens people are used to eating today. From it, during the week, my mother would make soup and very good pâtés and terrines using the livers.

GÂTEAU DE FOIES DE VOLAILLE

•

CHICKEN LIVER PÂTÉ WITH TOMATO SAUCE

•

100 g / 3½ oz chicken livers, trimmed, sinews and
yellow gall stains removed
1 egg
2 egg yolks
2 teaspoons double cream
175 ml / 6 fl oz
¼ garlic clove, very finely chopped
½ teaspoon parsley, finely chopped
a tiny pinch of nutmeg
salt and freshly ground pepper
20 g / ¾ oz butter, for greasing
salt and freshly ground pepper
Tomato sauce, for serving (see opposite)

•

Preheat the oven to 180°C / 350°F / gas 4.

Push the chicken livers through a fine sieve. Add the whole egg, mixing well. Whisk in the egg yolks, cream and little by little, the milk. Season, then mix in the garlic and parsley. Pour the mixture into four buttered ramekins and stand them in a roasting tray. Half-fill with boiling water, cover with a piece of lightly buttered greaseproof paper and cook in the oven for 20 minutes, or until set. Turn out onto warm serving plates and serve with hot tomato sauce.

overleaf: *Making Consommé de Canard aux Betteraves (recipe p. 27)*

SAUCE TOMATE

•

TOMATO SAUCE

•

200 g / 7 oz tomato passata
100 g / 3½ oz butter
160 g / 6 oz carrots, finely diced
160 g / 6 oz onions, finely diced
150 g / 5 oz bacon, diced
1.5 L / 2½ pt hot water
4 cloves garlic, crushed
1 Bouquet garni (page 11)
a pinch of sugar
salt and freshly ground pepper

•

Melt the butter in a saucepan. Add the carrots and sweat for 5 minutes. Then add the onion and bacon and sweat for another 5 minutes. Stir with a wooden spatula, then mix in the tomato passata. Cook gently for about 5 minutes. Whisk in the hot water and add the garlic and bouquet garni. Season to taste with salt, pepper and sugar. Bring to the boil and simmer for 2 hours. Pass through a fine conical strainer.

TERRINE DE FOIES DE VOLAILLE

·

CHICKEN LIVER TERRINE

·

500 g / 1 lb 2 oz chicken livers, trimmed, sinews
and yellow gall stains removed
100 g / 3½ oz pork back fat, thinly sliced
1 garlic clove
500 g / 1 lb 2 oz butter melted and cooled
5 eggs
50 g / 2 oz soft sultanas
60 ml / 2 fl oz port
2 tablespoons armagnac
salt and freshly ground pepper

·

Preheat the oven to 170°C / 325°F / gas 3.

*Line a 32 × 11 cm / 12½ × 4½ in cast iron terrine
dish first with overhanging foil, then with overhanging
pork fat. Purée the chicken livers and garlic in a
blender, then add the eggs, one at a time, making sure
each is well incorporated before adding the next. Add
the port and armagnac little by little with the motor
running. Pour on the melted butter in a thin steady
stream, still with the motor running until the mixture is
homogeneous. Add the sultanas, and season with salt
and pepper. Check the seasoning at this stage, as it is
difficult to adjust once the terrine is cooked.*

*Pour the mixture into the prepared terrine dish and
fold over the overhanging fat and foil Put the dish into
a deep roasting pan and pour in hot water to come
halfway up the dish. Cook for 1 hour 40 minutes in the
preheated oven. After this time, check if the terrine is
cooked by inserting a larding needle into the centre.
Put the needle to your lips and if it feels hot, the terrine
is cooked. Allow to cool and refrigerate for several
hours.*

*Cut into 1 cm / ½ in slices and serve with a mixed
green salad and good crusty country bread.*

Good cooking and good food were important connecting links between the two different halves – town and country – of my childhood. We all had healthy appetites. My grandmother's country cooking at the farm was a decisive influence on my whole development as a cook; and I can never remember my mother happier than when she was either planning or preparing a meal, or eating it in the company of the family or friends, or even just standing in the middle of a large supermarket, radiant with joy at the thought of so much food spread out on every side of her. Both my sisters are good cooks; and my father, who cannot have eaten well when he was young, has always appreciated food, even though in his own rather eccentric and secretive way. He is the slowest eater I have ever known, and can take an hour to eat a dish which I would finish in ten minutes. If the food was something he liked, he never minded eating a lot provided nobody tried to rush him. If you offered him a large bowl of mayonnaise, for example, which was one of his favourites, he would eat all of it right down to the very last spoonful. He never paused for a moment but he never hurried. I well remember how, at lunch, if it was his day off, he would grumble when my mother started to do the washing-up at the end of the meal, because he was still only half-way through his soup. When she came back from work in the evening, she would find him still sitting at the table and just about to begin his apple tart. We were indeed a family who enjoyed food; but, as my mother has often said: '*Si on n'est pas gourmand, on ne peut pas faire la bonne cuisine*'. (If you don't enjoy food, you cannot be a good cook.)

One dish I specially enjoyed as a boy was her *brandade de morue*; even now, each time my wife Annie and I go to Tarbes, my mother invites us to a meal and cooks it for us. The occasion has become something of a family tradition. The brandade of salt cod is one of the old country dishes of southern France, and dates from the early middle ages when fishermen brought cod back across the Atlantic from the coastal waters of Newfoundland to be landed and sold at Bordeaux. Each region makes its brandade in its own way. My mother's recipe was the Gascon one, the one I have always liked the best. My mother enjoys telling people how once, when I was a small boy, I ordered brandade at a restaurant, but when it came I only ate half and left the rest. The waiter asked anxiously if there was anything wrong. It seems that I replied with dignified regret: 'No, there's nothing wrong. It's very good, but it is not like the brandade my mother makes at home!' *'Ce n'est pas la brandade de ma mère'* soon became my mother's favourite quote. She made her version with mashed potatoes as a main dish. The cod was soaked overnight to de-salt it, then poached with thyme and a bay leaf. My mother then fried it in oil with immense care, adding the fish morsel by morsel, until it was time to put in the garlic and parsley, and to mix the cod with the mashed potatoes. Another way, which is typically Provençal, is to put the cod into a mixer with extra garlic and oil and some milk and lemon juice, and to work it until it becomes a completely smooth cream. This is more of a starter than a main dish, but it makes a wonderful appetiser eaten on toasted bread just before a meal.

At La Tante Claire I have done a restaurant version of *brandade de morue* which appeared on some of our earlier menus and was very successful. The cod was mixed with mashed potatoes, exactly as my mother made it, but I added truffles and presented it to our customers surrounded by a circle of sliced, lightly fried red peppers. The scarlet ring and the white centre studded with the black morsels of truffle looked very effective and unusual. A *brandade de morue* can be elaborated in other ways as well. If you want to give it a delicious Alsatian character, you can combine it with *choucroute*; or, if you are in Brittany, you can make it into fritters or pancakes. But however you do it, the real heart of the dish is always the same: the traditional housewife's recipe from southern France.

MOUSSE DE BRANDADE DE MORUE

SALT COD MOUSSE

200 g / 7 oz salt cod
30 g / 1 oz butter
white part of 1 leek, chopped and washed
1 small onion, chopped
250 ml / 9 fl oz double cream
2 gelatine leaves, soaked in cold water and drained
200 ml / 7 fl oz whipping cream, lightly whipped
salt and freshly ground pepper

Put the salt cod in a bowl of cold water and leave to soak overnight under a trickle of cold water.

In a saucepan, melt the butter over gentle heat, then add the leek and onion. Cook slowly, add the garlic, pat dry the cod and add it to the pan with the double cream. Poach over slow heat until the fish is very tender. Remove the skin, put the cod back in the pan and dissolve the gelatine in the mixture, stirring well. Purée in a food processor and rub through a sieve. Leave to cool, then fold in the lightly whipped cream.

Line 4 ramekins with clingfilm, divide the cod mixture between them and leave to set in the fridge. To serve, turn out the mousses and peel off the clingfilm.

33

Brandade de Morue aux Truffes (recipe p. 35)

BRANDADE DE MORUE AUX TRUFFES

• —

BRANDADE OF SALT COD WITH TRUFFLES

— • —

500 g / 1 lb 2 oz salt cod, soaked overnight in
running water
250 ml / 9 fl oz milk
1 sprig of thyme
150 ml / 5 fl oz olive oil
50 g / 2 oz truffles, chopped
1 tablespoon chopped parsley
500 g / 1 lb 2 oz potatoes, boiled and mashed
freshly ground pepper
2 red peppers, thinly sliced and lightly fried in olive
oil, for serving

— • —

*Put the soaked cod in a saucepan and add the milk,
250 ml / 9 fl oz water, thyme and bay leaf. Bring to
the boil, take the pan off the heat and leave the fish to
cool in the cooking liquid. Strain off the cooled liquid
and reserve it.*

*Flake the cod. Heat the oil in a saucepan. When it is
sizzling, add a little of the cod and stir well with a
wooden spoon. Add a little more cod, stir well and
repeat until you have used all the cod. Make sure the
oil stays very hot and that the fish absorbs it all. Stir in
the chopped parsley and mix well.*

*Mix the fish into the mashed potatoes. The mixture
should be very creamy. If it is not, add some of the
cooking stock. Check the seasoning. The pepper flavour
should be very pronounced, but you will almost
certainly not need to add salt. Add the truffles and mix
well. Serve the brandade in a deep dish, surrounded by
the red peppers. (Photograph p. 34)*

Not far from the Tarbes flat, there was a little
garden. It belonged to us but neither of my
parents ever bothered to look after it, and when
I was about ten, I was the only member of the
family who took any interest in it. I loved
working there, and touching the earth, and
feeling the fineness of the soil on my hands. I
grew cabbages and tomatoes and radishes and,
occasionally, a triumphantly juicy cucumber or
two. In one part of the garden I even sowed
some grass seeds which I thought would one
day turn into a smooth, neat English lawn! I
intended to be a farmer, after all, and this
humble little plot was nothing less than my
first farm. When I brought my own tomatoes,
cucumbers and radishes home, my mother
would put them into stews, soups and salads,
and watching her do this, I would feel immense
pride in being able to play my part in feeding
the family. I was already well aware that both
my mother and my grandmother were good
cooks, and that food was not only enjoyable but
also rather interesting. On summer evenings,
as I walked home from school, I would pass
open kitchen windows while the evening meal
was being cooked, and I became expert at
knowing, just from the smell of the food, what
each family was going to have that night for
supper. I knew who was having *civet de lièvre*,
or whose dinner would be beef stew or roast
lamb, or which family would have to be content
with *confit de canard* and chips. I took a great
pleasure in visualising all these kitchens and all
these meals, and I was cheered on my way by
the knowledge that my mother's excellent
supper would be waiting for me at the end of
my journey.

SOUPE DE RADIS ET DE CONCOMBRE

•

RADISH AND CUCUMBER SOUP

•

400 g / 14 oz onions, thinly sliced
100 g / 3½ oz garlic, very thinly sliced
200 g / 7 oz carrots, thinly sliced
150 g / 5 oz radishes, with fresh leaves, very thinly sliced
350 g / 12 oz tomatoes, blanched, skinned, deseeded and diced.
2 basil leaves very finely chopped
1 sprig marjoram, very finely chopped
2 radish leaves, finely chopped
50 g / 2 oz cucumber, washed but not peeled, and cut into very thin julienne strips
30 g / 1 oz butter
salt and freshly ground pepper

•

Melt the butter over medium heat in a large saucepan. When hot, but not brown, put in the onions, garlic and carrots. Cover the pan and sweat gently for 15 minutes, stirring from time to time to prevent the vegetables from browning. Add 1.75 L / 3 pt water and salt and pepper to taste. Bring back to the boil, immediately add the radishes and simmer for 10 minutes, uncovered. Add the tomatoes, basil, marjoram and radish leaves and simmer for another 10 minutes. Garnish with the cucumber julienne and serve hot.

When at last the time came for me to leave school, it was made clear that I must now choose a proper trade. It would have to be something for which I could train at a local college in Tarbes, and that left me with a stark choice between two alternatives: the Tarbes arsénal or the *école hôtelière*. I had no aptitude for military engineering or for the manufacture of tanks, mortars or automatic weapons, so I settled on the catering college. When I say that I became a cook almost by chance, I am perhaps forgetting that I was already, without altogether realising it, starting to be fascinated by food and cooking, and also quite good at preparing certain elementary dishes. Even so, life as a *chef de cuisine* in a tall white hat was not quite what I had had in mind for myself!

It was with inward misgiving, therefore, that on a bright September morning in 1963, I walked for the first time through the gates of the Tarbes catering college and found myself standing in a vast courtyard, surrounded by tall buildings and divided at intervals by neat rows of trees. I was fifteen years old and slightly apprehensive. In front of me, the long, white, four-storey facade seemed as forbiddingly classical as the *haute cuisine* I was to spend the next three years of my life learning. The full name of the school was *Le collège d'enseignement technique Reffye*, though locally it was always just referred to as 'Reffye'. The military character of its buildings, and also its name, were due to the fact that the school was originally built in 1875 as an infantry barracks

under the supervision of Colonel Verchère de Reffye, who was also the creator and organiser of the Tarbes Arsenal. Even in the 1960s the former barracks still served in an official capacity, since a large part of the buildings housed offices connected with various departments of local government. There were nearly two thousand students, mostly girls; and the subjects taught included accountancy and secretarial work, welfare administration, dressmaking and hairdressing. In the catering college, which was only a small part of the school, the cookery section consisted of about three dozen students, twenty eight boys and just eight girls.

I shall always owe a debt of gratitude to the school for what it taught me. I still have my old text-books, which I glance at from time to time, just to admire their precision and clarity. The fundamental principles of my cooking at La Tante Claire are all ones I originally learnt at Reffye, who was the creator and organiser of the Tarbes arsenal. Even in the 1960s the their opportunity, and who had no intention of ever becoming chefs. They just wanted to pass the exam at the end of the course and get a job. Once the school day was over, their only thought was to escape and play rugby; they never felt the urge to rush home to the kitchen to put into practice what they had learnt that day in class. We were a wild bunch and we had a lot of fun; but that took nothing away from the quality of the training which was available to anyone who wanted to benefit from it. We

were quite proud of the fact that Reffye was not a specialised catering college, like those at Thonon or Toulouse, but just a straightforward *lycée* with a catering department attached to it. We regarded the other schools as snobbish affairs, fit only for the privileged sons and heirs of established family hotels and restaurants, where you learned how to tell other people to do things rather than do them yourself. The pupils might be smarter and more ambitious, we told ourselves, but we were the real cooks, who did the real work in a kitchen. Without us the whole gastronomic universe would collapse. We were its foundation. Our sentiments were probably not very objective; but, as far as my own career is concerned, I am sure that the professional training I got at Reffye could not have been bettered. Bernard Ramounéda, my oldest and best friend in the trade, and a contemporary at Reffye, would certainly agree with me. We are the only two people of our class who are today chef-proprietors of their own restaurants, I at La Tante Claire, and he at Le Florida at Castéra-Verduzan, not far from Saint Puy. As chefs of the 'old school', we look back with appreciation on what we learned from our teachers at Tarbes. On the foundations of his Reffye training, Bernard developed dishes like his delicious *croustade d'agneau* in which the lamb is cooked with cinnamon and tomatoes and covered with flaky Gascon pastry. Bernard and I would make this dish with *pastis* pastry (page 198), but filo pastry makes a good substitute.

CROUSTADE D'AGNEAU RAMOUNÉDA

•

CROUSTADE OF LAMB

•

500 g / 1 lb 2 oz neck of lamb, cut into
1 cm / 1½ in cubes
50 ml / 2 fl oz extra virgin olive oil
200 g / 7 oz carrots, diced very small
2 garlic cloves, crushed and very finely chopped
2 shallots, very finely chopped
2 tomatoes, blanched, skinned, deseeded and diced
250 ml / 9 fl oz dry white wine
2 basil leaves, finely chopped
¼ teaspoon cinnamon
200 g / 7 oz courgettes, diced very small
50 g / 2 oz butter, at room temperature
4 × 27 cm / 11 in squares of Pastis pastry
(page 198) or filo pastry
100 g / 3½ oz clarified butter
1 egg yolk mixed with 1 teaspoon water, for
eggwash
salt and freshly ground pepper

•

Preheat the oven to 230°C / 450°F / gas 8.

Heat the oil in a large shallow pan. When very hot, add the meat and season well with salt and pepper. Cook quickly until golden brown all over. Add the carrots, garlic, shallots and tomatoes and cook for 1 minute, stirring continuously. Pour in the white wine and add the basil, mint and cinnamon. Cook quickly until the liquid has reduced by half, then add the courgettes, cook for 30 seconds and pass through a fine sieve into a small saucepan.

Spread the meat and vegetables on a plate and leave to cool. Bring the sauce to the boil, whisk in the butter and keep warm. Spread the pastis or filo pastry squares on a work surface and brush with clarified butter. Cut each square in half and brush with the rest of the butter.

Butter four 10 cm / 4 in tartlet moulds and line with a double thickness of pastry. Divide the meat mixture between the moulds, pull the corners up together and press well in the middle to shape a little purse. Brush with the eggwash and bake in the middle of the oven, for about 15 minutes, until golden brown. Delicately take the croustades out of the moulds and place on warm serving plates. Serve the sauce separately.

I know too that by the end of my course I was far better equipped to start my first job as a *commis chef* in a big kitchen than young cooks are now. Besides learning how to cook, we learned how to work as waiters and how to serve our food to customers in the school restaurant, where the art of *la salle* was taught us by Monsieur Dibello, a dramatic, fiery Italian and a vintage *maître d'hôtel*. Each student could choose whether to specialise in *la cuisine* or *la salle*; but whichever branch he selected, he had to spend a certain amount of his course in learning something of the other. The would-be waiters formed a separate restaurant management class, which was larger than ours, and they spent the same amount of time in the restaurant as we spent in the kitchen. Other subjects included mathematics, which I rather enjoyed, and elementary English, which at first I disliked intensely. We had lessons in dietary theory and food hygiene; and we learned quite a lot about the maintenance and upkeep of kitchens and restaurants; about laundering and ironing; and cleaning and washing walls. We were also taught carpentry, with a view, I suppose, to being able to make or repair tables and chairs. One year, in the carpentry class, I was asked to make an electric guitar, which turned out to be a great success. I was very pleased with it and so was the teacher, but I could never quite discover what role it was intended to fill in a busy kitchen.

Since Reffye was mainly a girls' school, it is not surprising that most of the teachers were women, and the only male teachers were those connected with the catering department. Mademoiselle Victor, the headmistress, was small, plump, red-haired and bespectacled. I remember her well. She was a figure of authority, but one we all admired. She was one of those remarkable people who, naturally and quietly, manage to make you respect and like them at the same time. She ran the large school firmly and fairly; her personality alone was usually enough to keep us in order. Serving at her table in the restaurant, however, was always something of an ordeal. Although only the better students were chosen for the job, and it was an honour to be among those selected, you knew that she would be watching and noticing every single thing you did, and would tell you off sharply if you made the least mistake.

Mademoiselle Victor never shouted at us in temper as did some of the other mistresses, especially Madame Favier, whom none of us liked. She was always scolding and reporting and punishing; and her shrieks and shouts, followed by the sound of two sharp slaps, could be heard from a hundred yards away, right across the courtyard.

Monsieur Mégelas, our principal cookery teacher, was a tall, imposing figure with an imperious Escoffier-like moustache who ruled his class with a rod of iron. No fooling was allowed, and no jokes, though beneath his gruff, forbidding exterior he could turn out to be quite warm and friendly, once he had got to know you. All through the 1930s he had worked for important hotels and restaurants, and he had been *chef de cuisine* on board some of the old transatlantic liners. There was an air of faded international romance about him, which was certainly not the case with Monsieur Borde, the butchery teacher, who was as rough and square and solid as if he had been hewn out of the rock of his native Pyrenees. Surrounded by sides of beef and carcasses of lamb and pork, he would lecture us about meat in a thick peasant accent which at times was almost a sort of patois. He died while I was still at Reffye, and I still remember his funeral, which took place high up in the Bigorre mountains, at a remote village consisting only of a small, stone-roofed church and a surrounding handful of houses. Perhaps because he was buried in

November, or because of his love for a good piece of beef, I have always associated Monsieur Borde with a recipe for steak cooked with winter vegetables. In French we have a beautiful way of describing root vegetables: we call them 'forgotten vegetables' because they are hidden beneath the earth and nobody thinks about them. Another simple but favourite recipe of mine uses turnips with duck.

TOURNEDOS D'ECOSSE AUX LÉGUMES OUBLIÉS

·

TOURNEDOS WITH ROOT VEGETABLES

·

4 tournedos, about 175 g / 6 oz each
1 L / 1¾ pint Chicken stock (page 49)
400 g / 14 oz swede, turned or cut into bite-size chunks
2 Jerusalem artichokes, turned or cut into bite-size chunks
2 parsnips, turned or cut into bite-size chunks
2 carrots, turned or cut into bite-size chunks
100 g / 3½ oz pumpkin flesh, diced
100 ml / 4 fl oz whipping cream
1 teaspoon English mustard
2 tablespoons vegetable oil
salt and freshly ground pepper

·

Bring the chicken stock to the boil and cook the vegetables in it, one variety at a time. Cover and keep in a warm place. Cook the pumpkin last, mash it in the stock and reduce to about 200 ml / 7 fl oz. Add the mustard, salt and pepper to taste. Pass through a fine conical strainer and keep warm.

Season the meat. Heat the oil in a frying pan. When very hot, add the tournedos and cook to your taste. Spoon the sauce over the warm plates and arrange the meat and vegetables on top.

CANARD RÔTI AUX NAVETS

—————— • ——————

ROAST DUCK WITH TURNIPS

—————— • ——————

1 × 1.8 kg / 4 lb duck, with its giblets
75 g / 3 oz butter
100 g / 3½ oz *mirepoix* (diced onions, carrots,
celery, thyme, bay leaf)
150 ml / 5 fl oz dry white wine
250 ml / 9 fl oz Veal stock (page 49)
100 g / 3½ oz pearl onions
150 g / 5 oz button onions
150 g / 5 oz baby turnips
2 teaspoons sugar
salt and freshly ground pepper

—————— • ——————

Preheat the overn to 230°C / 450°F / gas 8.

Using a heatproof casserole about the size of the duck, melt 50 g / 2 oz butter, add the mirepoix *and place the duck on top with the giblets, heart and liver if possible. Season, cover the casserole and cook in the oven for 40-50 minutes, until the duck is done to your liking, spooning over the buttery juices every 10 minutes. Three-quarters of the way through the cooking time, remove the lid so that the duck skin browns.*

Remove the duck from the casserole and keep in a warm place. Leave the fat in the pan and deglaze with the wine. Reduce almost completely to a glaze, add the stock and boil gently for 10 minutes. Strain the sauce and spoon off the fat. Keep warm.

Meanwhile, half-cook the onions and turnips in the remaining butter and the sugar, then put them into the sauce to cook until tender.

Carve the duck, place it on a dish and arrange the vegetables around. Pour the sauce on top and serve immediately.

Our English teacher, Monsieur Victor, was utterly unlike either Monsieur Mégelas or Monsieur Borde. We were supposed to know something of the language, just to be able to talk to English or American customers in a restaurant, and to explain the menu to them; and we had an English test when the time came for us to qualify as waiters. Monsieur Victor was a brother of the headmistress; although he adored his subject, he was a completely ineffectual teacher. He was a dreamer, an eccentric, but he loved England and everything to do with it with a passionate ardour that was quite astonishing. He even went to the extent of trying to make himself look like an Englishman. He wore baggy trousers and tweed jackets with leather patches on the elbows; his hair was always wild and curly; and he affected a bluff, hearty manner which he probably considered very Dickensian. We used to have two consecutive hours of English every Monday, which we found very boring, because we only needed a smattering of the language to pass our exam. One day, however, we discovered that if we asked Monsieur Victor any question about England, his enthusiastic answer, in French, would spread itself comfortably over the entire lesson to the complete exclusion of any serious effort on our part. 'Do the English like music, monsieur?' could start him off on the Beatles for fifty minutes; or 'What is the food like in England, monsieur?' would launch him into an exhaustive, detailed lecture on plum pudding, fish and chips, Lancashire hot pot, and above all custard. His favourite topic was rugby. 'Where is Twickenham, monsieur?' would light such enthusiasm in him that when at last the English scene was exhausted, he would quite happily begin on the French. Only when the bell rang at the end of the lesson, would he suddenly spring out of his dream, and cry: 'To work! To work! Quickly, messieurs, we really must prepare next week's work!'

CRÈME ANGLAISE

·

CUSTARD

·

250 ml / 8 fl oz milk
4 egg yolks
60 g / 2 oz sugar

·

*Bring the milk to the boil. Whisk the egg yolks and
sugar together until thick. Pour the milk over,
whisking continuously. Return to the pan and cook
over gentle heat, stirring with a wooden spoon until the
custard thickens enough to coat the back of the spoon.
Pass through a fine conical sieve. Serve hot or cold.*

*This custard may be flavoured. Add your chosen
flavouring to the milk before bringing it to the boil and
follow the basic recipe.*

Vanilla:
*Split half a vanilla pod, scraping out all the seeds into
the milk.*

Cinnamon:
Add ground cinnamon to taste to the milk.

Coffee:
Heat the milk and add instant coffee to taste.

Chocolate:
Add 50 g / 2 oz grated bitter chocolate to the milk.

Hazelnut:
*Take 2 tablespoons hazelnut butter (available from
health food shops) and skim off the oil from the surface.
Whisk the hazelnut butter with the egg yolks and
sugar.*

Cardamom:
Add 3 finely-crushed cardamom pods to the milk.

The oldest teacher of all, and the one I think
everybody respected the most, was Monsieur
Hèche, who taught us *pâtisserie*. He was sixty
years old and was paralysed in both legs. He
could just walk very slowly, with two sticks, but
he could not stand, so his desk was raised up on
a little platform and he taught us from there.
We sat below him, round a big table, in groups
of three, each group having its own little stove
and oven. From his platform Monsieur Hèche
could watch and check everything we did. We
were better behaved with him than with
anyone else, and he, in his turn, took more
trouble with us than did the other teachers. He
was an excellent *pâtissier*; he had played an
important part in the Resistance during the
war; and he struck you as being a man of
tranquil, mature wisdom who had made his
peace with life, and who had no more need to
prove himself to the world.

PÂTE BRISÉE

·

SHORTCRUST

·

250 g / 9 oz flour
120 g / 4 oz butter, diced
1 egg yolk
50 ml / 2 fl oz iced water
¼ tablespoon salt
50 g / 2 oz caster sugar (for fruit tarts and sweet
flans only)

·

*Put the flour in a large bowl and make a well. Put in
the butter, egg yolk, water, salt and the sugar, if
making sweet pastry. Using the tips of your fingers,
mix the wet ingredients together first, then incorporate
the flour, little by little.*

*Knead lightly and quickly, pressing the pastry
downwards and away from you with the heel of your
hand. Wrap immediately in clingfilm and refrigerate
for 12 hours.*

PÂTE FEUILLETÉE

●

PUFF PASTRY

300 g / 11 oz plain flour
a pinch of salt
100 ml / 4 fl oz iced water
225 g / 8 oz butter

●

Make a dough with the flour, salt and cold water. Knead on a lightly-floured surface and form into a neat square. Dust with flour, wrap in clingfilm and refrigerate for about 30 minutes.

Meanwhile, dice the butter and knead it to make it soft but not oily; it should remain cold. Form into a square.

Roll the dough into a 25 cm / 10 in square. Place the butter in the middle and fold up the sides of the dough so that the 4 corners of the dough meet in the centre of the butter. Press together the ends of the dough over the butter to enclose it completely without stretching the dough.

Place this 'parcel' on a lightly-floured surface and start rolling into a 45 cm / 18 in strip. Fold this into 3 equal parts. Turn the folded dough and roll it in the opposite direction into another 45 cm / 18 in strip. Fold over the ends towards the middle, wrap in clingfilm and rest in the fridge for 10 minutes.

Repeat this operation twice more, always rolling the dough away from you. Chill for 30 minutes before using the pastry.

PÂTE À CHOUX

●

CHOUX PASTRY

250 ml / 9 fl oz water
½ teaspoon salt
100 g / 3½ oz butter, diced, plus extra for greasing
120 g / 4 oz flour, sifted
4 eggs, lightly beaten

●

Preheat the oven to 240°C / 475°F / gas 9.

Bring the water, salt and butter to the boil. Remove from the heat. Add the sifted flour all at once and beat it in with a wooden spatula until completely amalgamated. Return the pan to a moderate heat and beat continuously until the paste leaves the sides and bottom of the pan. Transfer to a mixing bowl and allow to cool slightly before adding the eggs gradually, beating well after each addition. The mixture must be homogeneous.

To bake, spoon 45 teaspoons of the paste on to 2 large, lightly buttered baking trays, making sure there is at least 4 cm / 1½ in space between each choux bun.

Bake initially at 240°C / 475°F / gas 9, then, as soon as the choux begin to puff, up, lower the oven temperature to 220°C / 425°F / gas 7 and cook for about 15-20 minutes, until the buns are golden brown and crisp. Leave to cool completely before filling.

This recipe will make about forty-five 5 cm / 2 in choux buns. Any that you do not need immediately can be placed in a plastic bag and frozen while still tepid. Reheat gently before using.

CRÈME PÂTISSIÈRE

PASTRY CREAM

500 ml / 18 fl oz milk
30 g / 1 oz flour
15 g / ½ oz cornflour
6 egg yolks
120 g / 4 oz caster sugar

*Bring the milk to the boil in a large saucepan.
Whisk the egg yolks and sugar together until thick and
pale, then stir in the flour and cornflour. Whisk the
boiling milk into the egg mixture and pour back into
the pan. Bring to the boil over medium heat and cook
for 5 minutes, stirring continuously.*

*Transfer the pastry cream to a bowl and cover with
clingfilm while hot, making sure the film clings to the
cream. This will prevent a skin from forming on the
surface of the cream. Cool and refrigerate until ready
to use.*

There was one little corner of the room which
Monsieur Hèche could not see from his
platform, and in this corner there was a small
hotplate. Whenever we had an early morning
pâtisserie lesson, this hotplate came into its
own. We would smuggle eggs and bacon into
the classroom and cook them, surreptitiously,
out of sight of Monsieur Hèche, to give ourselves a rather enjoyable extra breakfast. Though
the teacher could not see what was happening,
it is impossible to ignore the smell of fried eggs
in a pastry-making class, so he certainly knew
what we were doing. He never once mentioned
it, however, and never told us off. But if we
ever made the least mistake in a *pâtisserie*, he
would spot it and correct us immediately.
Whatever cake or pastry we were learning,
each member of each group would make it in
turn, and we carried on until everyone could do
it more or less correctly. A good student could
learn a lot from Monsieur Hèche.

TARTES FINES AUX POIRES

INDIVIDUAL PEAR TARTS

150 g / 5 oz Puff pastry (page 42)
6 tasty pears, peeled, cored and very thinly sliced
4 tablespoons butter
6 tablespoons caster sugar
Caramel sauce (see below), for serving

*Preheat the oven to 220°C / 425°F / gas 7.
Roll out the pastry very thinly and prick all over with a
fork. Use a small plate to mark four 17-18 cm / 7 in
circles on the pastry and cut them out with a sharp
knife. Arrange the pear slices on the top of each circle,
overlapping them closely. Dot with butter and sprinkle
generously with sugar. Bake in the oven for 20
minutes, or until the pastry base is golden brown. Serve
with caramel sauce.*

*In season fresh figs can be used very successfully instead
of the pears. You will need about 12 figs, depending on
their size. Serve the fig tarts with cinnamon-flavoured
Crème anglaise (page 41).*

SAUCE CARAMEL

CARAMEL SAUCE

200 g / 7 oz caster sugar
300 ml / ½ pint whipping cream

*In a 2 L / 4½ pt saucepan, melt the sugar over
medium heat until liquid and brown. Take the pan off
the heat, and bring the cream to the boil in a small
saucepan. Return the caramel to the heat and carefully
pour the boiling cream over it, whisking all the time
until homogeneous.*

*Serve the sauce hot or cold, thinning it down with a
little more cream if necessary.*

COULIS DE FRUITS

FRESH FRUIT COULIS

450 g / 1 lb raspberries or strawberries, washed and
hulled
100 g / 3½ oz caster sugar

*Purée the fruit in a blender, then pass through a fine
conical sieve. Whisk in the sugar until dissolved and
chill in the fridge. Make fruit coulis in larger quantities
during the summer when the berries are plentiful, and
freeze it. It can also be made during the winter with
thawed frozen berries.*

MARQUISE AU CHOCOLAT TANTE CLAIRE

CHOCOLATE MARQUISE

(Serves 6)

Sponge:
butter for greasing
flour for dusting
75 g / 3 oz icing sugar, sifted
3 egg whites
50 g / 2 oz cocoa powder

Chocolate mousse:
3 egg yolks
60 g / 2 oz caster sugar
60 g / 2 oz bitter chocolate, finely grated and
melted over a double boiler
100 g / 3½ oz butter, softened
50 g / 2 oz cocoa powder
150 ml / 5 fl oz whipping cream, lightly whipped

Preheat the oven to 180°C / 350°F / gas 4.

*Lightly butter a shallow baking tray (33 × 23 × 2 cm /
13 × 9 × ¾ in) and line it with greaseproof paper.
Butter and lightly flour the paper, shaking off the
excess flour.*

*First make the sponge layer: Whisk the egg yolks with
50 g / 2 oz icing sugar until thick and ribbon-like.
Whisk the egg whites until frothy, then gradually add
the remaining icing sugar and whisk until stiff. Fold
the whites into the yolks and sift and fold in the cocoa
powder. Spread the mixture evenly on the baking tray
and bake for about 12 minutes, or until a skewer
inserted in the middle comes out clean. Turn out the
cake onto a clean tea towel, remove the paper, fold the
tea towel over the sponge and allow to cool. Line a
500 g / 1 lb loaf tin with greaseproof paper.*

*Cut the sponge layer into two 17 × 5 cm / 7 × 2 in
pieces for the sides, one 15 × 7 cm / 6 × 3 in piece for
the bottom, two 5 × 7 cm / 2 × 3 in pieces for the ends
and one 17 × 9 cm / 7 × 3½ in piece for the top. Use
these sponge pieces to line the prepared loaf tin and set
aside.*

*To make the chocolate mousse filling: In a bowl, whisk
together the egg yolks, sugar and melted chocolate. In
another bowl, mix the soft butter and cocoa powder
until smooth. Mix the egg yolk and butter mixtures
together until homogeneous. Stir in one-third of the
lightly-whipped cream and fold the rest in very gently
but thoroughly. Pour the mousse into the sponge-lined
tin and fit the 17 × 9 cm / 7 × 3½ in sponge rectangle
on top. Wrap well with clingfilm and refrigerate for at
least 6 hours before cutting into slices.*

*Serve with chocolate Crème anglaise (page 41) or
Raspberry coulis (see previous column).*

At Reffye we were taught classical *haute cuisine* which, in my case, was an addition to the regional tradition I had already acquired from my mother and my grandmother. Our teachers told us to revere Escoffier's *Le Guide Culinaire* as a sacrosanct authority. None of them seemed to have heard about the new ideas which were just starting to impinge on the world of professional cooking, and which would, amid much publicity in the 1970s, culminate in the victory of *nouvelle cuisine* and *cuisine minceur* over the old guard of gastronomic classicists. The main difference between the two camps was that *haute cuisine* cooks worked to transform their ingredients into a dish which frequently bore little resemblance to the original, whereas the 'new' cooks sought to present ingredients which, as it were, had suffered only the barest minimum of culinary interference.

For our very first lesson at Reffye, we were shown the big professional kitchen where most of the food eaten in the school restaurant was prepared. We were told how cooks were divided up into *parties*, each responsible for a different variety of dish (fish, vegetables, meat, sauces), and how each *partie* had its own area for washing-up, and how each kitchen utensil should be washed immediately after use. In school we wore white coats and black trousers; our lessons took place in the classroom, where we were divided up into threes, each little group sitting at a separate table which was equipped with cooking implements. We were then told how to prepare some very simple recipes, just to start us off cooking; but, when we tried to do them, one or two people got into serious difficulties straight away. My friend Bernard Ramounéda was one of them. He and the two others in his group were told to do some provençal tomatoes and they all collaborated well until the tomatoes were sizzling away in the frying-pan. At this point, each of the three boys thought that one of the others was watching the food whereas, in fact, nobody was, and they were all three looking in other directions. Suddenly the blackened tomatoes went up in a cloud of smoke, and the cookery teacher descended on the incompetent little group in a rage that was almost as black as the contents of the frying-pan. The teacher was Monsieur Mégelas. He told poor Bernard off even more copiously than the others because he had worked with his father (who was also a chef) on board one of the pre-war liners, and thought that, having such a father, he really ought to know better. It is one lesson which Bernard says he has never forgotten.

The simpler recipes we learned at this stage included mousses, made from eggs and cream, and much easier to make with modern kitchen machinery than they used to be in the old days when all the grinding and pounding had to be done by hand. We started with the usual chocolate mousse, and then went on to other flavours such as chicken and fish. At La Tante Claire I serve a lobster mousse, and also a very good one made with game and ceps.

MOUSSE DE VOLAILLE

•

CHICKEN MOUSSE

•

500 g / 1 lb 2 oz white chicken meat, chopped
2 egg whites
500 ml / 18 fl oz whipping cream
salt and freshly ground pepper

•

Put the chicken meat in a food processor, add the egg whites, little by little and process until smooth. Push through a fine sieve and refrigerate until very well chilled. Return to the food processor and add the cream little by little. Season carefully at this stage, as it is difficult to improve the seasoning once the mousse is cooked. Shape into quenelles and cook as in the following recipe.

Fish mousse (e.g. salmon or sole) can be prepared by substituting the chicken meat with equal quantities of skinned fish fillet.

MOUSSE DE HOMARD

•

LOBSTER MOUSSE

•

200 g / 7 oz lobster meat, chopped, head and
all shells reserved
2 egg whites
200 ml / 7 fl oz whipping cream
24 asparagus tips, lightly cooked in boiling salted
water, drained and reheated in a little hot butter
salt and freshly ground pepper
Sauce Americaine (see next column), for serving

•

*Put the lobster meat in a food processor, adding the egg
whites little by little and process until smooth. Push
through a fine sieve and refrigerate until thoroughly
chilled. Return to the food processor and mix in the
cream little by little. Taste and season carefully at this
stage, it is difficult to improve the seasoning once the
mousse is cooked. Refrigerate until ready to cook.*

*Fill a deep roasting pan or large saucepan with water
and heat to 90°C / 194°F. Shape the mousse into 4
quenelles with 2 metal serving spoons and poach them
in the hot water. Cook for 5 minutes on one side, turn
them over gently and cook for 5 minutes on the other
side. Heat the sauce and pour it over 4 warm plates.
Place a quenelle in the centre and arrange the
asparagus tips around (Photograph p. 47)*

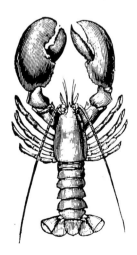

SAUCE AMÉRICAINE

•

AMERICAN SAUCE FOR FISH OR SHELLFISH

•

150 g / 5 oz butter, at room temperature
50 g / 2 oz onion, finely chopped
50 g / 2 oz shallots, very finely chopped
100 g / 3½ oz carrot, very finely diced
4 garlic cloves, peeled and crushed
1 small Bouquet garni (page 11)
1 tablespoon coarsely chopped tarragon
1 tablespoon coarsely chopped chervil
25 g / 1 oz tomato purée
250 g / 9 oz ripe tomatoes, washed and coarsely
chopped
50 ml / 2 fl oz armagnac
200 ml / 7 fl oz good quality dry white wine
400 ml / 14 fl oz Fish stock, (page 49)
salt and freshly ground pepper

•

*Melt 50 g / 2 oz butter in a large saucepan. If
preparing this sauce for a lobster dish, keep the skin,
bones and head. Add the chopped shells or bones to the
butter and sweat until no moisture is left. Add the
finely chopped onion, shallots and carrot and sweat for
5 minutes. Mix in the tomato purée and cook for 5
minutes, stirring all the time. Put in the crushed garlic
cloves. Flame with the armagnac, then pour in the
white wine and fish stock and deglaze well. Add the
tomatoes, tarragon, chervil and bouquet garni. Season
and cook, uncovered, for 20 minutes, skimming
whenever necessary. Pass through a fine sieve into a
pan and whisk in the remaining butter, cut into small
dice. Keep warm.*

Mousse de Homard (recipe p. 46)

MOUSSE DE GIBIER

—— • ——

GAME MOUSSE

—— • ——

200 g / 7 oz pheasant or hare meat, or a mixture of
the two, chopped
3 egg whites
200 ml / 7 fl oz whipping cream
500 g / 1 lb 2 oz fresh ceps, trimmed and wiped
with a damp tea towel
2 tablespoons vegetable oil
salt and freshly ground pepper
Red bordelaise sauce (page 51), for serving

—— • ——

*Put the chopped meat in a food processor, add the egg
whites little by little and process until smooth. Push
through a fine sieve and refrigerate until thoroughly
chilled. Return to the food processor and mix in the
cream little by little. Taste and season carefully at this
stage, as it is difficult to improve the seasoning once the
mousse is cooked. Refrigerate until ready to cook.*

*Fill a deep roasting pan or large saucepan with water
and heat to 90°C / 194° F. Shape the mousse into 4
quenelles with 2 metal serving spoons and poach them
in the hot water for 5 minutes on one side, then turn
them over gently and cook for 5 minutes on the other
side.*

*Meanwhile, heat the oil until very hot and sauté the
ceps until soft. Season with salt. Cover and keep warm.
Heat the bordelaise sauce and pour it onto 4 warm
plates. Put a quenelle in the centre and arrange the
ceps around.*

Before we went on to the more complicated recipes, we learned all the basic elements of classical restaurant cooking, the most important of which have always been the stocks or *fonds de cuisine*. These include all the liquids which we use in the kitchen other than water, wine, milk, and the various fruit juices and syrups. The *fonds* are the end product of the lengthy and laborious extraction of the innermost juices of meat and fish bones, and also vegetables, which can then be reduced further to produce glazes and essences. They provide a reservoir of rich, concentrated flavour which cannot be obtained in any other way. As their name implies, they are the foundation stones of *haute cuisine*; they find their way into every kind of sauce and preparation and recipe; and they mark the frontier between home cooking and the work of the professional chef for whom in the old days, the wide range of *fonds* and sauces, which was permanently at his disposal, was not unlike the varied array of stops available to an organist.

At Reffye we learned first the simple *jus*, and then we went on to the brown and white *fonds*, the chicken stock and the *fumets* of fish and game. At La Tante Claire we use only four *fonds de cuisine* which are prepared in two large, modern and very efficient French-made *chaudrons* or boilers. Every day we make some fish *fumet* and a vegetable *bouillon*. The veal and chicken *fonds* we make about once a week in larger quantities, about fifteen to twenty litres at a time. There is really no reason why an ordinary housewife should not make a *fond* like ours, if she respects the rules. She would have to roast bones in the oven, and scrape them, and simmer them with vegetables. It means quite a bit of extra work and time, but it is well worth the trouble, and all the stocks can be frozen to use another time.

FOND DE VEAU

VEAL STOCK

1 kg / 2¼ lb small veal bones chopped
150 g / 5 oz carrots, diced
200 g / 7 oz onions, diced
100 ml / 4 fl oz vegetable oil
100 g / 3½ oz pork rind
500 ml / 18 fl oz white wine
1 Bouquet garni (page 11)
salt and freshly ground pepper

Preheat the oven to 240°C / 475°F / gas 9.
Roast the veal bones in the hot oven until golden.

Sweat the vegetables in the oil, add the pork rind and
the roasted bones and cook slowly for 10 minutes.
Deglaze the roasting pan with the wine and pour the
liquid into the saucepan. Add 3 L / 5½ pt water and
bring to the boil. Skim the surface and add the bouquet
garni and salt to taste. Cook slowly for about 5 hours.

Strain the stock through a sieve. Let it rest for 10
minutes, then skim off all the fat from the top.

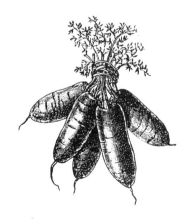

FOND DE VOLAILLE

CHICKEN STOCK

1 kg / 2¼ lbs chicken bones, chopped
150 g / 5 oz onions, coarsely chopped
150 g / 5 oz carrots, coarsely chopped
150 g / 5 oz leeks, coarsely chopped
1 celery stalk
4 garlic cloves
1 Bouquet garni (page 11)
coarse salt and coarsely ground pepper

Put the bones in a large pot and pour on 1.5 L / 2½ pt
cold water. Bring quickly to the boil over high heat.
Skim well. Add all the vegetables, the bouquet garni
and salt and pepper, to taste. Simmer gently for 1½
hours. Strain through a fine sieve.

FUMET DE POISSON

FISH STOCK

500 g / 1 lb 2 oz fish bones (sole, turbot or brill), cut
into small pieces
50 g / 2 oz butter
50 g / 2 oz carrots, thinly sliced
80 g / 3 oz onions, thinly sliced
200 ml / 7 fl oz dry white wine
1 small Bouquet garni (page 11)

Sweat the vegetables slowly in the butter until soft.
Add the fish bones and cook gently for 5 minutes. Pour
over the wine and cook for 5 minutes. Add 800 ml /
1½ pt cold water and bring to the boil, then skim the
surface. Add the bouquet garni and cook slowly for 20
minutes. Pass the stock through a fine sieve.

NAGE DE LÉGUMES

● ●

VEGETABLE STOCK

●

75 g / 3 oz onion, very finely chopped
65 g / 2½ oz leek, very finely chopped
30 g / 1 oz celery, very finely chopped
100 g / 3½ oz carrots, very finely chopped
2 garlic cloves, peeled and crushed
1 teaspoon coarse sea salt
250 ml / 9 fl oz white wine
6 pink peppercorns
1 star anise
4 parsley stalks
2 sprigs of tarragon
1 sprig of coriander
½ bay leaf

● ●

Bring 700 ml / 1¼ pt water to the boil, then add the vegetables and salt. Pour in the wine and bring to the boil again. Add the herbs and spices and leave the stock to steep off the heat. When cold, refrigerate. This stock will keep for 3 days.

One of the most vital ways in which the *fonds* have permeated French classical cooking has been through the part they played in the composition of sauces. Sauces are the crowning glory of traditional *haute cuisine*; and the system of sauces which we learned at Reffye was that evolved by Carême in the early nineteenth century, and then sustained and developed by the master chefs of the Second Empire and the Third Republic. At the head of the system you had the little group of *sauces mères*, principal sauces which were prepared regularly in advance, and which were always on hand in the kitchen, kept permanently warm, like the stocks themselves, in a spacious bain-marie. From them and with them, as though they were musical themes, you were able to produce an apparently endless line of separately-named variations which made up the long lists of sauces you find in the old cookery books. The principal sauces were always thickened with a roux of butter and flour. Their names are famous: the *espagnole*, *velouté*, *béchamel*, *allemande* and so on; but we never use them now at La Tante Claire. I may sometimes do a *béchamel*; but if I were to ask one of my young cooks to make me an *espagnole* or a *velouté*, he would have no idea how to do it, for he has never been taught. Nowadays you make a sauce by combining a basic *fond* with the juice of the meat; or, for speed you just take some chicken stock and mix it with double cream, and that's it. The 'new' cooking despises the old flour-thickened sauces as being too heavy, but the traditionalist in me regrets their passing. It is by his sauces that I judge the achievement and standing of a chef. I do not go to a three-star restaurant to eat a grilled sole; I go to taste the sauces, and very often now I am disappointed because what should have been a real sauce turns out to be no more than a fashionable *jus*. It may be good, but it is not what I was looking for. The crusade against flour, condemned as the enemy number one of good cooking by the early adherent of nouvelle cuisine, was far too sweeping in scope; although admittedly a wrong and careless use of flour in sauces had become widespread, and the whole classical tradition had, in many ways, become stale and uncreative. Bad cooks, as always, were cooking badly. The crusade was also sustained by fashionable medical theories and by the popular cult of physical slimness and lighter diet, phenomena which were as much sociological as culinary.

From a cookery angle, the most important thing to realise about flour-thickened sauces is that they are difficult to make. It takes a special skill and more time to make a roux than it does to make a sauce thickened in other ways. Nevertheless the old sauces, when they were prepared correctly, were very good indeed. To me a béchamel sauce is unthinkable without a flour roux. If you thickened it with cream, it would be a *béchamel-sauce crème*, quite another thing and not at all as good. And if you made a *boeuf bourgignon* or a *civet de lièvre* without

For the more complicated recipes, we were first given instruction cards, then each stage of a preparation was explained to us theoretically, and finally, still in groups, we carried out the recipe in practice. It was in this way, under the watchful eye of Monsieur Mégelas, that I first learned to make a fricassée of chicken. We had to cut a chicken into pieces, roll them in flour, and fry them. Then one of us had to sweat some onions in white wine, reduce it, add some chicken stock and put in the pieces of chicken so that they could go on cooking. When they were ready, we reduced the stock and put in some cream to make a sauce. When we were cooking for the school restaurant, we used to serve the fricassée with onions and mushrooms.

FRICASSÉE DE VOLAILLE À L'ANCIENNE

•

CHICKEN FRICASSÉE

•

1 × 1.5 kg / 3 lb 5 oz corn-fed chicken, with its giblets
75 g / 3 oz onions, coarsely chopped
75 g / 3 oz carrots, coarsely chopped
75 g / 3 oz leeks, coarsely chopped
1 small celery stalk
2 garlic cloves, peeled and left whole
1 small Bouquet garni (page 11)
120 g / 4 oz button onions, peeled
75 g / 3 oz butter
a pinch of sugar
1 teaspoon lemon juice
150 g / 6 oz button mushrooms, trimmed
50 g / 2 oz onions, finely chopped
30 g / 1 oz flour
150 ml / 5 fl oz double cream
a pinch of ground cloves
salt and freshly ground pepper
Pilaf rice (page 55), for serving

•

Cut off the chicken legs and remove the breasts from the carcass. Chop the carcass coarsely with a heavy knife. Put the chopped bones and giblets in a large saucepan with 1 L / 1¾ pt cold water. Bring quickly to the boil and skim. Add the coarsely chopped onions, the carrots, leeks, celery, garlic cloves and the bouquet garni. Cover and simmer this stock for 1 hour.

Meanwhile, put the button onions into a pan large enough to hold them in a single layer and pour over just enough water to cover them. Add 15 g / ½ oz butter, ½ teaspoon salt and ½ teaspoon sugar. Press a tight-fitting piece of greaseproof paper firmly over the onions. Bring to the boil, then simmer over very low heat until the water has evaporated and the onions are cooked and shiny but not brown. Keep warm.

In a small saucepan, put the lemon juice, a pinch of salt, 1 tablespoon butter and 100 ml / 4 fl oz water. Bring to the boil, then put in the mushrooms. Cover and cook for 5 minutes. Transfer the mushrooms and juices to a small bowl and keep warm.

Pass the chicken stock through a fine conical sieve and keep it very hot. Heat 50 g / 2 oz butter in a large pan. When very hot, but not brown, put in the chicken pieces, skin-side down and quickly seal them without browning. Add the finely chopped onion and sweat for 3 minutes. Sift the flour over the chicken pieces and stir gently with a large spoon. Pour over 1 L / 1¾ pint of the boiling hot stock and mix thoroughly to make a smooth sauce. Bring to the boil, add the pinch of cloves and check the seasoning. Simmer for about 25 minutes.

With a slotted spoon, take the chicken pieces out of the sauce and put them in a deep, warmed serving dish. Whisk the cream into the sauce and reduce it for about 5 minutes, stirring from time to time. If the sauce is too thick, thin it with the mushroom cooking juice. Pass the sauce through a fine conical sieve over the chicken pieces. Arrange the button onions and the drained mushrooms on top of the chicken.
Serve with Rice Pilaf (page 55), ommitting the diced red pepper and artichokes.

Making sauce

Riz Pilaf au Poivron Rouge et aux Artichauts

RICE PILAF WITH RED PEPPER AND ARTICHOKES

200 g / 7 oz long grain or basmati rice
50 g / 2 oz butter
50 g / 2 oz onion, very finely chopped
500 ml / 18 fl oz boiling Chicken stock (page 49)
1 teaspoon coarse sea salt
65 g / 2½ oz red pepper, skinned, deseeded and
finely diced
2 artichoke bottoms (see *Pavé de Loup Barigoule*,
page 110), cooked, trimmed and finely diced
1 small Bouquet garni (page 11)

Preheat the oven to 200°C / 400°F / gas 6.

*Melt the butter in a casserole. Add the onion and cook
for about 5 minutes, until transparent. Put in the rice,
stirring to coat it well with the butter. Pour in the hot
chicken stock and bring quickly to the boil. Add the salt
and bouquet garni, cover with buttered greaseproof
paper, transfer to the preheated oven and cook for
about 20 minutes, until the rice is tender and fluffy.
Discard the bouquet garni and gently mix in the finely
diced red pepper and artichoke.*

Since Reffye was an *école hôtelière*, the school restaurant was quite important. It was patronised by the teaching staff, but it was also used every day by the people who worked in the local government offices in the other parts of the Reffye buildings, and members of the public could eat there too. The customers knew we were still students, and they were usually very patient and understanding. The teachers, on the other hand, were much more vigilant. Once a waiter had to bring two cups of coffee to the same table, one of which was iced and the other hot. The cups were identical in appearance, and when he got to the table, he had completely forgotten which was which. Without hesitation he thrust his finger into one of the cups to test the temperature. The customers raised their eyebrows and said nothing, but Mademoiselle Victor had also noticed the incident, and Julien got a dreadful dressing-down in front of everyone, and for once he was quite taken aback. We began to cook for the restaurant in our second year. Each threesome of students cooked for two tables; but we operated a simple sort of *partie* system since one group did the soup, another the fish, another the meat, and so on. In that way it was not too hectic and nobody got into a panic; and each day the groups took their turn at doing different dishes. I remember once, when I was in the meat group, doing a *navarin d'agneau*, a lamb stew supposedly devised by a French naval cook to celebrate the victory of Navarino in 1827, though some say that the name derives rather more prosaically from the word *navet*, the French for turnip. In the aftermath of the battle the cook was probably unable to lay his hands on the brown stock and various other refinements which, since then, have raised the dish to the status of a culinary classic, and which, on the day I am thinking of, earned my group a special compliment. Another popular dish in the restaurant was a traditional *poulet en cocotte*, braised chicken with vegetables.

NAVARIN PRINTANIER

•

LAMB STEW WITH SPRING VEGETABLES

•

700 g / 1½ lb boneless lean shoulder of lamb, cut
into 2.5 cm / 1 in cubes
50 ml / 2 fl oz vegetable oil
75 g / 3 oz onions, finely diced
30 g / 1 oz plain flour
250 ml / 9 oz dry white wine
2 garlic cloves, crushed and chopped
1 Bouquet garni (page 11)
1 heaped tablespoon tomato purée
coarse salt and freshly ground pepper

Spring vegetable garnish:
120 g / 4 oz button onions
250 g / 9 oz baby carrots
250 g / 9 oz baby turnips
50 g / 2 oz fresh peas
50 g / 2 oz fine French beans
75 g / 3 oz butter

•

Preheat the oven to 200°C / 400°F / gas 6.
*Heat the oil in a large casserole. Season the meat and
brown it evenly in the oil. Strain off the fat and put the
meat back in the pan. Add the onions, cook for a few
minutes until soft and transparent. Then sprinkle over
the flour and stir to coat the meat well. Cook for about
5 minutes, then add 1 L / 1¾ pt cold water and the
white wine, stirring continuously. Put in the garlic and
bouquet garni and stir in the tomato purée. Season
with coarse salt and pepper. Bring to the boil, cover
and cook in the oven for about 45 minutes. Take the
pieces of meat out, pass the sauce through a fine sieve,
then pour it back over the meat. Keep warm while you
make the spring vegetable garnish.*

*Put the onions, carrots and turnips in separate small
pans, cover with water and add 30 g / 1 oz butter to
each vegetable. Season with salt. Cover, bring to the
boil and simmer until just cooked. Drain and keep
warm.*

*Bring 2 pans of salted water to the boil, drop the peas
into one and the beans into the other and cook quickly
until just tender. Drain.*

*Place the meat in the centre of each plate and cover
with sauce. Arrange the spring vegetables around the
edge.*

POULET EN COCOTTE
GRAND'MÈRE

•

BRAISED CHICKEN WITH VEGETABLES

•

1 × 2 kg / 4 ½ lb corn-fed chicken, cut into 4 pieces
100 ml / 4 lf oz extra virgin olive oil
12 baby new potatoes, peeled
2 artichoke bottoms (see *Pavé de Loup Barigoule*,
page 110), cut into 8
1 fennel bulb, trimmed and cut into 8
200 g / 7 oz courgettes, thickly sliced
400 g / 14 oz tomatoes, blanched, skinned,
deseeded and chopped
12 small mushrooms, trimmed
100 g / 3½ oz broad beans
12 mange-tout, trimmed
500 ml / 18 fl oz Chicken stock (page 49)
6 garlic cloves, peeled but left whole
2 sprigs of thyme
2 bay leaves
100 g / 3½ oz butter
salt and freshly ground pepper

•

*Season the chicken joints with salt and pepper. Heat
the olive oil in a large casserole. When very hot, brown
the chicken pieces in it quickly. Take them out with a
slotted spoon and lightly brown the potatoes, artichokes
and onions in the same casserole for 3 minutes. Put the
chicken pieces back in, with 250 ml / 9 fl oz chicken
stock. Cover and cook for 10 minutes.*

Add the other vegetables and herbs, season and pour in the rest of the stock. Cover and cook for another 15 minutes. Discard the thyme and bay leaves. Take the chicken out with a slotted spoon, place on a warm serving dish and arrange the vegetables around it. Whisk the butter into the sauce and pour it over the chicken and vegetables. (Photograph p. 58)

The students had their meals in the ordinary school dining-room. I only had lunch at Reffye, but I remember how good the food was. Some of it was cooked by first-year students, but most was prepared in a special kitchen with its own chef and a group of assistant cooks, mostly advanced students. One of the dining-room dishes which everyone enjoyed was fritters of calf's brains; we used to eat both halves of a brain at each helping, and they really were delicious.

PÂTE À FRIRE POUR BEIGNETS

FRITTER BATTER

120 g / 4 oz flour, sifted
2 tablespoons butter, melted and cooled
200 ml / 7 fl oz tepid water
2 egg whites, at room temperature
salt

Put the flour in a small bowl and make a well in the centre. Add a pinch of salt, then pour in the melted butter and tepid water. Mix quickly and avoid overworking this batter, or it will not cling properly to the foods dipped into it. Stiffly beat the egg whites, fold into the batter and use immediately.

BEIGNETS DE CERVELLE DE VEAU À LA ORLY

CALF'S BRAIN FRITTERS

2 calves' brains, membranes and sinews removed
1 teaspoon wine vinegar
1 bay leaf
100 g / 3½ oz seasoned flour
Fritter batter (see previous column)
2 L / 3½ pt vegetable oil, for deep-frying
salt and freshly ground pepper

Put the brains in a large bowl, cover with cold water and 2 teaspoons salt. Refrigerate for 1 hour. Rinse under cold running water and place in a pan. Cover with cold water and add the vinegar, 1 teaspoon salt, ¼ teaspoon pepper and the bay leaf. Bring to the boil, take the pan off the heat and leave the brains to cool in the stock.

Drain and cut into bite-size pieces. Roll in the seasoned flour and dip them into the batter. Heat the oil to 180°C / 350°F and drop the fritters into the hot oil, one at a time. Leave the fritters to rise to the surface before touching them, then turn them over and fry until golden all over. Take them out with a slotted spoon and lay them on several layers of kitchen towels to drain. Keep the cooked fritters warm in a low oven while you fry the rest. Arrange on a warm dish and serve.

Poulet en Cocotte Grand'mère (recipe p. 56)

During the Reffye holidays, we were sent out to do periods of practical training, called *stages*, during which we worked as waiters or cooks at local hotels and restaurants. It was a regular practice at all catering colleges; but though it gave us some valuable work experience, it also exposed us to a good deal of unscrupulous exploitation. We were only about sixteen or seventeen years old; we were paid very little; and it was sometimes very hard to know how to defend ourselves from overbearing *patrons* and managers. My very first *stage* was a Christmas one. I was sent to a hotel near Bagnères-de-Bigorre, together with nine other boys from Reffye and about the same number from the catering college at Toulouse. We were all employed as waiters in the restaurant, and everything went well until after the *réveillon*, the great midnight dinner on Christmas Eve. It had been clearly agreed with the management that those of us who served at the *réveillon*, and who would therefore be working until about five o'clock in the morning, could sleep late on Christmas Day, and need not report downstairs until midday. Instead, we were awoken unceremoniously at nine and told to go down and wash up all the dirty glasses left after the *réveillon* the night before. There were hundreds and hundreds of them. The agreement had been broken and we were furious. Sullenly we set to work, but the more glasses we washed, the more our fury grew until, somehow or other, one of the glasses got broken. Mysteriously, a few minutes later, this was followed by another, and then by another and by another until, quite soon, a considerable proportion of the hotel's stock of wine glasses lay in the rubbish bin. The manager was outraged and threatened to dock our pay, which was absolutely minimal, and probably totalled no more than the equivalent of about twenty pounds for two weeks' hard work. Our anger merely increased; and when we were told, on top of everything else, that we would be given no time to eat a proper meal before starting to serve Christmas lunch, it finally boiled over. We all threw down our dishcloths, refused to go on working, and went up to our rooms. We were on strike. In the evening the manager came up, and told us that if we did not work we would get no supper. We stayed where we were; we did not work; and we had no supper. Next morning we were very hungry but still unabashed. The manager came to see us again. We told him we would come down to work if he would apologise to us. He refused. The *maître d'hôtel* came to see us. Even the chef came to see us. But it was all to no avail; we still refused to work, and the manager still refused to apologise or to feed us. By the afternoon we were so famished that we all packed our suitcases and marched ostentatiously out of the hotel, our heads high and our stomachs empty, and made our way down to the town in search of something to eat and the first train home. It was a Christmas I shall never forget.

I did another holiday job at Argelès-Gazost. The hotel was run by a somewhat unusual couple, since the *patronne* was about seventy and her husband half that age. She was the one who owned the business and looked after all the money, and she was very strict about allowing her husband to have any. We used to hear him begging her for some pocket money; and each time he went to the market, he had to account to her for everything he had spent and give her back the change. Regularly, every three weeks, the *patronne* spent seven entire days in bed as part of her health cure. She covered herself with slices of raw meat and cucumber, saw and spoke to nobody, and drank nothing but orange juice. I remember it well because I was a cook there and, every morning of her week off, it was I who had to cut the escalopes of veal and slice the cucumbers.

The *stage* I liked most was a summer placement in 1965 at the Chalet Hotel at Cauterets, an important Pyreneean spa nestling in the bottom of a deep valley. It was known to the Romans, described by Marguerite de Navarre, and much visited by Chateaubriand, de Vigny and George Sand. It is an attractive town, full of steep little streets and unexpected corners; but it also contains the Boulevard Latapie-Flurin, a short, incongruously pompous thoroughfare of tall, balconied buildings and impressive facades. Here you will find the two gigantic caryatids which guard the entrance to the once-famous Hôtel de l'Angleterre; and facing you, at the very end of the street, the rather humbler Chalet Hotel, now turned into flats. It was a squat, white, broad-gabled building, decidedly Swiss in appearance, and, as you walked towards it, it seemed to crouch down as though overawed by the surrounding snowy peaks. It was quite an active hotel, however, whose forty rooms, were full all through the summer with people who were doing the cure. It was like a family *pension*. At lunch and dinner, all the guests came into the dining-room at the same time, sat at the same tables, and ate exactly the same menu. I was again working as a waiter, and this *pension* system meant that I had to do a good deal of rather quick walking twice each day. Normally this would not have worried me, but it so happened that the shoes I had brought with me turned out to be far too small with the result that very soon my feet became painfully swollen. The manager noticed I was limping, and was very kind and understanding, and gave me a lot of good advice about what I should do to get my feet back to normal again. I think he must once have been a waiter himself and may have suffered from the same trouble.

Another activity at Cauterets was the helicopter departure from the hotel grounds of hunting-parties going up into the mountains to shoot *isard*, the Pyreneean chamois. The hunting season is a very short one; and I remember the triumph which everybody felt, hunters, cooks and waiters alike, when a party returned with a chamois which was eventually cooked in the hotel kitchen. It was an old-fashioned, rather ramshackle kitchen with a large and ancient black cast-iron cooker in the middle of it. There was a brass rail running all round and brass handles to the oven doors. It was a handsome thing, but it threw out a lot of heat and it made for a lot of work because it was coal-burning. Every night the cooks had to empty its grates and clean them; and every morning one of them had to get up early to light it and get it hot enough to start cooking.

Eventually my course at Reffye came to an end, and I obtained the certificate which qualified me professionally as cook and waiter. On the morning of the examination we all assembled in our classrooms and each cookery student was given the menu of a three-course meal which he would have to prepare. Every menu was different, of course, and you were given half an hour to plan how you would do it. In that time you had to write out a concise, detailed recipe for each dish you were going to cook; then you had to write a *feuille d'économat*, a list of every single ingredient you would need; and finally you had to go the storeroom and collect the ingredients on your list. You were not allowed to go back there, so if you had forgotten anything, it was too late. Back at your table, sitting in front of your stove and surrounded by all your ingredients, you were now completely alone with no one to help you. You had three hours in which to cook the meal, which must be served punctually at a precise time in the school restaurant, where it would be carefully tasted by the examiners. The first course of my own exam menu was a quiche, and the second a *tournedos à l'archiduc*, one of the old, classical recipes whose very name makes you think of the *Belle Epoque* and the world of the palace hotels.

TOURNEDOS À L'ARCHIDUC

•

4 × 150 g / 5 oz tournedos
80 g / 3 oz butter
1 calf's brain, poached and cut into 8
20 g / ¾ oz truffles, sliced
100 ml / 4 fl oz dry sherry
100 ml / 4 fl oz Veal stock (page 49)
100 ml / 4 fl oz double cream
a pinch of paprika
Fritter batter (page 57)
oil for deep-frying
salt and freshly ground pepper

•

Season the tournedos and pan-fry them in 60 g / 2 oz butter. When cooked to your liking, keep in a warm place. Discard the fat from the pan, pour in the sherry and reduce by half. Add the veal stock and reduce by one-third. Add the cream and reduce until the sauce coats the back of a spoon. Check the seasoning and add the truffle slices to the sauce. Arrange the tournedos in a warm dish, pour the sauce on top and place the truffle slices on the meat.

Heat the deep-frying oil to 180°C / 350°F. Roll the pieces of brain in the batter and deep-fry them in the hot oil. Season. Arrange the brain around the dish and serve with Pommes dauphine *(see below).*

POMMES DAUPHINE

•

DAUPHINE POTATOES

•

250 g / 9 oz potatoes, peeled and cut in large pieces
2 L / 3½ pt vegetable oil, for deep-frying
½ quantity uncooked Choux paste (page 42)
a pinch of ground nutmeg
1 teaspoon coarse salt
fine salt

•

Put the potato pieces in a saucepan and cover with cold water. Add the coarse salt. Cover the pan and cook until the potatoes are tender. Drain them in a colander immediately. Place in a small roasting pan and warm in a slow oven for a few minutes to get rid of any excess water. Push the dried potatoes through a sieve into a bowl, mix in the choux pastry and season with fine salt and nutmeg.

Heat the vegetable oil to 180°C / 350°F.

Using a spoon, shape the pommes dauphine *into walnut-sized pieces. Drop them one at a time into the hot oil and leave them to rise to the surface before touching them. Turn them over and fry until golden brown all over. Take the potatoes out with a slotted spoon and lay them on several thicknesses of kitchen paper to drain. Arrange on a warm serving dish and serve immediately.*

For the dessert course I was very lucky because I just had to make some pancakes, which was not hard to do, though, of course, they had to be cooked to perfection and be ready on the dot. I could well have been set something like a *bavarois* which is much more difficult. The cookery test was my principal exam as cooking was my main subject; the waiter's exam, which I took the following day, serving the food cooked by the other examinees whose main subject had been the *salle*, was much less arduous. Early in the morning we all assembled in the restaurant, where each of us was allotted a *rang* of three completely bare tables. We were told how many people were going to sit at them, and were given until lunchtime to prepare the tables and lay them. The laying had to be faultless; and everything from tablecloths, napkins and flowers to serving tables, wine, cutlery and glasses, had to be organised in exactly the right way and in the right position. At one o'clock the examiners walked into the restaurant, and our efforts were duly judged and criticized. We then had to serve a four-course meal without any mistakes or accidents.

Looking back at it now, the whole examination seems to have been very easy, of course, but at the time it struck me as being quite a searching test. When the results were finally published, and I knew I had passed, I was overjoyed.

Gruss aus Strassburg

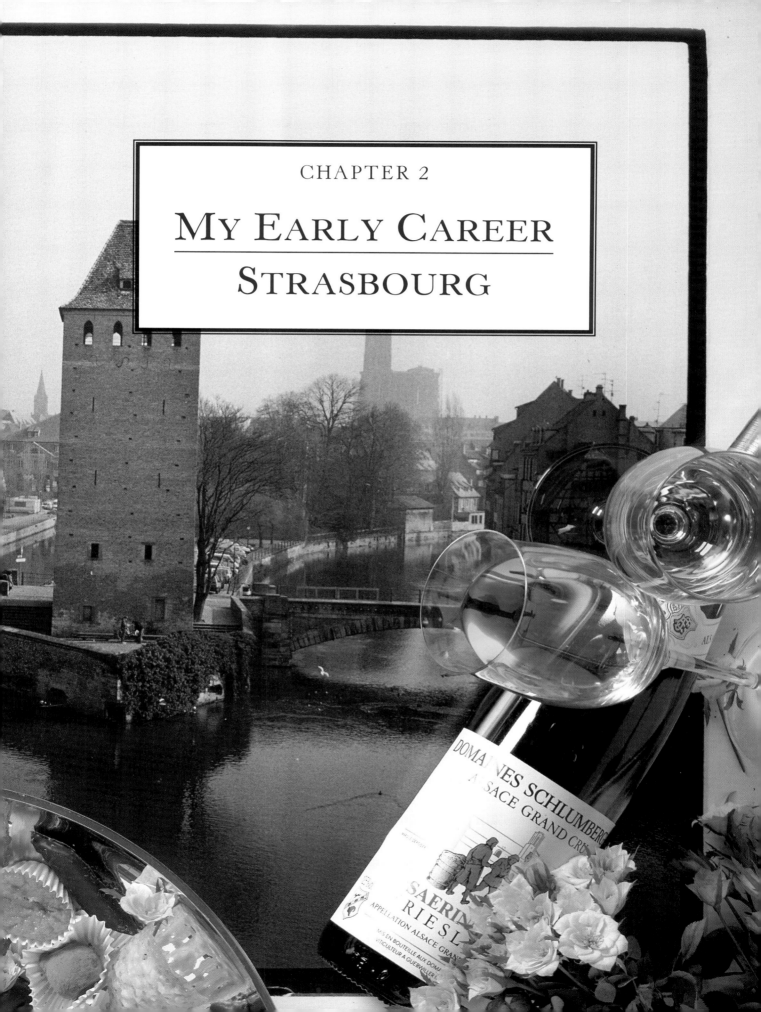

CHAPTER 2
MY EARLY CAREER
STRASBOURG

In June 1966 I started my first full-time job as a commis cook in the kitchen of a large and prestigious restaurant in Strasbourg. This was a good placement which the catering college had found for me. The restaurant was called the Aubette, had two stars in the Michelin guide, and it was considered something of a privilege to be sent there. It meant that Mademoiselle Victor regarded you as being one of her better and more promising pupils. Strasbourg and Tarbes lay in diametrically opposite corners of France with some five hundred miles between them; but this hardly worried me, even though I had never before travelled so far from home. Of course we had been taught at school about Alsace and the old city of Strasbourg; about 1870 and the Prussians, and the old songs, and storks and *choucroute* and all that sort of thing, but I never thought that I would one day go there myself. Strasbourg was also the place where my grandfather had been stationed during the war; and his happy memories of a city consisting almost entirely of warm, cosy bars and surrounded by a countryside teeming with game and wild mushrooms were not only typical of his own private vision of paradise, they were just about the only thing I had ever heard about the capital of Alsace which actually made it seem real.

I was not alone. There was one other cook with me, whom I had known at Reffye, Julien. He, like me, had been selected for a job at the Aubette; although, as it turned out, he did not stay there long, and after he left I never saw him again. We decided to take the night train from Tarbes, travelling via Toulouse, Marseilles, Arles and Lyons. It seemed more exciting and adventurous than taking the usual day train via Paris. Well settled into our second class corner seats, which in those days were a good deal harder than they are now, and with our suitcases firmly stowed on the racks above our heads, we peered into the evening gloom as the train pulled out of Tarbes. It was already dark, and beneath the yellow glare of the street lights of the Avenue Maréchal Joffre we had one final glimpse of the Reffye gates and the long facade of the school looming behind them.

We must both have been silently wondering about the future. I had known Julien by sight at Reffye, but he had never been a close friend, and was virtually a stranger to me. As the lights of Tarbes disappeared and the train plunged on into the blackness of the open country, I remember feeling confident that I was going to do well in my chosen trade, that one day I would be successful; but I was not going to worry about that just yet. My immediate wish was to be free from school and to enjoy myself. The rest would come later.

We changed trains at Lyons where there was just time for a steak and *pomme frites* and a bottle of red wine; then finally, at about eight in the morning, we arrived at Strasbourg. The restaurant where we were to work was not too far from the station, so we at once set off, lugging our suitcases and not knowing at all what to expect. It turned out to be even larger than we had imagined, and the kitchen clearly was going to be an extremely busy one. We were directed to the office of the *chef de cuisine*, who looked at us briefly, grunted, and told us to go and find somewhere to live, then to report back at once to start work. Nowadays when a young cook arrives at a good class restaurant straight from college, accommodation is usually arranged for him in advance, but twenty-five years ago things were rather different. You were left to look after yourself and to find your own lodgings, and nobody went out of their way to help you. In the end it was a *plongeur*, a lean, pale, tousle-headed man wearing a long leather apron buckled round him like a piece of armour, who came to our aid. He was scrubbing away at a huge copper casserole, using, I remember, the traditional mixture of lemon juice, flour and sand, which is recommended in the old cookery books, and which, incidentally, we still use at La Tante Claire. He had a great tub of this next to the sink, and the lemon skins immersed in the white paste made the mixture look like some delicious, expensive dessert. The *plongeur* stopped his hard work for a moment to tell us of an address where we would almost certainly find rooms. We set off again with our suitcases, and I remember hearing one of the *chefs de partie* calling out to us not to be too long because there was already plenty of work waiting for us.

When we saw the place where we were to live, we stopped and looked at it in complete silence. I think it was the saddest building I have ever seen. It was five stories high, blackish-grey in colour, with rows of small, shabby windows which extended all the way down one side of the narrow street. If the outside made you think of a prison, the inside was even worse. The rooms were just like cells. They were minute, all exactly the same size, and each contained a chair, a small cupboard, and a narrow bed which folded up against the wall during the day, because once you put it down there was hardly any space left in which to move about. There was no water in the rooms, and in order to wash or shave you had to go outside into the passage where there was a row of cracked, dirty basins fitted with just a cold tap. To get any warm water you had to be first in the queue for the showers which opened off another part of the passage. The place was run like an army barracks, though in some ways it was even stricter. In the army you cannot be given notice until your time is finished, and even if they put you in detention, you know they still have to feed you and shelter you. At the Strasbourg *pension* you were turned straight out into the street at the least murmur of a complaint or even a request. The bespectacled old harridan with a red wig, who lurked in the dark little office near the entrance, only consented to speak to you when you were paying her. At other times she regarded even a simple '*bonjour*' with deep suspicion.

Julien was completely cowed by the heartless inhumanity of the *pension*, and perhaps it was this which soon induced him to disappear from Strasbourg. I myself soon got used to the place, especially when I became accustomed to the work I was doing and began to enjoy it. The restaurant was in the Place Kléber, the city's largest square, which lay to the north-west of the cathedral and the old town. In those days it was still paved with cobblestones; one-way traffic roared and hooted it way round the statue of the eponymous Napoleonic general, and on the north side it swept past the long, classical facade of an elegant building known as the Aubette. This had been built in the eighteenth century, but it was damaged during the bombardment of 1870, then painstakingly re-built by the Germans after the annexation of Alsace. The restaurant occupied the three lower floors of the right hand wing of the building, and actually consisted of three separate establishments all run by the same owner. First there was a big brasserie which occuped the middle of the ground floor and which could seat about a hundred and fifty people, though in summer the tables spilled out on to the pavement and the number of customers was even higher. To the left of this was the high class rôtisserie which had won the Aubette's two Michelin stars. One of its specialities was salmon cooked in champagne, a dish which, with one or two variations, I featured on the early Tante Claire menus.

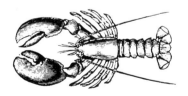

Escalope de Saumon au Champagne

SALMON FILLETS COOKED WITH CHAMPAGNE

4 × 150 g / 5 oz thin salmon escalopes
75 g / 3 oz butter
30 g / 1 oz shallots, finely chopped
300 ml / ½ pt champagne
12 button mushrooms, trimmed
150 ml / 5 fl oz double cream
12 baby new potatoes, cooked, lightly buttered and
kept warm
1 tablespoon finely snipped chives
salt and white pepper

Preheat the oven to 170°C / 325°F / gas 3.

Season the salmon fillets with salt and pepper. Smear the bottom of a flameproof dish with 30 g / 1 oz butter. Sprinkle over the chopped shallots and put the salmon fillets on top. Pour over the champagne and add the mushrooms. Bring to a simmer, cover with a piece of buttered greaseproof paper and cook in the preheated oven for about 8 minutes, until you can insert a larding needle into the fish with no resistance. Arrange the fish on a warm serving plate. Cover with the greaseproof paper and keep warm.

Reduce the cooking juices to 50 ml / 2 fl oz. Add the cream and reduce by three-quarters. Whisk in the remaining butter. Pass the sauce through a fine sieve and keep warm. Place the salmon fillets on warm serving plates. Arrange 3 mushrooms and 3 baby potatoes on each plate and pour the sauce around. Sprinkle with the chopped chives.

On the far right of the building there was a café and snack bar with which I never really had any contact. Although later on I worked in the special ground floor kitchen of the more expensive *haute cuisine* restaurant, which seated about sixty people, I first started in the big upstairs kitchen which cooked the food for the brasserie. It occupied most of the mezzanine floor which ran down the whole length of the building, and during the service periods it was a hive of activity and animation. Despite all the complicated interweavings of the work of the different *parties*, and the clash of temperaments and personalities, I do not remember a single serious or violent fight. The *chef de cuisine* was a local man in his mid-forties, who ran the kitchen very well indeed. Everyone worked in a quiet, disciplined way; and the chef was always quick to notice if any cook was cutting corners. He never wasted words but he somehow managed to be aware of everything that was going on. I have always remembered him, and I think that in many ways he has been a model I have tried to emulate. He was not very impressive to look at, however. He was short and fat, rather bald, and he had a large, very bushy moustache which seemed much too large for his face. He spent the morning doing his paper work in a little office with a panelled mahogany door and a large window through which he could look out into the main part of the kitchen; but as soon as the really busy part of the work started, at mid-day or in the evening, he would emerge from his office to supervise the cooks and to check every dish before it was carried away by a waiter.

The brasserie kitchen at the Aubette was the largest kitchen I have ever worked in. In all there were about forty cooks, not counting the washers-up and kitchen porters who were there to clean and carry. It was ideal for me, and I gained a lot of good experience there. The kitchen premises consisted of four main interconnecting rooms situated immediately above the restaurant. The rooms were not very high, but they were well lit during the daytime by the row of rather grandly arched windows which ran down the outer wall and looked out over the Place Kléber. The largest room was that immediately in front of the chef's office, and in the centre stood the massive, free-standing, cast-iron cooker, the *fourneau*, which must have measured about ten feet by twenty, and had eight pairs of ovens and a whole variety of hotplates and cooking rings. It was coal-burning and very hot. Even the brass rail which ran all round it got hot in places, and you had to be careful where you touched it. The cooker was lit every morning, and its ashes were cleaned out every night by the kitchen porters. Otherwise the work of the kitchen was organized according to the traditional *partie* system, consisting of groups of five or six cooks, each headed by their own *chef de partie* and doing just one particular category of the cooking. It is a system which goes right back to the early history of French classical cooking; and around the turn of the century, it was reckoned that there should be sixteen *parties* working together in a really big kitchen. At the Aubette we had about nine. The huge *fourneau* was divided up into four imaginary quarters each of which was the province of a different *partie*, who had the exclusive use of the ovens and hotplates near to them. The section of the cooker closest to the chef's office belonged to the fish cooks; behind them was their big wooden working-table, and beyond that the doors of the refrigerator where all the fish was kept. Next to them stood the sauce chefs who were primarily responsible for all the sauces which were served separately in sauce boats; on their hotplate there simmered perpetually the big, rectangular, copper bain-marie which warmed and cossetted the saucepans of *espagnole*, *velouté*, *allemande* and other basic sauces. Another important job of the sauce chefs was the production of the all-important stocks – veal, chicken and so on. They also made all the dishes in which meat or poultry is cooked in a juice or a sauce, such as *daubes*, *civets*, *blanquettes* and the *pot-au-feu*. Game dishes were always very important in Alsace, and I remember how good the Aubette terrines of venison and game tasted.

Terrine de Chevreuil

— • —

VENISON TERRINE

— • —

1 kg / 2¼ lb shoulder of venison
800 g / 1¾ lb hand and belly of pork
50 g / 2 oz pistachios, skinned
120 g / 4 oz shallots, chopped and sweated in butter
50 ml / 2 fl oz brandy
50 ml / 2 fl oz madeira
20 g / ¾ oz salt
a large pinch of freshly ground pepper
25 ml / 1 fl oz double cream
6 egg yolks
1 thin slice of pork back fat, about 10 × 25 cm /
4 × 10 in
2 bay leaves
2 sprigs of thyme

— • —

Preheat the oven to 180°C / 350°F / gas 4.

Finely mince the venison and pork and place in an electric mixer fitted with a dough hook. Add all the other ingredients except the back fat and herbs and mix thoroughly. Place the mixture in a terrine dish, cover with the slice of back fat with the bay leaves and thyme on the top. Place in a bain-marie – half-filled with hot water and cook in the oven for 2 hours.

Let the terrine rest for 1 hour, then place a light weight on top. When cold, chill in the fridge for 24 hours.

BLANQUETTE DE VEAU À L'ANCIENNE

•

BLANQUETTE OF VEAL

800 g / 1 ¾ lb boned shoulder of veal, cut into
50 g / 2 oz chunks
1.5 L / 2½ pt Chicken stock (page 49)
coarse salt
3 onions, peeled, one stuck with a clove
3 carrots, kept whole
3 leeks, split lengthways and washed thoroughly
thoroughly
1 small celery stalk
2 garlic cloves, peeled
1 small Bouquet garni (page 11)
150 g / 5 oz button onions
100 g / 3½ oz butter
a pinch of sugar
juice of ¼ lemon
200 g / 7 oz button mushrooms
40 g / 1½ oz flour
1 egg yolk
10 ml / 4 fl oz double cream
salt and white pepper

•

Cover the veal with cold water, bring to the boil and blanch for 2 minutes. Refresh under cold running water and drain thoroughly in a colander. Put the meat into a large saucepan, add the stock, some coarse salt, the larger onions, carrots, leeks, celery, garlic and the bouquet garni. Bring to the boil and skim the surface. Cover and simmer for 1 hour.

Put the button onions into a pan large enough to hold them in a single layer. Add just enough water to cover them, 30 g / 1 oz butter and a good pinch each of salt and sugar. Cover tightly with foil so that the liquid does not evaporate too quickly. Simmer slowly until all the water has evaporated. Make sure the onions do not brown, as they are traditionally kept white in this recipe. Keep warm.

Combine the lemon juice, a pinch of salt, 25 g / 1 oz butter and 75 ml / 3 fl oz water in a small saucepan. Bring to the boil, add the mushrooms and cover. Cook gently for about 10 minutes, then take off the heat and keep warm.

Melt 40 g / 1½ oz butter in a saucepan, then mix in the flour to make a smooth roux. Cook slowly for 3-4 minutes, until the roux becomes frothy. Leave in the pan until ready to use.

Transfer the meat from the stock to a deep dish, using a slotted spoon. Drain the mushrooms, reserving the cooking juices and put them and the button onions with the meat. Keep warm. Pass the stock through a fine sieve into a clean saucepan and bring back to the boil. Pour it over the cold roux and whisk thoroughly until perfectly smooth. If the sauce seems too thick, add the cooking juices from the mushrooms. Bring to the boil and simmer for 10 minutes, stirring constantly.

In a large bowl, whisk together the egg yolk and the cream. Little by little, pour on the sauce, whisking continuously. Check the seasoning. Pass the sauce through a fine sieve over the meat, mushrooms, and onions and mix gently. Reheat without boiling if necessary.

TERRINE DE GIBIER À PLUMES

•

TERRINE OF GAME BIRDS

•

2 pheasants, plucked and cleaned
2 wild duck, plucked and cleaned
120 ml / 4½ fl oz madeira
120 ml / 4½ fl oz port
80 ml / 3 fl oz armagnac
120 g / 4 oz shallots, very finely chopped
400 g / 14 oz chicken livers, trimmed, sinews and
yellow gall stains removed
350 g / 12 oz butter, melted and cooled
3 eggs
225 g / 8 oz Parma ham, thinly sliced
4 sprigs of thyme
2 bay leaves
salt and freshly ground pepper

•

The night before you are going to make the terrine, bone the pheasants and wild duck. Keep the 8 breasts whole and reserve all the flesh from the thighs. Put the breasts, the thigh meat and the chicken livers in a large container. Pour over the madeira, port and amagnac. Add the shallots, garlic, thyme and the bay leaves and mix well with your hands. Cover with clingfilm and leave to marinate in a cool place (outside or in a cool larder, but not in the fridge) for 12 hours.

Preheat the oven to 170°C / 325° F / gas 3. Line a 28 × 11 × 8.5 cm / 11 × 4½ × 3½ in loaf tin or terrine dish first with overhanging foil, then with the Parma ham slices and refrigerate.

Chop the pheasant and duck thigh meat and the livers. Place in a food processor with the alcohol marinade, and purée until smooth. With the motor running, add the eggs one by one, making sure each is well incorporated before adding the next. Pour in the cold melted butter in a steady trickle, keeping the motor running, until the mixture is completely homogeneous.

Season well and taste the raw mixture to check the seasoning, as it is difficult to rectify it after cooking.

Wrap the pheasant and duck breasts individually in a slice of ham. Pour half the puréed meat mixture into the foil-and-ham-lined tin. Lay a pheasant breast next to a duck breast in each end of the tin, and spread over the remaining puréed meat mixture. Arrange the 4 remaining breasts in the same way, pushing down gently to make sure the terrine is compact. Cover with the rest of the ham slices. Fold over the foil. Place the terrine in a deep roasting pan, fill the pan with hot water to come halfway up the sides of the terrine, and cook for 1 hour 40 minutes in the preheated oven. Allow to cool and refrigerate overnight.

Cut the terrine into 1 cm / ½ in slices. Serve with a chicory salad, tossed with a little walnut oil and vinegar. Add salt to taste and sprinkle with chopped walnuts. (Photograph p. 70)

The *partie* which occupied the corner of the cooker opposite the *sauciers*, or sauce chefs, was that of the *entremettiers*, named after the cooks who prepared the *entremets*, the dishes which were arranged round and between the roasts of the second service of the formal banquets of the *ancien régime*. At the Aubette they were responsible for all the vegetables, for the garnishes that accompany meat dishes, and for the soups. In Alsace, the *entremettiers* make the *choucroute*, and they also traditionally do all the egg dishes and cook the omelettes. The lakes and ponds of Alsace abound in frogs, and frog dishes are another local favourite. The *sauciers* made a very good dish of frogs' legs cooked with riesling, cream and herbs; and I remember the *entremettiers* making generous quantities of a frog soup which always sold well, and which was not unlike the one I sometimes do at La Tante Claire.

Terrine de Gibier à Plumes (recipe p. 69)

SOUPE DE GRENOUILLES AU CRESSON

•

FROGS' LEGS SOUP WITH WATERCRESS

•

24 frogs' legs
150 ml / 5 fl oz dry white wine
20 g / ¾ oz shallots, thinly sliced
1 sprig of thyme
1 sprig of parsley
1 bay leaf
20 g / ¾ oz butter
500 ml / 18 fl oz light Chicken stock (page 49)
3 bunches of watercress, washed and trimmed
50 ml / 2 fl oz double cream
salt and white pepper

•

Sweat the frogs' legs gently with the wine, shallots, thyme, parsley, bay leaf and butter until cooked, about 4 minutes, depending on the size of the legs. Take the legs out of the stock and debone them with your fingers. Set the meat aside.

Return the cooking liquid to the heat and add the chicken stock and watercress. Bring to a simmer and cook for 10 minutes. Purée the soup in a blender, then pour through a sieve. Check the seasoning and reheat the soup if necessary. Put the frogs' legs into a tureen, pour in the soup and stir in the cream.

The fourth and last corner of the *fourneau* was occupied by the *rôtisseurs*, who prepared all meat dishes which had to be either roasted, grilled or fried. The roasting was done in the ovens allotted to them, and they used the top of the cooker for frying. A long grill, which was always glowing with red-hot charcoal, was built into the wall near the big stove, and on it were cooked the steaks and chops and other cuts of meat requiring the addition of vegetables or a special garnish which would have to be provided by the neighbouring *entremettiers*. Sometimes, when the sauce was an integral part of a meat dish rather than an added extra, as in the case of a *tournedos à la béarnaise*, it would be made by the *rôtisseurs* and not by the *sauciers*. Though the *chef rôtisseur* worked in the kitchen in the same way as the other *chefs de partie*, watching over his oven and the meat sizzling on the hot charcoal and keeping an eye on his cooks, he was the only chef whose domain extended out of the kitchen and into the brasserie dining room. Here he was responsible for the great open grill with its ornate chimney-piece and its imposing hood, which was built against one of the end walls and always inspired much interest and admiration amongst the customers. This grill was wood-burning; and there was fire not only under the horizontal bars at the bottom but also at the back behind sturdy upright bars which faced you like those of a manger. The all-round heat which resulted from this meant that food could be roasted on spits as well as grilled over the bars at the bottom. As the *chef rôtisseur* had to be in the kitchen, he used to put his best *commis* in charge of the dining-room grill; a job which necessitated a great deal of care, experience and skill. People sitting at their tables were protected from the fire by a thick glass screen; but the *rôtisseur*, working in the intense heat on the other side, was sometimes, especially in summer, almost as well grilled as the steaks and chickens. The basting, the turning speed of the different spits, and their proximity to the fire all needed continual checking and adjusting; and meantime the cook had to remember and satisfy ceaseless orders from a hundred and fifty diners called out to him by the waiters. Above all, he must never allow anything to burn, for if that had ever happened, the whole restaurant would have been filled with the smell and the smoke. As Brillat-Savarin so aptly put it: '*On devient cuisinier, mais on naît rôtisseur*' (one can learn to be a cook, but you must be born a grill chef.) Besides the usual chickens and rabbits we regularly spit-roasted woodcocks, hares, ducks, partridges, and all sorts of other game. At La Tante Claire we have no open fire and all our game and ducks are roasted in the oven.

PIGEONNEAU RÔTI AUX POMMES FRITES

• —

ROAST PIGEON WITH FRENCH FRIED POTATOES

• —

4 young pigeons
150 ml / 5 fl oz vegetable oil
30 g / 1 oz shallots, finely chopped
16 neat potato sticks 6 × 1 cm / 2½ × ½ in, patted
dry
700 ml / 1¼ pt vegetable oil, for deep-frying
2 tablespoons brandy
200 ml / 7 fl oz Chicken stock (page 49)
2 sprigs of thyme
50 g / 2 oz butter, at room temperature
4 cherry tomatoes
12 button mushrooms
4 smoked bacon rashers
4 quail's eggs
salt and freshly ground pepper

— •——

Preheat the oven to 230°C / 450°F / gas 8.
Heat 2 tablespoons vegetable oil in a roasting pan.
When very hot, quickly brown the seasoned pigeons on
both sides, then roast in the oven for 12 minutes. The
flesh should remain very pink and juicy.

While the pigeons are roasting, start cooking the french
fries. Heat the oil to 200°C / 395°F then plunge in the
potato sticks for just long enough to cook them without
browning. Drain and set aside on several layers of
absorbent kitchen paper. Keep the frying oil hot.

Remove the pigeons from the oven and keep them
warm. Lower the oven temperature to 130°C / 250°F /
gas ½. Discard the cooking fat from the roasting pan.
Put in the shallots and sweat for 1-2 minutes until soft.
Lay the pigeons on top and flame with the brandy.
Remove the pigeons, cover with foil and keep warm.
Add the chicken stock and thyme to the roasting pan,
and deglaze well. Reduce by two-thirds, whisk in the
butter, season and pass the sauce through a fine sieve.
Keep warm.

Place the tomatoes in a lightly buttered ovenproof dish
and heat in the warm oven for 10 minutes. Put the
french fries back into the hot oil and brown them.
Drain, sprinkle with salt and place in the warm oven.

Heat 2 tablespoons oil in a saucepan and quickly sauté
the mushrooms. Season and keep warm in the oven.
Heat another 2 tablespoons oil in a frying pan. When
very hot, fry the bacon rashers until just golden and
crisp. Discard the fat and keep the bacon in the oven.

While the bacon is frying, quickly fry the quail's eggs
in hot oil. Season with salt and pepper, and keep in the
oven while you carve the pigeons. Arrange 2 thighs and
2 breasts on each serving plate. Surround them with a
quail's egg, a bacon rasher, a cherry tomato, 3 button
mushrooms and 4 french fries, neatly piled in pairs.
Pour the sauce over the pigeon and serve immediately.

DOS DE PETITS LAPINS FARCIS AU FOIE GRAS, AUX ARTICHAUTS ET TRUFFES

• —

*SADDLES OF YOUNG RABBIT STUFFED WITH FOIE
GRAS, ARTICHOKES AND TRUFFLES*

— • —

4 saddles of rabbit 300 g / 11 oz each, boned
4 teaspoons armagnac
1 truffle, diced
200 g / 7 oz foie gras, diced
2 artichoke bottoms (see *Pavé de Loup Barigoule*,
page 110), cooked and diced
3 tablespoons vegetable oil
200 ml / 7 fl oz Chicken stock (page 49)
a knob of butter
salt and freshly ground pepper

—— • ——

Preheat the oven to 220°C / 425°F / gas 7.
Mix the armagnac with the diced truffle, foie gras and

artichoke bottoms. Divide this mixture between the 4 saddles. Pull the overhanging skin over the stuffing and secure each end with string. Season.

Heat the oil over a high flame in a cast iron roasting dish until very hot. Put in the saddles and seal quickly until just golden. Transfer to the oven and roast for 20 minutes. Remove the rabbit from the pan and keep it warm while you make the sauce.

Skim off all the fat from the roasting dish, add the chicken stock, bring to the boil and reduce for 2 minutes. Season and whisk in the butter.
Remove the string from the rabbit and slice each saddle into six pieces. Serve on warm plates, pouring the sauce around the edge.

———————————

The glowing grill was the only direct contact the brasserie customers had with the work of the cooks. Because the kitchen was on another floor and there was no lift or hoist, the chief link between it and the restaurant was a constant traffic of tray-carrying waiters pushing and thrusting their way up and down a steep wooden staircase. At the top of the stairs, during the *service*, they always found a kitchen seething with hectic activity. Clutching their trays and their *bons de commande*, the little slips of paper on which they had scribbled down the customers' orders, the waiters entered the kitchen near the chef's office, and stood beside the hot counter while the *aboyeur* called out the contents of the *bons* to the kitchen. In the world of cooks the *aboyeur* has always been something of an archetypal figure. Nowadays he usually talks into a microphone, and is often more of an announcer than a real 'barker'; but in the past he had no mechanical aid, and much depended on the strength of his personality and on the power and quality of his voice. At the Aubette it was the *sous-chef*, the second in command, who acted as *aboyeur*. He was a robust, thick-set man who wore a white hat which was halfway in height between the caps of the cooks and the tall *toque* of the *chef de cuisine*. His fine voice was exceptionally clear and precise, and it was easily heard above all the scraping and clattering. He had to scrutinize the waiters' *bons*, and then he would start to cry out something like: *'Ça marche, deux soupes, quatre choucroutes!'* This would be answered by a yell of: *'Oui! Oui, ça marche!'* from the *chef entremettier*. If the *aboyeur* called out: *'Ça marche, un gratin et un filet de porc!'* there would be two answering shouts of *'Oui!'* – one from the *chef rôtisseur* for the meat, and another from the *chef entremettier* for the vegetables and the garnish. And so the voices would go on, all through the cooking like a sort of litany. Normally the *aboyeur* never had to repeat himself; and the chefs of each *partie* remembered all the orders without ever writing anything down on paper. Everybody had to learn to concentrate hard on this particular work, just as the waiters had to calculate how much cooking time to allow between ordering a particular dish and coming up to the kitchen to collect it.

FILETS DE PORC AUX PETITS OIGNONS

FILLETS OF PORK WITH BABY ONIONS

4 pork fillets, about 250 g / 9 oz each, trimmed
120 g / 4 oz butter
50 ml / 2 fl oz vegetable oil
300 g / 11 oz baby onions, peeled
200 ml / 7 fl oz Chicken stock (page 49)
juice of ½ lemon, strained
1 tablespoon finely chopped parsley
salt and freshly ground pepper

Preheat the oven to 200°C / 400°F / gas 6.

Heat 25 g / 1 oz butter with the vegetable oil in a cast-iron pan. When very hot, brown the seasoned pork fillets evenly. Transfer to the oven and cook for 12 minutes, basting the meat twice during cooking. Take the cooked fillets out of the pan, put them into a warm serving dish, cover tightly with foil and leave to rest in a warm place.

Tip off the fat from the pan. Put in the onions and brown them over medium heat, stirring frequently, to loosen the cooking juices. Then add 100 ml / 4 fl oz water, the stock and 20 g / ¾ oz butter and cook over low heat for about 20 minutes. With a slotted spoon, take the onions out of the pan and put them on top of the pork fillets. Cover tightly with the foil.

Reduce the cooking stock from the onions by half and set aside. In a small saucepan, cook the remaining 80 g / 3 oz butter until golden. Take off the heat and add the lemon juice and parsley. Mix this butter with the cooking stock, check the seasoning and simmer for 2 minutes. Pour over the meat and serve.

GRATIN DE POMMES DE TERRE ET DE POIREAUX

POTATO AND LEEK GRATIN

450 g / 1 lb potatoes, very thinly sliced
¾ teaspoon salt
150 g / 5 oz white of leeks, trimmed, chopped and washed
300 ml / ½ pint milk
300 ml / ½ pint double cream

Preheat the oven to 180°C / 350°F / gas 4.

Sprinkle the salt over the potato slices and mix well with your hands. Leave to rest for 10 minutes, then squeeze out the excess water. Boil the milk and cream, add the potato and leek and mix well. Transfer to a small ovenproof dish and bake in the oven for 40 minutes.

Of the other rooms which opened off the main kitchen, the first was the *plonge*. This was equipped with deep sinks running all the way down one of its walls, and, opposite them, deep wooden shelves for storage purposes. The *plonge* was divided into two principal parts: one in which all the copper cooking utensils, saucepans and casseroles were washed and cleaned and stored, and another where all the plates, glasses and cutlery of the restaurant were washed. The *plongeurs* always wore their long leather aprons; but though they were the lowest in grade of all the *parties* who worked in the kitchen, they usually seemed to be good-natured and hard working people, and their relationship with the cooks was normally a very happy one. On the opposite side of the kitchen to the *plonge* was the large pastry area where the *pâtissiers* worked away in cool, silent peace, like scholars in a library.

PAVÉ AUX CHOCOLATS

· — ·

*CREAMY WHITE AND BITTER CHOCOLATE
MOUSSE*

· — ·

Sponge layer:
3 eggs, separated
75 g / 3 oz icing sugar, sifted
50 g / 2 oz cocoa powder, sifted, plus extra for
dusting

Chocolate cream:
100 g / 3½ oz bitter chocolate, finely chopped
50 ml / 2 fl oz strong black coffee
2 egg yolks
200 ml / 7 fl oz cream, lightly whipped
100 g / 3½ oz white chocolate, finely chopped
1 gelatine leaf softened in 25 ml / 1 fl oz cold water,
then heated gently to dissolve.
Coffee *Crème Anglaise* (page 41), for serving

· — ·

Preheat the oven to 180°C / 350°F / gas 4.

*To make the sponge: Lightly butter a shallow 33 × 23
× 2 cm / 13 × 9 × 1 in baking tray, line it with a
sheet of greaseproof paper, and lightly butter and flour
the paper, shaking off the excess flour.*

*Whisk the egg yolks with 50 g / 2 oz icing sugar until
thick and ribbon-like. Whisk the egg whites until
frothy adding the remaining icing sugar gradually and
whisking until stiff. Mix the whites into the yolk
mixture, and fold in the cocoa powder. Spread the
mixture evenly on the baking tray and bake for about
12 minutes, or until a skewer inserted in the middle
comes out clean. Turn out the cake onto a clean tea
towel; remove the paper and fold the ends of the tea
towel over the sponge. Leave to cool.*

*Using a 20 cm / 8 in round cake tin, cut out a circle
from the sponge. Line the cake tin with clingfilm; then
put in the sponge.*

*To make the chocolate creams: Melt the bitter chocolate
with the coffee over a double boiler. Cool slightly then
mix in the egg yolks and fold in half the lightly-
whipped cream. Pour into the cake tin over the
chocolate sponge and refrigerate. Melt the white
chocolate. Whisk in the dissolved gelatine and fold in
the remaining whipped cream. Pour this white
chocolate cream over the bitter chocolate cream and
refrigerate until set. Invert the mousse onto a plate and
peel off the clingfilm. Dust with cocoa powder and serve
with coffee* crème anglaise. *(Photograph p. 78)*

===

TUILES AUX AMANDES

· — ·

THIN ALMOND BISCUITS

· — ·

200 g / 7 oz icing sugar, sifted
75 g / 3 oz plain flour, sifted
200 g / 7 oz flaked almonds
120 g / 4 oz butter, plus extra for greasing
100 ml / 4 fl oz freshly squeezed orange juice

· — ·

Preheat the oven to 200°C / 400°F / gas mark 6.

*Melt the butter and set aside to cool. In a bowl, mix
together the icing sugar, flour and almonds. Make a
well in the centre, pour in the melted butter and orange
juice and mix thoroughly. Lightly butter an oven tray.
Put small teaspoons of the* tuile *mixture on the tray,
flattening them out with a fork dipped in water. Bake
until golden brown, about 7 minutes.*

*Have ready a rolling pin and another similar-shaped
implements, such as empty milk bottles. When the
tuiles are ready, remove each one quickly with a palette
knife and drape over the rolling pin. The tuiles will
take their traditional curved shape and harden as they
cool down.*

Next to the *pâtisserie* was the larder, which was also a separate room with a door opening into the kitchen near the chef's office. In my memories of the Aubette, the larder looms rather large because it was the place where I first started working.

It was here that all the restaurant's raw ingredients (with the exception of the fish which went straight to the *poissonniers*) were first delivered, then prepared for the stove or the oven and kept cool until they were required by the cooks. The larder was an excellent vantage point for a beginner, and while I was there I picked up a very good notion of the varied interaction of supply and demand which are such a basic aspect of the work in any kitchen.

The chef at the Aubette, was about fifty, and his very first job, after leaving college had been as a commis waiter at the Savoy Hotel in London. That was in 1938; and the stories he used to tell us about working in the big hotels of those days were like a miniature archive of pre-war catering history. The novice commis waiters were on the lowest rung of the whole professional ladder; and as a result they were ground between the two millstones of the *chefs de rang* (senior waiters) upstairs in the grill room and the *chefs de partie* and the other cooks in the kitchen downstairs. The chef remembered being particularly in awe of the bullying *aboyeur*, an irascible, unpredictable old Breton, who wore a flat bonnet-like cap and was swathed in a strange, white cloak which was a cross between a Roman toga and a priest's chasuble. He would call out the orders in a rasping, stentorian voice; and woe betide any waiter who came to collect his fish dishes too early or too late after taking away his soups, or any cook who was too slow in producing them. The *aboyeur* had a long stick, and he would bring it down with a sharp crack over the offender's knuckles.

It was a time-honoured tradition for hotel waiters to regard all the food which was left in the dish after the customers had been served as being their own special perks, but officially this was not allowed, and it was regarded as pilfering. At the end of the day nevertheless, they filled the pockets of their black trousers and waiter's jacket with chicken legs and *pommes parisiennes* and fragile portions of sole Walewska, and set off hopefully for home and a good supper. On the way to the staff entrance, however, they passed through the long, badly-lit stone corridors of the Savoy Hotel basement. Here the *chefs de rang*, hiding like policeman operating a speed trap, would suddenly spring out of the shadows and clap their hands against the waiters' pockets with enough strength to squash any packet of food they might be hiding there, and to make a real mess of their jacket and trousers. It meant that next day the waiters had to take their clothes to be cleaned, and to pay for it with their own money; if they were caught twice in the same week, it meant losing a sizeable amount of their wage. Another thing which the larder chef remembered was the appearance of the Savoy's senior *plongeurs*, the men who looked after all the hotel silver, and who were almost as dignified and as impressive as the maître d'hôtel. When they were walking down the Strand, they wore dark suits and ties and bowler hats; they had a favourite pub in Covent Garden where they used to meet for a drink and where no mere commis waiter ever dared to show his face.

The butcher was the oldest man in the Aubette's kitchen and was by far the slowest worker, but for all that, everybody liked him. His name was Charles. He had once owned his own butcher's shop, but it had failed and he had had to take a job at the Aubette. Nobody ever grumbled about him or told him off because the older hands in the kitchen were fond of him and remembered his shop well. Apparently his principal aim as a retail butcher had been to sell the best possible meat at the lowest possible price. Inevitably he had ended up with a shopful of very happy customers and a business with an inexorably mounting deficit. Even as an old man at the Aubette, he was still generous in his own fashion. He had built a secret still in the cellar of his house, and he spent all his free time there, distilling illegal schnapps, which I think he made from fermented potatoes. He was never without a bottle or two of the stuff, and his great joy was to invite you to have a glass. It was real firewater, which burnt the skin off your throat as it went down, and it had a kick like a mule. But we had to be very tactful about refusing a second glass, because it was all too easy to hurt Charles's feelings and to make him think that you were casting undeserved aspersions on his skills as a distiller.

The *garde-manger* was long and rather narrow. All down one wall you could see the doors of the refrigerators which were like little rooms into which you could actually walk. From hooks and rails hung carcasses of meat and rows of poultry and game; on the shelves were arranged items prepared and ready for the cooks; and in another area were all the fruit and vegetables. Back in the main room, beneath a long rail from which hung a bewildering profusion of Alsatian sausages and Ardennes hams, there was a table at which we worked to transform the raw materials into forms and shapes which could be immediately used. This meant peeling and cleaning all the vegetables and plucking, cleaning and trussing the poultry and game, while the butcher had to do the cutting, chopping and general preparation of all the meat. If the *chef entremettier* suddenly wanted a couple of partridges or the *chef-rôtisseur* called out for four tournedos and a *carré d'agneau*, we either had to have them ready and available on our shelves, or else produce them very quickly. We also made all the salads, though at that time these were nowhere near as varied or as imaginative as they are now. For example, though we prepared a good deal of game when it was in season, we never thought of making even the sort of simple game salad I prepare at La Tante Claire.

SALADE RETOUR DE CHASSE

—— • ——

GAME SALAD WITH WILD MUSHROOMS

—— • ——

1 cooked pheasant, or any game bird carved into thin slices
90 g / 3 oz French beans, cooked
Vinaigrette (page 25), made with walnut oil
12 walnuts, shelled
200 g / 7 oz cooked foie gras
30 g / 1 oz truffles, thinly sliced
100 g / 3½ oz girolles or chanterelles, cooked in butter

—— • ——

Dress the pheasant and beans with the walnut Vinaigrette. Place in the centre of a plate. Arrange all the remaining ingredients around the edge to make an attractive dish.

77

Pavé aux chocolats (recipe p. 75)

Sandre Rôti, Pâtes Fraîches à la Sauge et Coeurs d'Artichauts (recipe p. 83)

Another very important part of our work was the making or preparing of everything that would be eaten cold, with the exception, of course, of the desserts and the pastry which were made by the pâtissiers. In the traditional language of the kitchen, we were responsible for *le froid*. We cooked and prepared the fruit for the fruit pies, which we kept cool until the pâtissiers were ready to add the crusts. We made all the aspics and meat jellies, the cold hors d'oeuvre such as *aubergines à la grecque* and Russian salad, which in those days were still popular and important items, pushed round the brasserie on a burnished trolley. We made the cold sauces like mayonnaise and sauce tartare, plus all the galantines, pâtés and terrines. One of the culinary links between Alsace and Gascony which made me feel quite at home in Strasbourg when I first arrived there, was the Alsatian love of foie gras. There were differences, however, because the Alsace foie gras is made from goose livers and is always eaten cold, whereas in the south-west we eat a great deal of duck foie gras, and we love to eat it hot. At La Tante Claire, accordingly, my terrines are normally made from duck, though I like to combine the foie gras with other meats, such as calf's tongue.

TERRINE DE FOIE GRAS ET LANGUE DE VEAU

•

TERRINE OF FOIE GRAS AND CALVES' TONGUES

•

(Serves 8)

800 g / 1¾ lb foie gras
2 cooked calves' tongues
500 ml / 18 fl oz sweet white wine
salt and freshly ground pepper

•

Soak the foie gras in tepid water (less than 37°C / 98.6°F) for 3 hours and remove all the nerves and blood. Season with salt and pepper. Cut the tongues in half lengthways and use only the best part. In a terrine dish or loaf pan make layers of foie gras and tongue to give the terrine a marbled effect. Pour over the wine and cover with foil.

Preheat the oven to 200°C / 400°F / gas 6. Place the terrine in a bain-marie half filled with hot water, bring to the boil and place in the preheated oven. Immediately, switch off the oven and leave the terrine to cook for 40 minutes. Leave to cool. Place a small board on top with a 500 g / 1 lb weight on top, and refrigerate for at least 12 hours.

The *pâté de foie gras en croûte* is another Strasbourg speciality. It is said that, towards the end of the eighteenth century, the military governor of Alsace offered a superb *foie gras en croûte* to the king, Louis XVI, who so appreciated it that he rewarded the governor's cook with enough money for him to start his own pâtisserie in Strasbourg whence his pâtés and terrines carried the city's fame all over France. In my own kitchen I may be said to combine my fidelity to Gascony with a little bit of my memories of the Aubette because, in my duck *terrine en croûte*, I do sometimes include some goose liver, pork and veal.

Terrine de Canard en Croûte

•

DUCK AND PORT TERRINE EN CROÛTE

•

800 g / 1¾ lb duck meat, cut into chunks
700 g / 1½ lb hand and belly of pork, cut into
chunks
75 g / 3 oz veal, cut into chunks
75 g / 3 oz chicken livers, trimmed, sinews and
yellow gall stains removed
50 g / 2 oz pig's liver, trimmed, sinews removed
100 g / 3½ oz carrots, chopped
70 g / 3 oz onion, chopped
1 sprig of thyme
2 bay leaves
4 sprigs of parsley
2 tablespoons brandy
80 ml/ 3 fl oz madeira
80 ml / 3 fl oz dry white wine
butter for greasing
400 g / 14 oz Shortcrust pastry (page 41)
2 egg yolks
175 ml / 6 fl oz double cream
175 g / 6 oz raw or cooked foie gras, thinly sliced
50 g / 2 oz truffles, grated
30 g / 1 oz pistachios, skinned
30 g / 1 oz hazelnuts, skinned
150 g / 5 oz Puff pastry (page 42)
salt and freshly ground pepper

•

*Put all the meat except the foie gras in a large bowl.
Add the carrots, onion, thyme, bay leaves, parsley,
brandy, madeira and white wine and mix thoroughly
with your hands. Cover and refrigerate for 12 hours.*

*Grease a 2 kg / 4½ lb rectangular tin (about 27 × 10
× 9 cm / 10½ × 4 × 3½ in). Roll out the shortcrust
pastry thinly and use it to lin the tin. Refrigerate.*

Preheat the oven to 200°C / 400°F/ gas 6.

*Drain the meat in a colander, keeping the liquid.
Discard the vegetables and herbs. Mince the meat
finely. Add the egg yolks, cream, truffles, pistachios
and hazelnuts and season with salt and pepper.*

*Mix thoroughly with your hands. Check the seasoning
at this stage, as it is difficult to improve once the
terrine is cooked.*

*Spoon half of the meat mixture into the pastry-lined
tin. Lay the slices of foie gras on top, then spread over
the rest of the meat mixture. Roll out the puff pastry
very thinly and use it to cover the meat. Bake in the
oven for 1½ hours, leave to cool overnight and serve
cold.*

After I had been *commis garde-manger* for about
four months, it was decided that I should move
to another *partie*, and I became a fish cook. I
was now working in the midst of all the heat
and bustle of the main kitchen, at the corner of
the stove nearest the chef's office and the hot
counter at which the waiters collected their
orders. We were five fish cooks including the
chef de partie, and we were responsible for the
preparation of all the fish dishes, and for
making the fish fumet from the fish bones and
heads which trembled and bubbled nearby in a
great copper cauldron. Next to our working
table was the big refrigerator where early each
morning the day's supply of fish was delivered
and duly stored away. The first part of our
morning was spent in cleaning, washing,
filleting and generally preparing our 'catch' so
that everything was ready to be cooked as soon
as the heavy work started at lunchtime.

Traditional Alsatian cooking contains many
fish recipes. All of them, of course, are for
freshwater fish which have always been
plentiful in the numerous lakes and little rivers
and streams of the area. Carp, pike, perch and
trout, for example, are cooked in typical local
ways with riesling or beer. At the Aubette, carp
was a special favourite; and we used to fry it,
roast it in the oven, stuff it *à la juive*, or serve it

filleted and coated with a batter made from beer and flour. Inspired by my time in Alsace, I did a carp dish for some of the early menus at La Tante Claire, which was rather more Gascon than Alsatian, since it was cooked in red wine instead of riesling.

CARPE À LA BIÈRE

•

CARP BRAISED WITH BEER AND POACHED ROES

•

1 × 1 kg / 2¼ lb carp, scaled, cleaned and filleted
200 g / 7 oz carp roes
150 g / 5 oz onion, very thinly sliced
2 sprigs of thyme
1 small bay leaf
1 small celery stalk
5 peppercorns, coarsely crushed
1 clove
75 g / 3 oz plain gingerbread, cut into small dice
500 ml / 18 fl oz stout
juice of ½ lemon
30 g / 1 oz butter, at room temperature
salt and freshly ground pepper

•

*Preheat the oven to 180°C / 350°F / gas 4.
Melt 15 g / ½ oz butter in a large, deep roasting pan.
Sweat the onion until soft, then add the thyme, bay leaf, celery, peppercorns, clove and the diced gingerbread. Place the seasoned carp fillets on top, cover with the beer and cook in the oven for 10 minutes.*

Meanwhile heat a panful of salted water with the lemon juice to 80°C / 170°F. Poach the fish roes for 3 minutes, drain and keep warm.

Arrange the carp fillets on warm serving plates. Pass the cooking juices through a fine sieve into a small pan. Reheat gently, whisking in 15 g / ½ oz butter. Pour over the carp fillets and garnish with the poached roes.

CARPE AU VIN ROUGE

•

CARP IN RED WINE

•

1 × 2 kg / 2¼ lb carp, scaled and cleaned
160 g / 5½ oz butter
50 g / 2 oz carrots, sliced
50 g / 2 oz onions, sliced
1 bottle red wine
1 garlic clove, crushed
1 Bouquet garni (page 11)
20 button onions
a pinch of sugar
20 button mushrooms
salt and freshly ground pepper

•

Heat 40 g / 1½ oz butter in a pan large enough to hold the fish. Add the sliced carrots and onions and sweat gently for 10 minutes. Put the fish on top and add the wine, garlic, seasoning and bouquet garni. Cover the pan with a lid and simmer for 18 minutes. Pass the sauce through a sieve and incorporate 80 g / 3 oz butter.

Cook the button onions slowly in the remaining butter, adding a pinch of salt and sugar. When the onions are tender, add the mushrooms and cook for a few seconds. Place the fish in a dish. Arrange the garnish around the edge and pour over the sauce.

Another fish which was very common in Alsace, and which I often cook at the restaurant, is the zander, which I serve with my own freshly-made pasta, flavoured with sage, and garnished with artichoke hearts.

SANDRE RÔTI, PÂTES FRAÎCHES À LA SAUGE ET COEURS D'ARTICHAUTS

———— • ————

PAN-FRIED ZANDER WITH HOME-MADE SAGE-FLAVOURED NOODLES AND ARTICHOKES

———— • ————

4 zander fillets, 150 g / 5 oz each
100 g / 3½ oz flour
1 tablespoon coarsely ground black pepper
15 g / ½ oz shallots, very finely chopped
50 ml / 2 fl oz brandy
200 ml / 7 fl oz Veal stock (page 49)
4 sage leaves, very finely chopped
4 artichoke bottoms (see *Pavé de Loup Barigoule*, page 110), thinly sliced
50 ml / 2 fl oz vegetable oil
150 g / 5 oz butter
salt
300 g / 11 oz Home-made noodles (page 196), for serving.

———— • ————

Season the zander fillets with salt on both sides and roll them in the flour, then in the coarsely ground pepper. Heat the vegetable oil in a pan until very hot, then put in the fish fillets skin-side down and cook for 7 minutes. Turn over the fish and cook for another 3 minutes. Carefully lift the fish out of the pan, transfer it to a plate, cover with foil and keep warm.

Discard the cooking oil from the pan and put in 25 g / 1 oz butter. Sweat the chopped shallots for 1 minute. Pour in the veal stock and reduce by one-third. Check the seasoning and whisk in 40 g / 1½ oz butter. Pass the sauce through a fine sieve, cover and keep warm.

Melt 25 g / 1 oz butter in a pan and gently cook the artichokes until tender. Season with salt and set aside. Bring a pan of salted water to the boil. Cook the noodles until tender, drain and refresh under cold water. Melt 50 g / 2 oz butter ina pan, put in the noodles and reheat quickly adding the chopped sage.

Season with salt. Divide the noodles between the centre of four warmed serving plates. Place the fish fillets on the noodles and pour the sauce over. Arrange the artichokes around the fish and serve.
(*Photograph p. 79*)

══════════════

I have mentioned that salmon cooked in champagne was a speciality of the Aubette rôtisserie. Although neither champagne nor salmon is a typical product of Alsace, and the dish seems quite out of place in Strasbourg, its presence is not quite as extraordinary as you might think. Until well into the nineteenth century, before the general onset of industrialisation and pollution, salmon, coming up from the North Sea, were frequently found in the waters of the Rhine; and somewhere in the popular local imagination there is still an obscure corner in which salmon swim about in the guise of typical, well-established local fish. I always associate Strasbourg salmon with the Aubette's banqueting hall which filled most of the *piano nobile*, the floor immediately above the kitchen. The ceiling was very high, and the whole room was resplendent with gilt, neo-baroque embellishments, mirrors and chandeliers which dated from the Prussian reconstruction of the building after the 1870 bombardment. If required, the long tables could seat as many as fifteen hundred people, and an important banquet involved much special organising. Even a smaller banquet always meant a lot of work for the fish cooks and the *garde-manger* down below because the fish course nearly always consisted of salmon, and that meant not just a few fish, but sixty or seventy at least! Furthermore it was stipulated that every salmon should be decorated differently; this job took a long time, but it was quite fun. For each fish we would have to design new shapes and themes, make different flowers or leaves, and find new colours, mayonnaises and sauces.

Sometimes we would bone a salmon, poach it carefully in a court-bouillon, skin it, and then replace the skin with row upon row of artificial scales made from slices of courgette and cucumber which were given a touch of colour by the addition of little rounds of smoked salmon. The scales were attached to the fish with a mixture of gelatine and court-bouillon, and eventually it was served with three different sauces: a *sauce andalouse*, a courgette mousse, and an excellent cream sauce made with mustard and horseradish. At La Tante Claire my salmon dishes are usually more straightforward than this, though I do make one with wild mushrooms, which remind me of my grandfather's wartime mushroom hunts in the forests near Strasbourg.

PAUPIETTES DE SAUMON, CHAMPIGNONS DES BOIS

●

PAUPIETTES OF SALMON WITH WILD MUSHROOMS

●

4 × 100 g / 3½ oz salmon escalopes
250 g / 9 oz Salmon mousse (see Chicken mousse, page 45)
20 g / ¾ oz butter
200 g / 7 oz wild mushrooms
20 g / ¾ oz shallots
500 ml / 18 fl oz dry white wine
100 ml / 4 fl oz Chicken stock (page 49)
1 tablespoon chopped parsley
salt and freshly ground pepper

●

Place 60 g / 2 oz salmon mousse on each escalope. Roll and wrap in clingfilm to make neat paupiettes. Prepare a steamer, and steam the paupiettes for 12 minutes.

Heat the butter in a pan and cook the mushrooms until all their moisture has evaporated. Add the shallots and cook for 3 minutes. Deglaze with the wine, reduce it completely, then add the stock and parsley. Bring to the boil and season. Place the paupiettes on a plate, arrange the mushrooms around and pour over the sauce.

Nearly all of the Aubette's *chefs de partie* were slightly unusual. I particularly remember our *chef poissonnier*, for example. He was a small, bandy-legged man in his late twenties, and I think he was the ugliest person I have ever seen in my life. He had a low forehead, slightly heavy lips and huge, round, black eyes that protruded from his face like those of some tropical insect. His curious way of moving them around in circles while he was talking to you made him seem quite grotesque, but he personally thought himself extremely hand-some, and he used to tell us how irresistible he was to women. In reality, though he spent all his spare time trying to pick up girls, he never actually seemed to have much success. He would sit for hours in a bar until he found a girl alone at a table, then he would send the waiter over to offer her a drink. Usually, as soon as the girl saw the ugly creature who had made the offer, she left at once in horror; at least, that was what happened whenever, at the chef's own request, two other commis chefs and I sat in a corner of the café and watched. We always found the whole thing rather sad.

The Aubette closed every Monday, but our weekly holiday began effectively on the preceding Sunday evening. This was the *chef de cuisine*'s night off, and, in place of his normally quite strict control over everything we did, we found ourselves enjoying comparative freedom. Since there were usually very few customers on Sunday night, we had not too much work on our hands. It was the moment for the musical sauce chef to spring into action. He had been a drummer in a dance band before becoming a cook, and he would now jump up on one of the tables, hang a whole array of saucepans and casseroles from the waterpipes which ran round the kitchen, and start to beat out hectic, wild rhythms with an extraordinary assortment of knives, ladles, whisks and anything else he could get hold of. The effect was brilliant, and it was more than completed by a *plongeur* who could imitate the trumpet, a *commis rôtisseur* who was good at turning himself into a saxophone and an *entremettier* who could actually sing. In the end everybody joined in the singing and banging and stamping and dancing, until the waiters could only stand and stare at us in amazement. Nobody paid any attention to the orders, and one can but imagine the sort of complaints they were getting from the hungry customers downstairs in the brasserie.

We spent most Mondays walking round the old town of Strasbourg. I loved the narrow streets with their ancient, half-timbered houses, their high gables, and their red-tiled roofs. The admonishing, solitary finger of the cathedral tower presided over buildings and little squares whose names have always remained in my mind because of their curious connections with food. There was the Rue de l'Ail, for example, Garlic Street, the Vieux Marché aux Poissons, the Grande Boucherie and the Marché aux Cochons de Lait. The evenings we used to spend at La Petite France, a delightful old quarter of the city full of twisting alleys, old houses, and hidden, unexpected canals and waterways, softened by arching bridges and the tumbling branches of willow trees. There were also good little restaurants and bars, and you could drink beer and schnapps sitting at thick, wooden tables in shadowy, panelled *bierstuben*.

At Le Lièvre Amoureux there was a dance band which cannot have changed much since the 1930s, and which was almost as good as our own band on Sunday nights. The musicians were as old as our parents. They had large moustaches, and wore collars and ties and blue jackets with brass buttons. There was an accordion and a trumpet, and the drummer sat on a chair near his big drum and thumped away at it with an outsize, round-headed drumstick which he activated with a pedal. It was terribly old-fashioned, but somehow this was the secret of its charm; and, in any case, we liked the place because, unlike the *chef poissonnier*, we never had any difficulty in finding girls there. L'Ours Blanc was open all through the night, and at any hour you could eat a huge meal of *choucroute garnie* or sausages with *spätzle*, the local noodles, or a pork or hare stew followed by *kugelhopf*, the round, crown-like Alsatian cake with which we generally used

to drink a glass or two of the local gewürztraminer. I always enjoyed choucroute dishes. A love of cabbage is certainly something I have inherited from my Gascon background; and even now I often ponder over new ways of presenting or cooking it. Here, for example, is my variation on a traditional cabbage dish, and one of my Tante Claire dishes, in which I wrap a truffle in a humble cabbage leaf.

CHOU FRISÉ AU LARD FUMÉ

•

SAVOY CABBAGE WITH SMOKED BACON

•

1.5 kg / 3¼ lb savoy cabbage
50 ml / 2 fl oz vegetable oil
2 cloves garlic, crushed and very finely chopped
350 g / 12 oz smoked bacon rashers, halved
3 carrots, diced
200 g / 7 oz celeriac, peeled and diced
salt and freshly ground pepper

•

Discard the tough dark green outer cabbage leaves. Stack the leaves in threes and remove the large middle veins with a sharp knife. Chop coarsely. Heat half the oil in a large frying pan. Put the carrots and cook until tender, then stir in the garlic and cook for a few minutes, stirring continuously. Transfer the vegetables to a bowl, using a slotted spoon.

Fry the bacon in the same pan until brown and crisp, then lift it out with the slotted spoon and put with the carrot. Cook the celeriac in the bacon fat until lightly brown and tender and put with the carrots and bacon.

Add the remaining vegetable oil to the pan. When hot, put in the cabbage, season with salt and stir well so the cabbage does not burn. Cover with a tight-fitting lid and cook over high heat, shaking the pan briskly. The heat will make the cabbage shrink and lose volume. Cook until tender, then mix in the bacon and the other vegetables, check the seasoning and serve.

Truffes en Habit de Choux (recipe opposite)

TRUFFES EN HABIT DE CHOUX

—— • ——

TRUFFLES WRAPPED IN CABBAGE LEAVES

—— • ——

4 × 20 g / ¾ oz truffles
8 cabbage leaves
200 g / 7 oz Stuffing (see *Cou de Carnard farci*, page 28)
50 g / 2 oz butter
50 g / 2 oz carrots, finely chopped
50 g / 2 oz onions, finely chopped
100 ml / 4 fl oz madeira
200 ml / 7 fl oz Veal stock (page 49)
salt and freshly ground pepper

—— • ——

Preheat the oven to 200°C / 400°F / gas 6.

Blanch the cabbage leaves and refresh them. Lay the leaves flat on the table. Spread the stuffing on four of the leaves and wrap the truffles in the other four. Now wrap the wrapped truffles in the leaves spread with the stuffing. Set aside.

Heat 20 g / ¾ oz butter in a shallow pan, add the carrots and onions and sweat for 5 minutes. Add the madeira and bring to the boil. Pour in the veal stock. Put the little cabbage parcels into the pan, season and cover. Bake in an oven for 15 minutes.

Transfer the wrapped truffles to warm plates. Pass the sauce through a sieve into a saucepan. Bring to the boil and whisk in the remaining butter. Pour the sauce over the parcels and serve. (Photograph opposite)

Nearly all the cooks at the Aubette were native Alsatians who looked upon us French almost as foreigners. In the kitchen they talked to each other in the local patois which was a sort of German dialect. They made a great point of not letting us know what they were saying. Sometimes on Monday afternoons, we used to go out to villages in the country, and if we got lost and asked our way, people always replied in Alsatian and never in French; or they said nothing at all and simply walked away, an experience I found rather strange and disturbing. Though there were one or two boys in our little group who were Alsatian, and with whom we got on very well, the majority of us were French, some of us being cooks and others waiters.

Feelings of antagonism between cooks and waiters, between kitchen and dining room, have never really affected me, even though they are supposed to be traditional in the catering world. Cooks think that waiters, the *loufiats* as they used to call them from an old word for a server in a tavern, have an easier life than they do and that they do less work. They always look clean, unhurried and neatly dressed. When they arrive in the morning, they seem to have all the time in the world to hoover the restaurant, to spread the clean tablecloths, and to lay the tables. Then they dress up in their white jackets and black ties, and they move about the dining-room in quiet dignity, talking directly to the customers, chatting with them, advising them about food, receiving the compliments and getting all the tips. They work comfortably without any pressure. Of course this is a ridiculous generalisation, especially since, during the serving of a meal, the waiters are often under very great pressure indeed, but nevertheless it is the picture which the kitchen staff traditionally has of them. Cooks do not realise that whatever the waiter's panic or crisis may be, he must always appear pleasant and efficient and unruffled in the eyes of the customer at the table. In the kitchen, if something goes wrong, you can shout or push or rush from one side of the room to the other without anybody minding, but if a waiter started behaving like that in the middle of a dining room, it would be disastrous.

It is true, however, that cooks work under pressure the whole time. In the old days it was even worse. They worked downstairs in obscure basement kitchens; they had no contact at all with the glittering world of the dining-room above their heads; and they laboured long hours in continual dirt, noise and high temperatures. The old coal-burning *fourneaux* were always very hot; early flue-pipes used to leak so that many cooks died from the fumes before they were fifty; stoves had virtually no insulation; ventilation was poor and air-conditioning was non-existent. All of this led to cooks taking to drink while they worked and thus to getting a bad reputation on that account – particularly from waiters. I have never worked in a really rough kitchen, but I have always thought that a kitchen in which the cooks persistently behave badly must be one with a poor *chef de cuisine*. In the 1820s Antonin Carême described a large, well run kitchen as a place where everyone worked diligently and quietly, and where no voice was heard except the authoritative voice of the chef himself; and by the end of the century one of Escoffier's main concerns was to ameliorate working conditions in hotel and restaurant kitchens, and, in this way, to do all he could to improve the image which the cook had of himself and to curb his tendency towards drinking.

But old traditions and habits die hard. My wife Annie, who studied at the Bellegarde *école hôtelière* remembers with bitterness one fat, vulgar old chef who taught cookery there and who was hardly ever completely sober, even during lessons. I too remember that none of the *chefs de partie* at the Aubette was ever very far away from a bottle of red wine. The musical sauce chef, in particular, was always sipping a glass of cognac or calvados, which was easy for him as he always had open bottles in front of him, ready to be used in his sauces. These old-fashioned cooks were rarely obviously or violently drunk; they were never incapable of working, but it was easy to sense that they were completely macerated in alcohol; and by the time they retired they were often worn-out alcoholic wrecks. Today cooking is still thirsty work because you are always tasting sauces and seasonings and are probably taking in a good deal of salt as you do it. But at the same time there has been an immense improvement in kitchen conditions over the last twenty years and drinking habits have begun to change drastically. Cooks of the younger generation drink coca cola or fruit juice in the kitchen, and never touch any wine while they are working.

When I think of the *chefs de partie* and their surreptitious bottles of wine, I am reminded of the lugubrious features of the Aubette's storekeeper, the *économe*. This man never smiled. He wore a grey overall coat, and was the only person in the kitchen who was not dressed in white. He controlled the store cupboards with the assiduity and purpose of a born jailer and would allow nothing to be removed from them whose liberation could not be proved to be absolutely necessary. Every morning each *chef de partie* had to calculate what ingredients he would need during the day, and submit a *bon d'économat* to the storekeeper. If you thought you would use a litre of oil, you filled up a *bon* for it and you would be given this quantity from the stores. You had to say how much sugar you would need, how many bottles of wine, how much salt and pepper, and so on. It was essential to remember everything, because if you forgot anything and requested it in the middle of the day, the *économe* became furious. Even in the morning he was never exactly pleasant; he was always austere and miserable and only happy when you told him you did not require anything. Perhaps he assumed his misery in order to save himself work; but one day the management of the Aubette took a decision to curtail the habitual drinking of the cooks. This had unavoidable consequences for the *économe*, and must have plunged him into the very depths of depression. In order to try to curb the continual disappearance of wine, it was decided to offer all cooks a free daily ration of drink which, it was hoped, would satisfy them and stop them from wanting any more. It meant, however, that every morning the *économe* had to go round the kitchen, pushing a large drinks trolley, and ask everyone what they wanted. Then, grimly, he had to hand over their choice as a free gift. We were allowed to choose one bottle of wine, two bottles of beer or two bottles of lemonade. In 1966 I do not remember many people choosing the lemonade; but even a miraculous outbreak of teetotalism amongst the kitchen staff would not have made the *économe*'s job more cheerful.

The question of tips was another traditional bone of contention between kitchen and dining room. Not only did the cooks feel that the waiters worked less hard than they did, they also resented the fact that they earned more money. They were paid a better wage, and they got all the customers' tips as well. Nowadays tips are often shared amongst the whole staff, but at the time I started at the Aubette, such a thing was unheard of. Cooks felt that it was they who had toiled to produce the food which the customers made a special point of coming to eat; the waiters claimed that the customers would never stay to order it if they had not been charmingly received and welcomed.

Sometimes at the Aubette there were quarrels between individual cooks and waiters which seemed to go on for ever. I remember one in particular which made me realise that even if waiters are the first to receive all the customers' praises, they also have to cope with their complaints, which are not always unjustified. One evening a customer, who was a retired banker and quite well known at the restaurant, ordered a tournedos Rossini, and specified that he wanted it well cooked. When it was brought to his table, the steak was absolutely *saignant* and the centre had hardly been cooked at all. The banker was furious, told the waiter off, and made him take the plate back to the kitchen. Here the waiter, who was French, complained to the offending *commis rôtisseur*, who was Alsatian, and ordered him to grill another steak and judge the cooking correctly. The *rôtisseur* refused to do it; an argument began and finally the chef de cuisine

intervened, discovered what had happened, and gave the *rôtisseur* a good dressing down and told him to do another tournedos. The waiter now had the *commis rôtisseur* as an enemy for life, and the cook took his revenge in a time-honoured fashion. During the height of the *service*, when the kitchen was particularly busy, he began handing the waiter plates which looked quite innocent, but which were in fact so hot that they burnt his fingers as soon as he touched them. The subtlety of the *rôtisseur*'s revenge was that he did not give the waiter an overheated plate every time, so the poor man never knew for certain whether his fingers were going to be burnt or not, especially as each time the cook approached him, he gave him a confusingly mischievous smile. The waiter was always telling us that he had thought up a brilliant way of getting his own back on the *rôtisseur*, but I never did discover what it was or whether he acted upon it!

I had been in Strasbourg for about a year when I decided to leave the Aubette. It had been a very good first job for me and I had enjoyed myself, but I had learned all I could from that particular kitchen, and it was time for me to move on. From Alsace I went south again to Juan-les-Pins, on the Côte d'Azur between Nice and Cannes, where for almost another year I worked in the kitchen of the Grand Palace Hotel. It was here in 1968 that my cooking career was temporarily halted, for I received papers calling me up to do my national service in the armed forces. I was told to report immediately to Brest where I was to join the French navy.

CHAPTER 3
NATIONAL SERVICE
FROM BREST TO TOULON

It was in the late summer of 1968 that my national service papers arrived, and I had to say goodbye to Juan-les-Pins. I was sorry to go. The Palace Hotel was in a wonderful position facing the blue waters of the bay, and only the road and a garden of pine trees lay between it and the beach; and the weather was the weather of the south of France which has always suited me. The hotel was a large modern building with a magnificent open-air swimming pool, nearly a hundred rooms and a restaurant which served about eighty covers. Despite all that, however, the kitchen was comparatively small and difficult to work in. It was very long, quite narrow, rather like a corridor, and a total contrast to the big kitchen I had got so used to at the Aubette. The cooking stove was not free-standing as it had been at Strasbourg; it was installed against one wall, and the working tables and the refrigerators stood on the opposite side of the room against another wall. The staff consisted of a *chef de cuisine*, six cooks and a *pâtissier* who worked in a separate room opening out of the kitchen.

The *pâtissier* was one of the two people I remember best from Juan-les-Pins. He must have weighed about a hundred and forty kilos; he was the fattest man I have ever seen, but at the same time he was one of the friendliest and most generous, and I always got on well with him and liked him. He suffered a lot on account of his size. Even though he worked in a cool place away from the heat of the stove, he found the heatwaves of July and August almost unendurable, and sometimes he was so exhausted by them he could hardly move. In addition to suffering from the heat, he had, of course, to suffer all the teasing and the jokes of the other cooks. They were all much younger than he was, and because the *pâtissier* had difficulty in moving, they were always bullying him and hiding his tools and moulds so that he would have to walk about to find them. I did my best to defend him from the unkindness of the cooks, and on two occasions I nearly had a fight with the worst of them. Not surprisingly, perhaps, the *pâtissier* was a man who had lost

hope, though as far as his work was concerned he was an absolute master. He was up early every morning to make the croissants and the brioches for the hotel breakfasts, and during the day he made all the sweets and desserts for the restaurant. Everything he did was in the old classical style (he had no knowledge of *la nouvelle pâtisserie* which was then just on the verge of becoming popular), and he was a specialist in confections like *millefeuilles* and *chaussons* and *mirotons*. Whatever he made, he made with the skill of a real craftsman. He never told me much about his life, but somehow you knew he was a broken man. One day he confided to me that for years his one and only ambition had been to become an author and to write a book about pâtisserie: that he had spent all his spare time collecting, inventing, testing and writing out recipes; but that he knew he would never have the energy or the determination to bring the book to a conclusion or to get it published before he died. He showed me some of these recipes which were very good indeed and then, not long before I left to start my national service, he gave me the whole of his manuscript, and asked me to complete it one day and to get it published; to do, in his memory, the thing which he knew he was incapable of doing for himself. The manuscript is still in my possession, but I have never tried to publish it. The whole approach to restaurant *pâtisserie* has changed enormously since it was written; and, excellent as my friend's recipes were, some of them might seem a little old-fashioned today. Certainly at La Tante Claire, our approach to *pâtisserie* is more modern.

FEUILLETÉ TIÈDE AUX FRUITS DE SAISON

————— • —————

PUFF PASTRY CASE FILLED WITH CREAM AND WARM BERRIES IN THEIR COULIS

————— • —————

250 g / 9 oz Puff pastry (page 42)
1 egg yolk mixed with 1 teaspoon water, for eggwash
butter for greasing
300 g / 11 oz mixed summer berries (strawberries, blueberries, raspberries, red or blackcurrants etc)
150 ml / 5 fl oz Strawberry coulis (page 44)
100 ml / 4 fl oz whipping cream, lightly whipped
100 g / 3½ oz cold Crème patissière (page 43)
icing sugar, for dusting (optional)
Mint leaves, for garnish

————— • —————

Preheat the oven to 220°C / 425°F / gas 7.

Roll out the pastry to a thickness of 1 cm / ½ in and cut into four 4.5 cm / 2 in rectangles. With the back of a knife, mark out a smaller rectangle 1 cm / ½ in in from the edge of each case. Put the cases onto a lightly-greased baking tray and brush with eggwash, taking care not to drip any down the sides of the pastry, or it will not rise properly. Refrigerate for 30 minutes.

Brush the pastry cases lightly with eggwash again and bake in the oven for 20 minutes, or until well risen and golden brown. Allow to cool slightly, then with a sharp knife very gently cut away the marked-out rectangles and set them aside.

Remove all the soft inner layers of pastry from each case and discard them. Keep the pastry cases in a warm place. Mix together the pastry cream and the whipped cream and chill. Gently heat the berries in the coulis. Spoon some prepared cream into each case and top with the berries and coulis. Arrange more berries around the edge of the cases. If you like, sift some icing sugar over the pastry lids and place on top of each pastry case. Garnish with mint leaves.

My earliest memory of national service is one of noise, chaos and bewilderment outside the main railway station of the port of Brest. Crowds of boys and young men spilled out of trains, and petty officers shouted and gesticulated in the direction of large naval lorries drawn up in a long row to receive us and carry us off. I scrambled aboard one as best I could, and found myself wedged into a hot, tight, swaying crowd of recruits.

We were taken to some large barracks which had been rebuilt after the war, and there we stayed for about a month. Our heads were clipped and shaved until we were all as bald as convicts; we had medical examinations; we were fitted out with uniforms and other bits of naval equipment; and then we started on a long series of interviews with busy personnel managers who preferred to call themselves psychologists. They were supposed to be able to judge your character and to decide which branch of the service you were best fitted for. In the meantime, while they were making up their minds about this, we were put through a lot of physical training and drill. At last I was told that I had been selected as having great aptitude for becoming a radio operator, and I immediately started on an intensive course of lessons in Morse code; but whatever the psychologists may have thought, my own impression was that I had no aptitude whatsoever in this particular direction. However I was now starting to understand how you survived in the navy. Whatever you were told to do, you just did, and everyone was pleased. It was fatal to ask any questions about an order because that might just show you were a little more intelligent than the petty officer who had given you the order in the first place. So I just went on obediently tapping away at my Morse and trying to understand radar, things which really did not interest me in the least.

It was at Brest that I first walked in the streets wearing a sailor's uniform: blue bell-bottomed trousers and jumper with white lapels, a blue and white striped shirt and a round blue cap with a large red tuft on top of it. I felt as if I had been transformed into an entirely different being, and that there was a sort of special aura about me which set me quite apart from ordinary civilians. This feeling soon disappeared, of course, but for the moment it was rather pleasant. During the war Brest had been almost completely destroyed by bombing and, in comparison with the old town of Strasbourg, it was hard to find anything interesting or attractive. Only the castle at the mouth of the river and the seventeenth-century fortifications built round it by Vauban seemed to have survived more or less intact. Nevertheless, when we were allowed out of barracks in the evenings and at week-ends, I still managed to find a few restaurants serving local dishes which were quite new to me, and I had never been in Brittany before. I enjoyed sampling kidneys cooked in cider or with beetroot, and an apple eau-de-vie called *lambig*. Kidneys have since become a favourite dish of mine; I like to make them into a *fricassée* with sweetbreads and wild mushrooms.

ROGNONS DE VEAU AUX BETTERAVES

VEAL KIDNEYS WITH BEETROOT

2 veal kidneys, trimmed and chopped
1 tablespoon oil
75 g / 3 oz butter
4 shallots, finely chopped
2 × 150 g / 5 oz beetroot, cooked and sliced
100 ml / 4 fl oz double cream
4 tablespoons white wine
100 ml / 4 fl oz Veal stock (page 49)
2 tablespoons wholegrain mustard
salt and freshly ground pepper

Trim the kidneys, remove the sinews and core and chop the kidneys into pieces. Heat the oil and 25 g / 1 oz butter in a frying pan. When hot, add the kidneys, salt and pepper and cook to taste. Drain them in a sieve, discarding the cooking fat.

Using the same pan, add 25 g / 1 oz butter and the chopped shallots. Stir well and cook until soft. Add the white wine and beetroot, and reduce the wine completly. Pour in the stock and reduce it by half, then add the cream and cook until the sauce coats the back of a spoon. Take off the heat and whisk in the mustard and the remaining butter. Mix the sauce well with the kidneys and check the seasoning.

FRICASSÉE DE RIS ET ROGNONS DE VEAU AUX CHAMPIGNONS DES BOIS

FRICASSÉE OF VEAL KIDNEYS WITH WILD MUSHROOMS

1 veal kidney, cleaned and cut into slices 1 cm / ½ in
300 g / 11 oz veal sweetbreads, cleaned and cut into slices 1 cm / ½ in thick
100 g / 3½ oz butter
750 g / 1½ lb wild mushrooms (chanterelles, ceps, horns of plenty), cleaned
20 g / ¾ oz shallots, finely chopped
50 ml / 2 fl oz oil
1 tablespoon finely chopped parsley
salt and freshly ground pepper

Melt half the butter in a shallow pan. Add the mushrooms and cook until all their water evaporates. Add the shallots, season and keep hot.

Season the kidney and sweetbreads. Heat the oil in a frying pan until very hot and cook the kidneys very quickly for about 20 seconds on each side. Remove from the pan, put in the sweetbreads and cook them for about 2 minutes on each side. Discard the fat from the pan and deglaze with 100 ml / 4 fl oz water. Reduce by half and whisk in the rest of the butter. Check the seasoning. When everything is ready, mix it all together and arrange in the centre of each plate. Sprinkle with chopped parsley.

I think it was during my month at Brest that I first acquired my taste for shellfish. These, of course, constitute some of the most famous delicacies of the Breton coast, especially the lobsters and crayfish and the mussels and prawns. At the little restaurants near the barracks we used to get a whole variety of lobster dishes; we had them grilled, boiled, braised in cider, served with different sauces, sautéed with sorrel, and made into soups. These are all fine, traditional ways of cooking lobsters, simpler perhaps than some of our recipes at La Tante Claire, but good nevertheless. They inspired me to experiment with lobsters, and to evolve an excellent mousseline, which is served with a sauce made from the coral.

GÂTEAU DE HOMARD SAUCE CORAIL

•

LOBSTER MOUSSELINES WITH CORAL SAUCE

•

1 × 500 g / 18 oz female lobster, with her eggs
2 egg whites
300 ml / ½ pt double cream
3 tablespoons extra virgin olive oil
30 g / 1 oz shallots, finely chopped
2 tablespoons brandy
100 ml / 4 fl oz French dry vermouth
3 sprigs of tarragon
16 spinach leaves, trimmed
40 g / 1½ oz butter softened
salt and freshly ground pepper

•

Preheat the oven to 150°C / 300°F / gas 2. Bring 4 L / 7 pints water to the boil. Plunge in the lobster for 30 seconds, lift it out and place in a sink full of cold water until cooled.

Cut up the lobster, keeping all the flesh in one bowl and the eggs in another. Coarsely chop all the shells and carcass and set aside.

Following the instructions on page 46, prepare a Lobster mousse, using 200 ml / 7 fl oz cream. Refrigerate until ready to use.

Blanch the spinach leaves in boiling salted water, refresh in iced water and drain. Spread out the leaves in a single layer on a tea towel.

To make the sauce: Heat the olive oil in a shallow pan. When very hot, add the chopped lobster shells and carcass and cook until very red. Add the chopped shallots and sweat for 3 minutes. Flame with the brandy, then add the vermouth and mix in the remaining cream, lobster eggs and tarragon. Cook for 5 minutes over low heat, then season. Pass the sauce through a fine sieve into a small pan and reduce it to the consistency you prefer. Check the seasoning and keep warm.

Butter 4 dariole moulds and line them with the prepared spinach leaves, leaving an overhang. Spoon in the lobster mousse and fold over the overhanging spinach leaves.

Put the dariole moulds into a deep roasting pan and half-fill with boiling water, being careful not to splash any onto the darioles. Cover with lightly-buttered foil and bake in the oven for 8 minutes, or until set.

Unmould onto warm serving plates and pour the sauce around the mousselines. (Photograph p. 98)

Nor shall I easily forget the Brittany clams, eaten raw with a squeeze or two of lemon juice, or served with a cream sauce, or in the guise of wonderful *palourdes farcies*, stuffed with herbs and cooked in the oven. The locally-caught scallops were another variety of sea food which I often had at Brest and which I have liked ever since. They make an excellent start to a meal, and I love to think of new ways in which to serve them: flavoured with orange, for example, or presented on a bed of spinach with little pieces of diced bacon, or making a marriage with succulent oysters.

In another scallop recipe I detach them completely from their natural seaside setting and transport them in my imagination to inland Gascony where I cook them with a sweet white wine and a slice of hot, fresh foie gras such as my grandfather would have delighted in, though whether he would have appreciated the unfamiliar scallops quite as much is another question.

GRILLADE DE ST JACQUES AUX EPINARDS ET LARDONS

•

GRILLED SCALLOPS WITH SPINACH AND BACON

•

12 large scallops
4 tablespoons olive oil
20 g / ¾ oz shallots, finely chopped
150 g / 5 oz spinach, cooked and coarsely chopped
4 bacon rashers, cut into thin strips
500 ml / 18 fl oz double cream
salt and freshly ground pepper

•

Preheat the grill. Halve the scallops lengthways. Heat 1 tablespoon oil in a frying pan. Add the shallots and sweat for 1 minute. Add the spinach, season and heat through. Place on a plate and keep hot. Heat 1 tablespoon oil in the pan and fry the bacon until crispy. Transfer to a plate and keep hot.

Season the scallops and brush them with oil. Bring the cream to the boil and put in the spinach. Grill the scallops for 1 minute on each side. Put some spinach on each plate and place the scallops on top. Scatter over the bacon and serve immediately.

FEUILLETÉ D'HUÎTRES ET ST JACQUES AUX ASPERGES ET AUX NOIX

•

FEUILLETÉS OF OYSTERS AND SCALLOPS WITH ASPARAGUS AND WALNUTS

•

8 oysters, shelled, juices reserved
8 large scallops, shelled and halved lengthways
175 g / 6 oz butter
20 g / ¾ oz shallots, chopped
1 tablespoon snipped chives
2 tomatoes, blanched, skinned, deseeded and finely diced
4 cooked Puff pastry cases (page 93)
1 tablespoon double cream
8 cooked asparagus spears
50 g / 2 oz shelled walnuts
salt and freshly ground pepper

•

Put the oysters and their juice in a small pan and heat to 60°C / 140°F for about 2 minutes. Lift out the oysters with a slotted spoon and keep the juice in the pan. In a frying pan, heat 20 g / ¾ oz butter and pan-fry the scallops for 30 seconds on each side. Keep in a warm place with the oysters.

Add the shallots to the oyster juice and bring to the boil. Add the cream and beat in the remaining butter. Add the chives and tomatoes to the sauce.

Place a pastry case in the middle of each plate and put 2 hot asparagus in each case. Put some of the scallops and oysters and their sauce into the cases and spoon the rest around the edge. Sprinkle with the walnuts and serve immediately.

Escalope de Foie Gras et St Jacques au Sauternes

— • —

ESCALOPE OF FOIE GRAS AND SCALLOPS WITH SAUTERNES SAUCE

— • —

4 × 80 g / 3 oz slices of foie gras, 2.5 cm / 1 in thick
4 scallops, halved horizontally
16 carrots, cut into batons and cooked
350 ml / 12 fl oz Sauternes
50 g / 2 oz butter, softened
salt and freshly ground pepper

— • —

Season the foie gras and scallops. Put the foie gras in a cold, heavy frying pan and place over high heat. When the foie gras start to turn golden, reduce the heat to low. Leave the foie gras for 30 seconds, then turn it over. Cook for 1 minute, remove from the pan and keep in a warm place.

Put the scallops into the same pan and cook for 1 minute on each side, then place with the foie gras. Discard the fat, then pour half the wine into the pan. Reduce completely, then add the rest of the wine. Reduce by half and whisk in the butter. Put the sauce into a blender and mix for 15 seconds. Keep the sauce hot and do not season it. Arrange the foie gras, scallops and carrots attractively on a plate and pour the sauce around. (Photograph p. 99)

Note: When buying foie gras, make sure it is good quality. Touch the foie gras with your finger. If it is very hard, it is too fatty and will lose a lot of fat when cooking. If it is too soft, it will desintegrate while cooking. A good foie gras must be slightly soft to the touch like butter.

The harbour of Brest lies near the tip of the Breton peninsula as it juts out westwards into the grey distance of the Atlantic. Its inhabitants have always known and enjoyed the fish which came from the ocean. They have known salt cod for as long as we have known it in Gascony, but they have different ways of preparing it; the people of Brest, as I discovered, like to bake it on a bed of sliced potatoes and serve it with leeks and onions. It may not be the same as my mother's *brandade de morue*, but for me it was a new dish and I liked it. Of the finer fish of the Atlantic, I remember that menus in the town usually listed sole, brill, and, above all, turbot. I find this a really excellent fish, and very often serve it at La Tante Claire.

═══════════

Coquilles St Jacques à l'Orange

— • —

SCALLOPS WITH ORANGE AND GRAND MARNIER SAUCE

— • —

16 scallops, halved
1 teaspoon finely chopped shallots
25 ml / 1 fl oz Grand Marnier
100 ml / 4 fl oz freshly squeezed orange juice, strained
100 ml / 4 fl oz double cream
salt and freshly ground pepper

— • —

Halve the scallops lengthways and season with salt and pepper. Melt the butter in a frying pan until very hot but not burning. Add the scallops and cook for 1 minute on each side. Place on a plate, cover and keep warm. In the same pan, sweat the chopped shallots, then add the Grand Marnier, orange juice and cream. Leave to reduce until the sauce is shiny and coats the back of a spoon. Check the seasoning. Arrange the scallops on a warm serving plate and pour the sauce around them.

Gâteau de Homard, Sauce Corail (recipe p. 95)

Escalope de Foie Gras et St Jacques au Sauternes (recipe p. 97)

FILETS DE TURBOT AUX GRAINES DE MOUTARDE

•

FILLETS OF TURBOT WITH WHOLEGRAIN MUSTARD SAUCE

4 fillets of turbot, 150 g / 5 oz each, seasoned
30 g / 1 oz shallots, very finely chopped
100 ml / 4 fl oz white wine
250 ml / 9 fl oz Fish stock (page 49)
120 g / 4 oz butter, at room temperature
1 tablespoon wholegrain mustard
1 large tomato, blanched, skinned, deseeded and diced
1 teaspoon finely chopped parsley
salt and freshly ground pepper

———— • ————

Preheat the oven to 150°C / 300°F / gas 3.

Lightly butter an ovenproof pan or gratin dish and sprinkle on the shallots. Place the turbot fillets on top and pour the white wine and fish stock on to the fillets. Cover with a piece of buttered foil. Bring to the boil on the hob, then transfer to the preheated oven and cook for 8-10 minutes. Arrange the fillets on warm serving plates, cover and keep warm.

Reduce the cooking stock by three-fifths and whisk in the remaining butter, little by little. Mix in the mustard and check the seasoning. Sprinkle over the diced tomato and chopped parsley.

TURBOT À L'OS, JUS DE COQUILLAGES PERSILLÉ

•

BAKED TURBOT ON THE BONE, WITH MUSSEL AND VEGETABLE SAUCE

1 × 1.5 kg / 2¼ lb turbot
500 g / 1 lb 2 oz mussels, cleaned
100 ml / 4 fl oz dry white wine
20 g / ¾ oz butter
20 g / ¾ oz shallots, chopped
1 tablespoon chopped parsley
50 g / 2 oz peas, cooked
50 g / 2 oz French beans, diced and cooked
50 g / 2 oz tomatoes, skinned, deseeded and diced
salt

———— • ————

Preheat the oven to 180°C / 350 °F / gas 4.

In a large saucepan, cook the mussels with the white wine, butter, shallots and parsley for about 5 minutes, shaking the pan from time to time until all the mussels are open. Shell the cooked mussels, place in a bowl and pour over the cooking juice.

Cut off the head and fins of the turbot, then halve the fish lengthways. Cut widthways into four steaks of equal weight. Pour the mussel juice into a flameproof shallow dish, taking care not to use the lower part of the juice, as it is normally sandy. Place the fish on top. Do not season yet, as the mussels are already salty. Bring to the boil, cover with greaseproof paper and place in the oven. Cook for about 12 minutes, depending on the thickness of the fish, turning it over halfway through cooking. Transfer the fish to a dish and keep warm. Bring the cooking juices to the boil. Add the cream and boil again, but do not reduce the sauce too much; it must be quite thin. Add the vegetables, chives and mussels, place a piece of turbot on each plate and pour over the sauce. Serve immediately.

My first two or three weeks at Brest were passed easily enough in naval routine. Then an incident took place which unexpectedly and quite suddenly altered the whole course of my short naval career. One evening, when it was not my night off and I had to remain in barracks, a petty officer walked into the big dormitory where I was quartered and called out 'Does anyone here know how to cook?' There was the usual awkward silence and then the petty officer began again with 'All right, all right! Don't all answer at once!' Another silence, then he bawled out for the last time 'Can anybody here cook?' Things were clearly getting desperate. For a moment I considered the hoary advice given by old navy hands, 'never volunteer', but that moment soon passed, and I found myself taking one momentous step forward and saying, yes, I could cook. The petty officer was a thin, weedy little man with a small moustache. He looked hungry, and I thought at first that it was he who needed the cook and the good meal. But I was wrong. Off I was marched, left, right, left, right, down passages, up stairs, down other passages and up other stairs, until at last we came to a closed but imposing door. 'Hold yourself straight, lad,' snapped out the petty officer, 'you're going before the commanding officer now.' In an instant we were inside a large, comfortable office in the centre of which stood a table covered with papers and telephones, and sitting at it was a grey-haired, intellectual-looking man in an immaculate blue and gold uniform. 'This man here says he knows how to cook, sir.' shouted the petty officer after saluting. The commanding officer gave me a look of immense relief and slowly murmured 'Really? How absolutely wonderful!'

As soon as we were alone, he began to pour out a whole sequence of worries and mishaps to do with an important dinner he had to give the next evening. The guests were to include an admiral, a government minister and his wife, and two leading figures from the steel industry. It was essential that everything should go well, but up to now all preparations had ended in disaster. The commanding officer's chef was a long service man but he had turned out to be lazy, dishonest and often drunk (I nodded understandingly). The only people the commanding officer now had in his kitchen were two boys who had not even completed their training and so could not be relied on; the food had to be of a high standard because the minister's wife had a great reputation as a cook and her Paris dinner parties were prestigious; *une bonne table* had always been one of the most vital assets of any senior officer in the French navy (I nodded discreetly); a good *chef de cuisine* filled one of the most important roles in society (I nodded again); in short, he was in a desperate state over it all, and could I possibly help him? I could see that calming the poor man's nerves was going to be a far harder task than planning and cooking the dinner. I was shown the kitchen and met the two young cooks who were not, after all, so very much younger than I was, but who were very pleased to feel that the main responsibility for the meal was going to be taken off their shoulders. I had all next day to order my ingredients and prepare the work; but already, as we were talking, I was thinking out the menu, and making sure that the commanding officer would approve of it.

The oysters of the northern coast of Brittany have been famous for centuries, so, as a starter, I suggested an unusual oyster soup. For the fish course, I thought of fillets of John Dory served with a sauce and a ragoût of vegetables. The principal meat course would make the most of the tender lamb for which Brittany is famous; I planned to serve this encased in puff pastry to keep the delicate meat juicy. For the dessert at the end I would poach some pears in red wine which would be accompanied by one of my own ices. The commanding officer was delighted by my suggestions; he gave me full permission to go ahead, and I have the impression that he slept better that night than he probably had done for a day or two.

SOUPE AUX HUÎTRES

•

OYSTER SOUP

•

24 oysters
75 g / 3 oz butter
30 g / 1 oz flour
750 ml / 1½ pt milk
200 g / 7 oz mushrooms, washed and finely
chopped
2 tablespoons finely chopped parsley
100 ml / 4 fl oz sour cream
3 egg yolks, beaten
100 g / 3½ oz fine breadcrumbs
salt and white pepper

•

Open the oysters over a bowl to catch their juices. Shell them and strain the juices through muslin. Keep the oysters and juices in a bowl.

Prepare a béchamel sauce with the butter, flour and half the milk: melt the butter, mix in the flour and cook until froth. Whisk in the milk and cook over medium heat, stirring all the time, for abour 5 minutes or until smooth and thick. Add the mushrooms and the parsley along with the oyster water. Season and simmer for 15 minutes.

Heat the sour cream with the rest of the milk and mix into the prepared mushroom béchamel. Check the seasoning and keep hot.

Heat the remaining butter in a large shallow pan. Season the oysters, dip them into the egg yolks and roll them in the breadcrumbs. When the butter is very hot, quickly put in the oysters and brown them. Pour the soup into hot bowls and garnish with the fried oysters.

GRILLADE DE ST PIERRE À LA NAGE DE LÉGUMES

•

GRILLED FILLETS OF JOHN DORY WITH VEGETABLES

•

4 John Dory fillets, 150 g / 5 oz each
75 g / 3 oz butter, at room temperature
16 carrot sticks, about 5 cm / 2 in long, 0.5 cm /
¼ in thick
16 courgette sticks about 5 cm / 2 in long, 0.5 cm /
¼ in thick
12 leeks, white part only, cut lengthways into eight
20 fine French beans
12 mange-tout
50 g / 2 oz plain flour
40 ml / 1½ fl oz extra virgin olive oil
1 large tomato, blanched, skinned, deseeded and
diced
salt and freshly ground pepper

•

Bring 1 L / 1¾ pint water to the boil. Add 1 teaspoon salt and cook the vegetables, one variety at a time until just tender. Keep warm.

Make sure your grilling pan is spotless before heating it. Season the fish fillets, dust them with flour, shaking off the excess and smear with olive oil on both sides. Cook in the very hot grilling pan for 3 minutes, giving the fish a quarter-turn after 1½ minutes. Repeat on the other side of the fillets. Keep warm.

To make the sauce: Bring the stock to the boil, then liquidize in a blender, adding the butter a little at a time. Place the fish fillets on warm plates. Pour the sauce around and arrange the vegetables to give a contrast of colours. Sprinkle with diced tomato.

FILET D'AGNEAU EN CROÛTE

•

FILLET OF LAMB EN CROÛTE

———— • ————

2 × 120 g / 8 oz fillets of lamb
2 lambs' brains
1 bay leaf
1 sprig of thyme
50 g / 2 oz shallots, finely chopped
40 g / 1½ oz butter
400 g / 14 oz mushrooms, finely chopped
2 tablespoons breadcrumbs
1 tablespoon chopped parsley
300 ml / ½ pt vegetable oil
350 g / 12 oz Puff pastry (page 42)
1 egg yolk mixed with 1 tablespoon water, for
eggwash
salt and freshly ground pepper
Béarnaise sauce (page 52), for serving

———— • ————

Preheat the oven to 230°C / 450°F / gas 8.
First prepare the stuffing. Clean the brains and poach
them in cold water with a bay leaf and thyme. Bring to
the boil and drain. Sweat the shallots with 20 g / ¾ oz
butter for 1 minute. Add the mushrooms and cook until
all the water has evaporated. Add the brains
breadcrumbs and parsley and mash with a fork. Season
and cook in the remaining butter for 5 minutes. Place
in a bowl and leave to cool.

Season the lamb fillets. Heat the oil until very hot and
seal the lamb on all sides. Cut the pastry in two. Roll
out each piece of pastry into a rectangle large enough to
wrap the meat. Spoon some stuffing lengthways down
the middle of the pastry. Place the lamb on top and
cover with the rest of the stuffing. Wrap in the pastry,
sealing the joins with eggwash. Turn the croûtes over
and brush with eggwash. Place on a baking sheet and
bake in the hot oven for 20 minutes. Slice and serve
with a Béarnaise sauce (page 52).

POIRE AU VIN EPICÉ, GLACE AU MIEL

•

*PEARS POACHED IN SPICED WINE, FILLED WITH
HONEY ICE CREAM*

———— • ————

4 ripe pears
1 bottle red wine
150 g / 5 oz sugar
1 clove
1 star anise
1 cinnamon stick, broken into small pieces
1 slice of lemon
rind of 2 oranges
300 g / 11 oz Honey ice cream (page 104), for
serving

———— • ————

Put the red wine in a saucepan with the sugar, spices,
lemon and orange rind, and bring to the boil. Peel the
pears and add them to the wine. Simmer for 10
minutes or until tender. Transfer the pears to a dish
and leave to cool.

Reduce the cooking liquid until slightly syrupy and
leave to cool. Trim a slice from the bottom of the pears
so that they stand firmly, and with a melon balle scoop
out the cores and pips carefully. Fill the pears with
some of the ice cream and place one pear on each plate.
Add one scoop of ice cream on the side and pour the
syrupy wine over the pears. (Photograph p. 106)

GLACE AU MIEL

•

HONEY ICE CREAM

•

0.5 L / 1 pt milk
6 egg yolks
80 g / 3 oz sugar
150 g / 5 oz clear honey
100 ml / 4 fl oz double cream

•

Boil the milk. Whisk together the egg yolks, sugar and honey until very pale. Pour on the hot milk, whisking quickly. Pour the mixture into a saucepan and cook over medium heat, stirring with a wooden spoon. When the custard starts to coat the spoon, pour it into a bowl and let it cool down completely.

Churn the cold custard in an ice cream maker until it starts to solidify. Add the cream and continue to churn until the ice cream is hard. Place in a container and freeze.

The next morning I was again summoned into his presence. He was radiant with pleasure and satisfaction. All had gone well; the guests had praised everything they had eaten; and he himself could not remember when he had last enjoyed a meal so much. Where had I learned to cook? Where had I worked? What branch of the navy was I going to join? As soon as he realized that I was toiling several hours a day to learn Morse code, he threw up his hands in horror at the thought of such a waste of a good cook. He regretted deeply that he was unable to keep me with him at Brest, but he would recommend me to other senior naval officers who, like himself, were great gastronomes and would appreciate my cooking. He would at once take full charge of my service career, and send me to a very good, quiet post where I would find food and good cooking were taken seriously. There must be no more radar or Morse code. I nodded once more, thanked him for his kindness and help, and said *oui, d'accord,*

I would be very pleased to go wherever he suggested as long as I could go on cooking as I liked.

Four days later I again found myself crossing France by train, south-eastwards this time, in the direction of the port of Toulon. As the train drew close to the Mediterranean and began to roll along with sea on the right and, on the left, the red earth, the vines, the olive trees, the dark hills and the long, tile-roofed farms of the Provençal landscape, I began to feel at home again because I am after all a southerner. On arrival at Toulon I was taken in a naval van, along with several other sailors who had arrived by the same train, to my final destination at the fort of Cap Brun. The van jolted through the streets of Toulon, crossed the busy suburb of Le Mourillon and then began to climb uphill beside a wide, curving beach where the last of the summer bathers shouted and splashed, and brightly coloured sailing boats were drawn up in neat rows. We took a sudden, sharp turn to the right to climb even higher up a steep, dusty, twisting little road which brought us at last to the very top of the hill of Cap Brun. The views out to sea and along the coast were astonishingly beautiful. You seemed to soar above the Mediterranean like a gull. On one side you could see for miles across the intricate pattern of capes, islands, inlets and distant, blue hump-backed lines of hills which made up the great outer harbour of Toulon. The silhouettes of headlands showed jet black against a sea turned dazzling silver by the light of the afternoon sun; and here and there you could pick out the blurred, somnolent form of a warship or an aircraft carrier lying at anchor. In the opposite direction the bay was bounded by the lumpy hills and yellow beak of the Pointe de Carqueiranne and, in the further distance, by the Hyères peninsula and the island of Pourquerolles. Straight ahead, the open sea stretched to meet the sky in a haze of heat which made the horizon difficult to define. I was overwhelmed by the sheer splendour of it all, an unusual reaction since despite the fact that I was wearing a sailor's uniform, I am not by nature a man of the sea. I have never really liked it or been interested in it; I am easily seasick, and I would never go anywhere by boat if I could possibly fly. For me the sea is really just a lot of water, nothing else. I am fascinated by the things it cannot show you: the land beyond the horizon and the new and unknown things to be discovered there. When later on I used to stand and gaze out to sea at Cap Brun, it was North Africa I used to dream about: Fez, Marrakesh, Tunis, Algiers. Crossing the sea to get there was a brief, unavoidable necessity, nothing more. The important things were the crowded souks and the minarets and the caravans which I liked to imagine making their romantic way across miles of sunburnt desert.

Behind me, the brown, massively hewn stones of the walls of the fort also burned in the sun, but I did not find them particularly romantic. On the side nearest the sea the land dropped sharply in a sort of cliff; but on the landward side the place was defended by a wide ditch and an escarpment of embanked earth kept in place by a thick retaining wall. To enter the fort you crossed the dry moat and passed through an impressive classical portico into a big central courtyard where all the buildings were painted white. These comprised the commanding officer's quarters, the officers' mess, dormitories, store-rooms, a bar selling soft drinks and fruit juice, a recreation area and a large dining-hall. Indeed the whole atmosphere at Cap Brun was far more like that of some large hotel and restaurant than of an ordinary naval establishment. The reason was that though the fort formed part of the *école des timoniers*, the training school for signallers, radar operators and naval air-pilots, none of the two hundred or so long-service trainees or the thirty-odd national service conscripts actually worked there; they only used it for sleeping and eating. Every morning buses came to ferry them down to the main base at Toulon where they did their training, and every evening they were brought up again to have their supper and to go to bed.

The kitchen was in a small building standing on its own next to the dining-hall. It was not very big, and the main stove and all the other equipment was electrical. It was the first time I had ever cooked with electricity, but the experience failed to impress me favourably, and I have always preferred the quick, reliable response of a good gas flame. Of course the kitchen was a typical service kitchen; everything was a bit old and shabby, and there was probably a good deal in it which would have surprised a conscientious health inspector, if ever one had visited it. When it was my turn to get up early to start the stove and get the breakfasts ready, I hated turning on the lights and finding the whole place black with cockroaches. I have never seen anything like it before or since. The creatures were huge; they covered everything, tables, sinks, walls, hobs, anything they could get on to; but the minute they saw the light, they scuttled away out of sight until another night came and whichever cook was first in the kitchen the following day found them again.

There were four other cooks in the kitchen besides myself and a *chef de cuisine*. During working hours we wore the usual white coats and blue trousers; but when we left the fort on leave we were always dressed in our sailors' uniforms. We cooked for the officers' mess and, of course, we cooked all the food eaten in the big dining-hall, which meant doing about a hundred and fifty covers every night. The *chef de cuisine* was the worst and most incompetent chef I have ever worked with. He seemed to know nothing about cooking; whenever he tried to do anything in the kitchen, which was not often, he always did it badly, and one of us had to help him. He was a short, dark-haired man with a long face and a prim, bad-tempered little mouth, who was perpetually grumbling. He walked about the kitchen complaining, criticising, and finding imaginary fault with every single thing we did. In a professional kitchen in civilian life he would not have lasted a week, but at Cap Brun he was a long-service man not far from the end of his time and he seemed to have lost interest in his work. The one thing he really did like, however, was praise; and, in the end, this was not only the factor which irritated us the most, but it also

Poire au Vin Epicé, Glace au Miel (recipe p. 103)

provided us with our opportunity for revenge. Each time we had prepared a good lunch for the officers' mess they would send for the chef and congratulate him on his food. He would then return to the kitchen and tell us everything the officers had said; how happy they were to have a first class chef in charge, how imaginative his menus were, how delicious everything tasted, how much we must be learning from him. The more he talked, the more pleased with himself he became, until in the end we got so fed up that we could stand him no longer. Never once was there the least hint of thanks or appreciation for what we had done on his behalf. After all, we were the people who had done the work, planned the menus and cooked the meals.

One evening we held a secret council of war at which we decided on the irrevocable sabotage of the chef's reputation in the eyes of the officers. We began next day by sending them up a thin, lukewarm version of their favourite mussel soup; this was followed later on in the week by a steak whose red wine sauce had mysteriously remained unreduced so that it had the consistency of bath water. For two days their main course at lunch was plain boiled spaghetti; and finally we subjected them to liver as officially issued by the French navy for consumption on the lower deck. This was a unique variety of frozen Argentinian ox liver; it must have been about fifteen years old when it was delivered to us, and it was the most unpleasant food I have ever cooked. You had to cut it when it was still only half defrosted since if you waited any longer it turned into a sort of brown mud which it was quite impossible to slice. As it cooked it took on all sorts of horrible colours, and when finally you served it, it was usually dull green – a far cry from the liver I serve at La Tante Claire.

FOIE DE VEAU AU CITRON VERT

—— • ——

CALF'S LIVER WITH FRESH LIME

—— • ——

4 slices calf's liver, 1 cm / ½ in thick
20 g / ¾ oz sugar
50 ml / 2 fl oz wine vinegar
juice of 1 orange, strained
juice of 1 lemon, strained
250 ml / 9 fl oz Chicken stock (page 49)
50 g / 2 oz butter
3 tablespoons vegetable oil
salt and freshly ground pepper
segments of 1 lime, for garnish

—— • ——

First make the sauce: Cook the sugar and vinegar together until thick and golden. Add the fruit juices, bring to the boil and skim. Add the chicken stock and reduce by three-quarters, skimming all the time. Whisk in the butter and keep the sauce hot.

Heat the oil in a frying pan. Season the liver and cook over medium heat to taste.

Arrange the liver slices on a warm serving plate with the lime segments on top. Pour over the sauce.

The *chef de cuisine*, of course, was quite unaware of this sabotage, and when, some days later, he was summoned to the officers' mess, he was overjoyed at the prospect of receiving more compliments. This time, however, he returned to the kitchen so shocked and crestfallen that we almost felt sorry for him. I cannot imagine that he had ever had such a telling-off in all his life; but at least we were now able to talk quite openly to him. He always wanted to get the best out of us, we said, but, at the same time, he never stopped nagging and interfering with what we did, and on top of that he insisted that he should receive all the credit. We made a pact. We would have no objection to his getting all the glory so long as he left us completely free in the kitchen to run it as we liked, and to do the menus we wanted. Otherwise, we told him, we would see to it that the standard of the officers' food got worse and worse until at last he really would receive a very severe reprimand indeed. The poor man had no alternative but to agree to our terms; but the final outcome of the whole affair was that the other boys in the kitchen said they thought that I was the best cook there, and asked me to act as the real *chef de cuisine* in place of the official chef who was now deposed. Actually, I think he was secretly very pleased with the new arrangement. He was the sort of man who revelled in the idea of receiving fulsome praise for work he did not have to do himself. As we say in Gascony, he was as lazy as a grass snake.

The commanding officer at Cap Brun did not eat with the other officers, but took his meals on his own in a private room. I think he may have heard about what had been going on from the petty officer in charge of the storeroom, who was in frequent contact with the kitchen and who was very much on our side against the chef. One day the commanding officer sent for me, told me of the excellent things he had heard about me from Brest, and asked if I was good at cooking fish. He had been born near Toulon and had always enjoyed the fish and shellfish of the coast, especially the mussels, which are larger than those of the north, though some people find their taste inferior. Those which grew on the rocks between Cap Brun and Lamalgue used to be highly prized, he told me, even thirty or forty years ago. I said that I enjoyed cooking fish and shellfish and would be pleased to show him what I could do. Over the next few weeks I prepared an interesting variety of mussel recipes, including a very good mussel risotto.

RIZOTTE DE MOULES TOULONNAISE

MUSSEL RISOTTO FROM TOULON

1.8 kg / 4 lb mussels, scrubbed
200 ml / 7 fl oz dry white wine
200 g / 7 oz long grain rice
100 g / 3½ oz onions, finely chopped
2 tablespoons chopped parsley
a pinch of saffron
1 small Bouquet garni (page 11)
50 ml / 2 fl oz olive oil
salt and freshly ground pepper

Put the onions, parsley and wine in a very large saucepan. Add the mussels and bring to the boil. Cook for about 5 minutes, shaking the pan at intervals, until the mussels are open. Take the mussels out of the cooking liquid and remove the top shells, leaving the molluscs on the half shell. Put them back in their juice.

Heat the oil in a saucepan until warm. Add the rice and stir until it becomes transparent. Add the saffron, bouquet garni and 400 ml / 14 fl oz of the cooking liquid. Bring to the boil, cover with a lid and cook gently for about 18 minutes. Do not stir during cooking. When the risotto is done, check the seasoning and add the mussels. Mix and serve immediately.

Sea urchins were another delicacy much appreciated by the commanding officer. The Toulon coast also used to be famous for them, especially around Balaguier, on the opposite side of the Grande Rade to Cap Brun. The flesh of these creatures can be strained through muslin and mixed with mayonnaise to make a sauce, or you can add some béarnaise sauce to turn it into an excellent purée which can be served with other fish such as sole or turbot or mullet. Usually, however, urchins are eaten raw straight out of their hard, black, spiky shells; and this is how we serve them in London, as an hors d'oeuvre.

Sea urchins, remind me of the young man who was perhaps the most surprising customer we ever had at La Tante Claire. He booked a single table for dinner, and arrived clutching an armful of restaurant and food guides, which he insisted on piling up in front of him as soon as he had sat down. At first the *maître d'hôtel* thought that he must be a journalist, though there was something strange about the man which after a while made him doubt it. He refused to order, and just sat with his books open on the table, reading them as though he was in a library. Every now and then he would call a waiter over and query or grumble about something, finding obscure faults with the laying of the table or the folding of the cloth or the arrangement of the menu or the description of a dish, and all the time he would refer to one of his books as though it was some hallowed authority. By now the waiters were quite sure he was mad, and began to think that the sooner he could be tactfully removed from the restaurant the better. At long last he decided to order, and to start his meal with a sea urchin hors d'oeuvre. It was duly brought to his table, and for some minutes no one paid any more attention to him, until suddenly the *maître d'hôtel* noticed with horrified amazement that not only had the man eaten the flesh of the sea urchin but that he had also eaten half of its prickly shell! He was already looking horribly ill, but before anybody could hasten to his table to suggest as diplomatically as possible that it might be wiser not to tackle the other half, our mysterious customer had jumped to his feet, seized his books, and fled away into the night, never to be seen again at La Tante Claire!

I have already mentioned that my commanding officer had a special liking for Mediterranean fish. The *loup de mer,* which is very like the bass of the North Sea or the Atlantic, was a favourite of his; sometimes he would ask me to prepare it quite simply though at other times he rather liked something a little more elaborate. At La Tante Claire I sometimes serve it *à la barigoule*, which today always implies a preparation of artichokes, though the original word in Provençal really referred to a certain species of wild mushroom. Fresh sardines, either grilled or cooked in the oven with a little dry white wine, or breadcrumbed and served stuffed on a bed of spinach, were another favourite dish; and then there was the red mullet, an excellent Mediterranean fish, which I also have on the restaurant menu, sometimes served with a delicate flavouring of cumin seeds.

PAVÉ DE LOUP BARIGOULE

SEA BASS STEAKS WITH ARTICHOKES

4 sea bass steaks, 150 g / 5 oz each
2 artichokes
4 anchovy fillets, chopped
4 tablespoons olive oil
100 g / 3½ oz carrots, thinly sliced
500 ml / 18 fl oz dry white wine
1 small Bouquet garni (page 11)
20 g / ¾ oz shallots, finely chopped
a pinch of thyme leaves
a few drops of wine vinegar
12 black olives, stoned and chopped
salt and freshly ground pepper

Soak the anchovy fillets in cold water for 15 minutes to remove the salt.

Using a very sharp knife, cut off all the artichoke leaves and trim, turning the artichokes as you work, until only the neat bottoms are left. Cut each into 6 pieces. In a saucepan, heat 2 tablespoons oil and sweat the carrots for 3 minutes. Add the artichoke bottoms and sweat for 3 minutes. Add the wine, some seasoning and the bouquet garni, cover with a lid and cook for 10 minutes, or until the artichokes are tender. Add the anchovies.

Season the fish and pan-fry it in the remaining oil for 10 minutes, turning it over half-way through cooking. Transfer to a dish and keep it warm. Put the shallots and thyme into the same pan and sweat for 1 minute. Add the wine and reduce completely. Add 100 ml / 4 fl oz water and bring to the boil. Check the seasoning and add a few drops of vinegar.

Place a fish steak on each plate and arrange the vegetables around. Pour the sauce over the fish and sprinkle the olives on top. Serve immediately.

FILETS DE ROUGET AU CUMIN

RED MULLET FILLETS WITH CUMIN SAUCE

4 red mullet, scaled and filleted, with their livers
200 ml / 7 fl oz Fish stock, made with the red mullet bones (page 49)
1 teaspoon cumin seeds
150 ml / 5 fl oz double cream
1 tablespoon olive oil
salt and freshly ground pepper

Preheat the oven to 220°C / 425°F / gas 7. Wash the red mullet fillets thoroughly to remove all traces of blood.

Reduce the stock with the cumin seeds by three-quarters. Pour in the cream and reduce until the sauce coats the back of a spoon. Add the mullet livers and simmer for 15 seconds. Purée in a blender and pass through a fine mesh strainer. Add salt and pepper to taste and keep warm.

Cut 8 pieces of foil, large enough to hold the red mullet fillets. Smear some olive oil on each and put them on a baking tray. Place the fillets on the pieces of foil, skin-side up and smear them with olive oil. Season with salt. Cook in the preheated oven for 4-5 minutes.

Place the fillets on a warm serving plate and pour the sauce around the edge.

Cooking for the commanding officer and the officers' mess was the most interesting part of our work (once we had managed to conquer the *chef de cuisine*), but of course it was by no means all of it. We still had the regular hundred and fifty covers in the main dining hall to cater for. Here the big occasion was a weekly Sunday lunch to which the petty officers were allowed to invite their wives and families. I have never forgotten two particular petty officers and their spouses. One was the medical officer, the *infirmier*. He was a lean little man who seemed never to be without a glass of pernod in his hand, and who, though he could never be described as completely drunk, could never be called completely sober either. Everyone liked him, largely because he was so good at giving painless injections, unlike many of the hospital staff who jabbed the needle into you without thinking or caring about what they were doing; and also because he was always willing to give you a sickness certificate if you needed one. He was so popular, in fact, that we felt it was a shame to see the way he arrived with his family for Sunday lunch. His wife was much taller than he was; she was a fine, good-looking, well-rounded, splendid sort of woman who strode into the restaurant as though she owned it, and it took you a moment or two to realize that she was actually being followed meekly by the diminutive *infirmier* holding two little girls by the hand and preceded by a third rather larger little girl who walked demurely in front of him. During the meal his cheerful friendliness (and also perhaps his pernod) disappeared; he lapsed into silence, and only the stentorian tones of his wife could be heard, choosing the table, discussing the menu, deciding on the wines and telling the children off. It was a total transformation of our poor friend, and we all held our breath until things came right again, much to our relief, on Monday morning.

The other petty officer I remember was the *policier*, the regulating petty officer, who was generally responsible for maintaining discipline in the fort. He was a complete he-man, a Tarzan, big, bronzed and bulging with muscles, and a good athlete who spent hours in the gym, practising every kind of difficult and ambitious exercise. All day he strode about the fort, swinging his arms and shouting at people. He was not really wicked, however, and at heart he was even quite good-natured, though not terribly intelligent. Every woman adored him, of course. He was full of stories intended to enhance the general picture of his potency and virility. He told us that he had once slept with Brigitte Bardot – entirely at her own request, naturally! Nobody believed him for a moment; we all laughed at him and made up songs about him and Bardot which we sang at the tops of our voices whenever we saw him swinging past the window, or if we were marching in a group through the streets of Toulon and happened to catch sight of him sitting at a café. He was always furious after these incidents, but he never managed to convince us about Brigitte Bardot. The girl friends he used to invite to Sunday lunch at the fort were always vulgar, tarty and full of noisy fun, but they could annoy people. Once the storeroom petty officer and the *policier* had a furious argument over one girl who was so drenched in cheap scent that it was impossible to taste the food because of the pervading aroma. Indeed the petty officers were mostly knowledgeable about food and they really enjoyed and appreciated what they ate, so we always took trouble on Sundays to provide them with a good menu. We often devised a fish or a shellfish starter, and followed this with a main course of lamb or beef. Of course, Sunday lunch always ended with a good dessert.

Assiette de Frivolités de la Mer

•

SEAFOOD FANTASY

•

Raw marinated salmon:
(to be prepared 12 hours in advance)
4 kg / 9 lb salmon
400 g / 14 oz coarse sea salt
100 g / 3½ oz black peppercorns, crushed
4 sprigs of dill
250 g / 8 oz best quality gravadlax, thinly sliced
or ½ quantity *Mousse de Brandade de morue* (page 33)

Tomato coulis:
500 g / 1 lb 2 oz tomatoes, blanched, skinned and
deseeded
3 tablespoons extra virgin olive oil
salt and freshly ground pepper

Langoustine salad:
8 langoustines
4 small bunches of cornsalad
4 red oak leaf lettuce leaves
4 radicchio leaves

Dressing:
6 tablespoons extra virgin olive oil
1 tablespoon lemon juice
1 teaspoon finely snipped chives
1 tomato, blanched, skinned, deseeded and diced

Scallops tartare:
4 scallops, cleaned under running water
100 g / 3½ oz carrots, finely grated
3 tablespoons extra virgin olive oil
lemon juice
soy sauce

•

The marinated salmon: Rinse the fish under cold running water, fillet it leaving the skin on and tweeze out the small bones. Sprinkle the coarse salt and crushed peppercorns over both sides of the fillets and lay them on a tray. Place the dill sprigs between the two fleshy sides of the fillets. Cover with clingfilm and place another tray on top to hold a weight (6 or 8 tins of tomatoes will do well). Refrigerate for 12 hours.

Rinse the fillets under cold running water and pat dry. Slice the salmon very thinly and arrange a portion on each plate, crumpling the slices decoratively.

The tomato coulis: Purée the tomatoes in a blender with the olive oil and salt and pepper to taste. Chill. To serve, pour a little tomato coulis onto each plate and top with a scoop of salt cod mousse or sliced gravadlax.

The langoustine salad: Pull off the langoustine tails and fry them quickly over high heat in olive oil for about 2 minutes. Take the flesh out of the shells and keep warm.

The dressing: Whisk the olive oil over the lemon juice, salt and pepper. Add the chopped chives and diced tomato. Mix some of the dressing with the langoustines, keeping the rest for the salad.

To serve, place one of each type of lettuce on each plate. Drizzle over the dressing and arrange 2 langoustines on the top of each mixed salad.

The scallops tartare: Using your hands, squeeze the juice out of the grated carrots into a small bowl and add the lemon juice, salt and pepper. Whisk in the olive oil and season the carrots with half this dressing.

Cut the scallops into very small dice and sprinkle with a little soy sauce and salt and pepper to taste. Put about 1 teaspoon grated carrot on each plate and top with one diced scallop. Pour a little dressing around the edge. (Photograph p. 14)

PARMENTIÈRE D'AGNEAU AUX TRUFFES

•

FILLET OF LAMB WITH MASHED POTATOES AND TRUFFLES

•

4 small lamb fillets
20 g / ¾ oz fresh truffles
300 g / 11 oz potatoes, mashed and kept hot
50 ml / 2 fl oz vegetable oil
20 g / ¾ oz shallots, sliced
50 ml / 2 fl oz dry white wine
200 ml / 7 fl oz Chicken stock (page 49)
20 g / ¾ oz butter
salt and freshly ground pepper

•

Preheat the oven to 230°C / 450°F / gas 8.

Heat the oil in a roasting pan. Season the lamb and seal it in the oil. Roast for 12 minutes in the hot oven, turning the meat over halfway through cooking. Transfer the lamb to a dish and keep warm.

Add the shallots to the pan and sweat for 2 minutes. Discard the fat, pour in the wine and reduce completely. Pour in the stock and reduce by one-third. Whisk in the butter, season and pass the sauce through a sieve. Keep hot.

Grate the truffles into the mashed potatoes. Place a mound of potato in the middle of each plate. Slice the meat and arrange it around the potato. Pour the sauce around the edge.

FONDANT AU CHOCOLAT SAUCE ORANGE

•

RICH CHOCOLATE MOUSSE WITH ORANGE SAUCE

•

120 g / 4 oz bitter chocolate
50 g / 2 oz unsalted butter, softened
2 eggs, separated
40 g / 1½ oz icing sugar
300 ml / ½ pt *Crème Anglaise* (page 41)
20 ml / ¾ fl oz Grand Marnier
grated zest of 1 orange

•

Melt the chocolate in a bain-marie. Work the butter with a wooden spoon and add the egg yolks one by one. Mix well. Beat the egg whites until stiff and add the sugar. Fold the egg white gently into the chocolate. Spoon the mixture into a terrine or four small soufflé dishes and chill overnight.

Stir the Grand Marnier and grated orange zest into the crème anglaise. Unmould the chocolate mousse onto a plate and pour some sauce around.

Assiette de Frivolités de la Mer (recipe p. 112)

At Cap Brun we also made an outstanding lamb and chicken couscous, which the petty officers enjoyed. They were always begging us for couscous for weekday lunches, and we soon realised that we had almost as good a weapon for controlling them as we had previously found for controlling the *chef de cuisine*. If the petty officers had been bothering us with extra parades and reprimands for minor breaches of regulations, we would just say no, no couscous this week. But when the petty officers had been obliging, and had overlooked a few lapses and allowed us an extra afternoon off, we gave them a really first rate couscous. They soon understood the situation, and in no time they were almost literally eating out of our hands. They adored couscous. They ate so much, and they drank so much wine with it, that they slept solidly all through the ensuing afternoon, and for one day at least they gave no trouble whatsoever.

I found another good way of adapting naval surroundings to my own lifestyle when I opened my own unofficial private restaurant in a small, unused canteen next door to the kitchen. One of our more bizarre pieces of equipment was an electrical omelette-maker; a huge, square pan which heated up when you plugged it in, and which was so vast that it could cook five hundred eggs at a time. When the eggs were ready, you tilted the contraption upwards so that the mixture all ran down to the bottom of the slope, and you could without too much trouble roll it up into one colossal omelette. When you had cut this up into sections, you would find yourself with a good many portions of *omelette nature* ready to be served, and it was this which gave me the idea of setting up a restaurant. In the evenings there were not many officers or petty officers in the fort, and those who were would be glued to their television screens, so they never discovered my clandestine establishment. My customers were the trainees, and besides my omelettes, I sold pancakes, fritters and fruit tarts.

OMELETTE SOUFFLÉE, SAUCE RHUBARBE

— • —

SOUFFLÉ OMELETTE WITH RHUBARB SAUCE

— • —

6 egg yolks
250 g / 9 oz caster sugar
finely grated zest of one orange, or the scraped seeds of 1 vanilla pod
8 egg whites
50 g / 2 oz butter

Sauce:
450 g / 1 lb young pink rhubarb, trimmed and chopped into 1 cm / ½ in pieces
150 g / 5 oz caster sugar

— • —

First make the sauce: Put the rhubarb and sugar in a pan over low heat. Allow the sugar to dissolve slowly before raising the heat to bring the rhubarb to a simmer. Cook for about 25 minutes or until the rhubarb is breaking down into fibres. Remove from the heat, transfer into a bowl, cool and refrigerate until thoroughly chilled.

Whisk the egg yolks with 200 g / 7 oz sugar and the orange or vanilla, until thick and ribbon-like. Beat the egg whites until very soft peaks form. Sift in the remaining sugar like rain and whisk until the meringue is very stiff. Fold it into the yolk and sugar mixture.

Heat the butter in a large omelette pan. When very hot, but not brown, add the fluffy omelette mixture and cook until well risen. Turn it over onto the other side, divide quickly into portions and serve with the rhubarb sauce.

CRÊPES FOURRÉES AUX MANGUES

•

PANCAKES WITH MANGOES

•

Batter
60 g / 2 oz plain flour, sifted
2 eggs
1 teaspoon vanilla sugar
180 ml / 6 fl oz milk
1 tablespoon melted butter

Sauce
2 large fragrant mangoes, halved and stoned
100 g / 3½ oz butter
4 tablespoons sugar
175 ml / 6 fl oz freshly squeezed orange juice, strained
2 tablespoons Grand Marnier
2 tablespoons brandy

•

First make the pancake batter: Sift the flour into a bowl and whisk in the eggs and sugar until smooth. Little by little, stir in the milk and melted butter until the batter is smooth. Cover with clingfilm and leave to rest for about half an hour.

Lightly grease a large shallow frying pan. Allow to get very hot before pouring in one-quarter of the batter, then rotate the pan quickly to make a very thin pancake. When golden brown, cook on the other side. Make 3 more pancakes in the same way and keep warm.

To make the sauce: Melt the butter and sugar together in a small pan, stirring with a wooden spatula until the sugar is golden brown. Add the strained orange juice and stir until the sugar has melted. Add the Grand Marnier and simmer for a few minutes. Take the pan off the heat.

Fold each pancake into four and stuff the opening with large pieces of mango. Return the pan containing the

sauce to the heat, put in the pancakes and heat until the pancakes are very hot all through. Serve on warm plates.

TARTE AUX ABRICOTS

•

APRICOT TART

•

200 g / 7 oz Shortcrust pastry (page 41)
butter, for greasing
350 g / 12 oz ripe apricots, halved and stoned
2 eggs
200 ml / 7 fl oz whipping cream
2 tablespoons cornflour
100 g / 3½ oz caster sugar
a few drops of natural almond essence

•

Preheat the oven to 200°C / 400°F / gas 6.

Roll out the pastry into a circle approximately 21 cm / 8½ in diameter. Butter a 20 cm / 8 in loose-based, fluted flan tin and line it with the pastry. Leave to rest in the fridge for 30 minutes while you prepare the filling.

Whisk the eggs and cream together. In another bowl, mix the cornflour and all but one tablespoon of sugar. Little by little, pour the eggs and cream over the sugar and cornflour, whisking well to get rid of any lumps. Add the almond essence.

Line the pastry case with greaseproof paper and fill with ceramic baking beans. Bake blind in the preheated oven until golden. Remove the beans, pour in the filling and arrange the halved apricots on top. Sprinkle with the remaining sugar and bake for 1 hour.

The "restaurant" was a great success; there was never any lack of customers late at night, and I quickly earned myself quite a lot of extra pocket money which I was able to put to good use early in the summer of 1969, when four of us cooks had enough saved to club together to buy an old blue Peugeot 203 for the princely sum of £35. On our free evenings, after five o'clock, or even earlier if we had made the petty officers a good couscous the day before, we would drive off into the hills wearing our white summer uniforms to find some remote village with tiled roofs, golden walls, and an iron bell hanging in the church tower. Most importantly, we would find a little restaurant where we could sit out to eat a daube of beef with herbs and olives and drink a bottle of good Provençal wine, or we would drive along the coast and spend the evening bathing and relaxing on one of the beaches near Toulon. We had some wonderful moments. We would light a fire, barbecue pork chops and sausages, chat and sing songs while the *poissonnier* played his guitar. Sometimes we would find some girls to come with us, and sometimes not.

I also played a lot of rugby at Cap Brun and even managed to get into three teams at the same time, since I played for the Fort of Cap Brun, for the Région Maritime, and for Toulon. It was one more way in which I managed to soften the rigours of service life. My rugby playing was due, too, to my cooking, since the commanding officer was so pleased with the meals I served him that he allowed me to be absent from the kitchen almost as often as I wanted. On some occasions I would be away a whole afternoon, and on others, when I had to play in different matches at different places, I would be absent for two or three days on end, though I always came back to the fort at night. My first commanding officer at Brest was proved entirely right about life at Cap Brun. I certainly had a very pleasant, easy life there; and, what is more, I was surrounded by people who all, in different ways, appreciated good food.

Curiously enough rugby played a conspicuous part during the last few weeks of my year of national service. I still had about a month more to do when, one Friday afternoon, I hurt my leg very badly in a match we were playing near Toulon. Even though walking was painful, I did not want to report sick because that very evening I was to start a weekend's leave, and I was planning to spend it at home at Tarbes. Before leaving the fort I had to be inspected by the *policier*, who was always trying to make trouble for me because of my teasing him about Brigitte Bardot. He noticed that I did not have the right stripe on my sleeve to show that I had just been promoted to a higher rating. I offered to get it put on when I returned to the fort on Monday, but he was furious with me (I think he was the only petty officer who did not like couscous), and he made me go all the way to Toulon to buy a stripe, sew it on, and then report back to the fort so that he could inspect me again to be sure that I was properly dressed. By the time I eventually got the eleven o'clock night train for Tarbes, my leg was in a dreadful state with all the extra walking I had had to do. It was so swollen that I could hardly get my shoe on, and as a result, at Tarbes I really did have to report sick to the military hospital. An X-ray showed that I had a fracture and I had to spend the next few weeks in bed, so my national service came to an end before I was allowed to leave the hospital. By a strange coincidence the man in the next bed to me was also a cook, who had exactly the same sort of fracture as mine, though in his case it was the result of a bad parachute landing. We became great friends, and later on he too came to England and opened his own restaurant at Kenilworth.

Once I was out of hospital I spent a few weeks at home, resting and taking things easy before having to think about finding a new job. Some people grumble about national service, but I have usually found these are the awkward ones who argue about everything, who refuse to fit in, and who object habitually to any order they are given. As far as I was concerned, I had had a very easy time as a naval cook. Looking back on that year, I regard it as a year's free holiday, and an enjoyable one too.

CHAPTER 4
ENGLAND
THE MAKING OF A MASTER CHEF

The autumn of 1969 was gloriously sunny and warm, and the thought of leaving Tarbes to start working again in the cold north, and of spending the whole of the winter there, did not appeal to me in the least; so I was very pleased to find a job at a restaurant in the old seaport town of La Ciotat, halfway between Marseilles and Toulon. It was odd to be going straight back in the direction of Toulon when I had taken so much painful trouble to get away from it only a short time before. The restaurant was not actually in the town but about ten minutes walk away down the coast. The October afternoon was bright and warm and my suitcase was not heavy, so it was a pleasure to find my way there on foot. The beaches and rocks and the lines of moored sailing boats stood out brightly against the sea haze and the dull green hills and capes receded away in the distance in the direction of Toulon and Cap Brun. I turned to the left up a wide but rather unkempt avenue bordered on each side by tree-filled gardens and large seaside villas long since past their heyday. A few seemed to be occupied, but most were closed up; their gardens had run wild and the white paint was peeling away from gates and shutters. There were holes in the road, and the whole suburb seemed to be basking in a somnolent but rather decrepit calm. At a corner between two intersecting avenues stood the Restaurant de la Plage.

It was a low, white building with blue shutters and a dining room which jutted outwards towards the pavement. The entrance led into a small bar containing low tables and some comfortable wickerwork chairs in one of which a dark, fat man with a bushy moustache was lolling back, resolutely asleep. His mouth was wide open and he was snoring. A half finished glass of pernod stood near him on one of the little tables. I spoke and coughed and shuffled about, but nothing I did seemed to wake him. At last I became aware of noises coming from beyond an open door on my left, and almost simultaneously I was further aware of the comforting smell of good cooking. I left my suitcase where it was and, walking down a passage, I found myself in a small kitchen. The cook, an active, good-looking woman, was busy scrubbing a copper casserole, while on the stove a large saucepan of fish soup simmered gently, and from the ovens there came a delicious smell of roast lamb. When I explained who I was and mentioned the man in the bar, she gave me a friendly smile and told me that he was her husband and to pay no attention to him. As I soon discovered, he was a man who fitted perfectly into the average northerner's image of a typical Provençal. He was as drowsy as a lizard in the sun, and spent most of his life in the bar, either sleeping or drinking Pernod. When he was awake his favourite occupation was to surround himself with his cronies and to talk. The only other thing he liked to do was to write the bills for the restaurant, and to count and re-count over and over again the little piles of banknotes and coins which were brought to him in the bar by the saucerful. His wife, the *patronne*, was his opposite in every way. She was the first to get up in the morning and the last to go to bed at night, and it was she who did all the work. Her kitchen was spotless; the stove, the working table and all the knives and saucepans were always clean and shining. She was an outstanding cook, but she had so much to do that she could not spend much time in the kitchen, which is why it was essential for her to have a good chef on whom she could rely and who would do most of the cooking.

CARRÉ D'AGNEAU À LA PROVENÇALE

•

RACK OF LAMB WITH A HERB CRUST

———— • ————

2 best ends of lamb, trimmed
50 ml / 2 fl oz olive oil
3 egg whites
1 teaspoon thyme
1 teaspoon rosemary
1 teaspoon oregano
1 teaspoon chopped parsley
1 small garlic clove, finely chopped
80 g / 3 oz breadcrumbs
20 g / ¾ oz shallots
20 g / ¾ oz butter
50 ml / 2 fl oz dry white wine
1 bay leaf
200 ml / 7 fl oz Chicken stock (page 49)
salt and freshly ground pepper

———— • ————

Preheat the oven to 230°C / 450°F / gas 8.

Season the meat, heat the oil in a roasting pan and seal the meat on both sides. Roast it for 18 minutes in the hot oven, then keep in a warm place.

Beat the egg whites until very firm and fold in the herbs and garlic. With a spatula, spread the egg whites over the meaty side of the lamb. Sprinkle the breadcrumbs on top and place under a hot grill until golden. Keep the meat warm.

Sweat the shallots in the roasting pan for 2 minutes. Discard the fat and deglaze with the wine. Add the bay leaf, reduce the wine completely, then add the chicken stock. Reduce by two-thirds. Whisk in the butter, then check the seasoning. Carve the meat and put it on warm plates. Pour the sauce around.

I soon got into the way of things. The restaurant could serve up to a maximum of fifty covers, but it was not often completely full. The customers were still mostly holidaymakers, as long as the good weather lasted, but otherwise they were people from the town or families living in the nearby villas. We specialised in local Provençal dishes, but most of the time I was free to arrange menus as I liked. The *patronne* and her husband lived in a flat above the restaurant which faced down the avenue in the direction of the beach; and I had a small room at the back of the building whose window looked out on to the pine trees of a neighbour's garden. The villa was shut up; last year's leaves still lay in corners of the terrace, and a child's swing, rusty and unused, hung forlornly in the middle of the grass. The quiet seemed strange after the shouted orders and general bustle of Cap Brun, and at times I felt rather lonely. The restaurant closed each Monday in the traditional French way, and I would walk along the beach to spend the day in the old town. The little harbour was surrounded on two sides by old houses, but the whole of the other side was taken up by the famous shipyards which, at that time, were still very active. It made an odd contrast to see tall cranes and gantries and the hulls of half-built ships so close to the simple walls and buttresses of the seventeenth-century church and the picturesque buildings which connect it to the towered *hôtel de ville* at the corner of the quay. Behind them lay the old town, a rectangular labyrinth of narrow streets, ancient houses and little squares which suddenly surprised you with sunlight and fountains and the pediment of a baroque church.

There were one or two nightclubs but they were nowhere near as exciting as the ones in Juan-les-Pins. Except when the *patronne* came to help me, I worked alone in the kitchen and there were no other young cooks with whom I could enjoy my days off. The most unusual thing I remember about La Ciotat was watching a fisherman repeatedly hurling a dead octopus on to the stones of the quayside in order to soften its tentacles, and to make them more palatable when they appeared on somebody's table. Each time the creature hit the pavement it made a noise like a revolver shot, and this was the sound which had first attracted my attention. A small crowd collected to watch the fisherman and to maintain a critical running commentary on his technique. A large, dead, wet octopus is very heavy, and its slime makes it difficult to grip. The man got hold of it, walked away a few yards, turned, and, with a great effort, threw it up into the air as high as he could. Down it came with its resounding crack. The fisherman then walked slowly round it, preparing himself for the effort of the next heave, and, like a skilled artist, gripped it again, braced himself, and hurled it up once more. Between each throw he did a slow, jaunty little walk which brought the whole thing into the realm of theatrical performance. That octopus must have soared up into the air and landed flat on the stones a good twenty or thirty times before the fisherman was finally satisfied.

The *patronne* of the Restaurant de la Plage never bought her fish directly from the market on the quay. If she wanted an octopus, she would get it from the excellent fishmonger who called regularly with his van and who bought his fish from the local fishermen. Her menus always included fresh mullet and bream, for which she had excellent recipes, and I like to think that it was she who really taught me how to make a *soupe de poissons*. I have always considered this to be a woman's dish – that is to say that it was made best by traditional housewife-cooks such as my mother and my grandmother. It is not a *haute cuisine* recipe, although I do serve it at La Tante Claire. I have noticed that in the restaurant kitchens I have known, there have been very few cooks who really had the knack of making a good fish soup and I nearly always discovered that they had learned it from a woman. The housewives whom I remember from Tarbes and Saint Puy would cook long-simmered dishes like a *daube* or a *civet* or a *boeuf bourgignon* with almost as much love and care as if it were a child they were bringing into the world. They let the dish

cook for as long as they felt it needed. They did not try to economise on the wine they put in, and they never took a short cut. They were not under pressure. The professional chef, on the other hand, is perpetually under pressure. He tries to make a *boeuf bourgignon* as quickly and economically as possible, perhaps using veal stock to give it a sort of instant taste and to cut down cooking time, and adding a thin wine instead of the thick peasant wine the housewife would have used. He is far too impatient to make the dish properly. Even when he sautés the meat, he may just give it a moment on one side before carelessly and quickly tossing it over to sauté it on the other.

A fish soup is a typical *plat de femme*, which partly explains why the *patronne* at La Ciotat made it so well. It is not a difficult recipe; but she had the patience, and could take the care and the time to cook the dish to its full, natural perfection. She used all those little fish you get on the Provence coast which are too small to eat on their own, so that their only use is for soup, for the taste of their bones. They were always absolutely fresh from the sea, and she used as many different varieties as she could get that day from the fishmonger. The more there were, the better the soup tasted. When I do a *soupe de poissons* at La Tante Claire, I begin it the day before, when I leave the fish to marinate then, when I cook the soup, I also use vegetables, garlic and saffron mayonnaise, which is put in at the very end. Through there are really a number of different flavours in the soup, those of the fish, the garlic and the saffron, the overall impression is of one single taste into which all the others have merged. This is what makes it typical of genuine, old-fashioned family cooking.

SOUPE DE POISSONS

•

PROVENÇAL FISH SOUP

•

(Serves 8)

1 kg / 2¼ lb mixed Mediterranean fish (rascasse,
red mullet, weaver fish, grondin, conger eel),
scaled, cleaned and rinsed under cold running water
to remove all traces of blood
8 garlic cloves, chopped
100 g / 3½ oz leeks, chopped and washed
100 g / 3½ oz carrots, sliced thinly
100 g / 3½ oz onions, sliced thinly
100 g / 3½ oz celery, sliced thinly
100 g / 3½ oz fennel, sliced thinly
500 g / 1 lb 2 oz tomatoes, quartered
2 star anise, crushed
6 basil leaves, snipped
3 sprigs of fresh thyme
50 g / 2 oz parsley
3 bay leaves
a good pinch of saffron threads
150 ml / 5 fl oz extra virgin olive oil
1 tablespoon tomato purée
150 ml / 18 fl oz dry white wine
3 L / 5 pt Fish stock (page 49)
200 g / 7 oz potatoes, cut into 2cm / 1 in chunks
3 tablespoons aniseed aperitif (eg: Pernod or
Ricard)
salt and freshly ground pepper

•

*One day in advance, cut all the fish into chunks,
including the heads. Place in a container with the
chopped garlic, all the vegetables, the star anise, basil,
thyme, parsley, bay leaves and saffron. Mix thoroughly
with your hands. Cover and refrigerate for 24 hours.*

*Remove all the fish pieces from the marinade and
season with salt and pepper. Heat 100 ml / 4 fl oz olive
oil in a deep frying pan and when very hot, add the
fish. Cook for about 5 minutes until golden on all sides.
Add the tomato purée and stir well. Deglaze with the
white wine, bring to the boil and transfer to a large
saucepan.*

*Heat the remaining olive oil until very hot, put in all
the drained vegetables and sauté until soft and golden.
Put into the saucepan with the fish. Pour in the fish
stock, bring to the boil and add the potatoes. Simmer,
uncovered, for an hour, skimming regularly. Add the
aniseed aperitif and simmer for another 30 minutes.
Check the seasoning.*

*Discard the larger fish bones and liquidise the entire
contents of the saucepan in batches in a blender. Pass
the soup through a fine mesh conical sieve, pushing
hard with a small ladle to extract as much liquid as
possible. Reheat before serving with small fried croutons
and Saffron mayonnaise (recipe below).*

This soup freezes well.

MAYONNAISE AU SAFRAN

•

SAFFRON MAYONNAISE

•

2 egg yolks, at room temperature
125 ml / 4½ fl oz extra virgin olive oil
a pinch of saffron threads, steeped in 20 ml /
¾ fl oz boiling water
salt and freshly ground pepper

•

*Put the egg yolks in a small ceramic or stainless steel
bowl. Mix in the saffron with its steeping water, salt
and pepper. Whisk in the olive oil, one drop at a time
at first, then in a thin trickle, beating constantly until
the mayonnaise is thick and glossy. Cover with
clingfilm and refrigerate until needed.*

The high point of the *patronne*'s cooking was
her bouillabaisse. It was really a development of
her *soupe de poissons*, but she made it so well
that ever since I tasted it at La Ciotat it has
been one of my favourite dishes. It was never
listed on the menu, however, but was only
prepared to order two or three days in advance.

Such was the *patronne*'s fame as a cook that hardly a week passed without at least four orders for her special dish. Because of the quantity and variety of fish needed to make it well and to give it a good flavour, it is hardly worth making bouillabaisse for fewer than six people, but we regularly had parties of ten or twelve who came to La Ciotat specially for it. And as the last stage of its cooking has to take place just before it is eaten, the customers had to arrive punctually at the agreed hour.

Bouillabaisse is probably the most famous *plat du terroir* associated with the Mediterranean coast near Marseilles and Toulon. It is said to have begun on the beaches when the fishermen's wives, waiting for their husbands' boats to return, would set big iron cauldrons on fires of driftwood, and in them heat up a mixture of wine, water and oil. As soon as the catch was landed, all the tiny fish which were too small to sell in the market were tipped into the furiously-boiling pots, and a delicious proto-bouillabaisse soup was produced. I have myself seen a modern bouillabaisse cooked in this way, in a huge iron pot with flames jumping up its sides and completely clothing it in fire, and it was a very dramatic sight.

For her bouillabaisse at La Ciotat, my *patronne* used all the little fish she would have put into a *soupe de poissons*: local Mediterranean rock-fish like *demoiselles* and *girelles* (wrasse), and she also used the heads and tails of eels, and tiny green crabs. All these she would boil for about half an hour in a mixture of oil, water and wine, together with onions, tomatoes, fennel, orange peel and garlic, until everything had disintegrated and was absorbed into the soup. In a separate pan, she made a bed of sliced potatoes on which laid the larger, firmer-fleshed fish which always included some red, spiky *rascasses*, gurnard, John Dory or bream, comber and some eels. These she would cover with soup, more oil and saffron, and leave to boil for twelve to fifteen minutes. Then the bouillabaisse would be served immediately with the soup in one bowl and the larger fish separately in another dish. There would also be a rouille and some pieces of toasted local bread, which are always put at the bottom of each plate and are an essential, traditional adjunct to any good bouillabaisse.

BOUILLABAISSE

•

(Serves 8)
Fish soup (page 123), boiling hot.
1 kg / 2¼ lb mixed fillets of Mediterranean fish
(weaver, rascasse, monkfish, John Dory, red mullet)
cut into 5 cm / 2 in in pieces
1 kg / 2¼ lb mussels, scrubbed and debearded
300 g / 11 oz potatoes, peeled and cut into 3 mm /
⅛ in slices
salt and freshly ground pepper

•

Lay the potato slices in the bottom of a large pan in a single layer. Scatter over the pieces of weaver, rascasse and monkfish and the mussels. Pour the boiling soup over, bring to the boil, cover tightly with a lid and simmer for 5 minutes. Add the John Dory and red mullet pieces. Simmer, uncovered for about 5 minutes more, skimming whenever necessary.

Serve with good crusty bread and Saffron mayonnaise (page 123). (Photograph pp. 126-7)

Although I enjoy eating bouillabaisse and have cooked it for friends several times at home in London, I have never served it at La Tante Claire. As I have explained, it would not be a suitable dish to prepare for only small groups of people. I have however had great success at the restaurant with a bouillabaisse of snails, which is my own rather unorthodox variation on the classical theme. It has a fish soup as its base in the usual way, but then, instead of using the larger fish from the Mediterranean, I finish it with shellfish, such as mussels, scallops and crayfish, and, of course, the unexpected snails. The addition of mussels and lobster to a bouillabaisse has been the subject of hot dispute among purists over the last hundred and fifty years or so, but I doubt whether any of them ever thought of adding snails as well.

BOUILLABAISSE D'ESCARGOTS

•

BOUILLABAISSE WITH SNAILS

•

40 cooked snails
1.5 L /2½pt Fish soup (page 123)
50 g / 2 oz Snail butter (page 24)
12 baby carrots, turned and cooked
12 baby turnips, turned and cooked
12 small courgettes, turned and cooked
salt and freshly ground pepper

•

Heat the fish soup to boiling point. Add the snails, then mix in the snail butter and the vegetables. Check the seasoning. Ladle into soup plates or shallow bowls and serve immediately.

My days of making bouillabaisse at La Ciotat were not destined to last for long, however. My first impression of the *patron* of the Restaurant de la Plage as he sprawled unreachably in the grip of his afternoon siesta did not alter much during the first few months I was working in the kitchen. He was always in the bar, talking to his friends and counting his money; he got up late in the morning, and he never really did any serious work. His wife, on the other hand, I got to like and admire more and more, and I was not surprised when one day she disappeared with one of the customers. He was a good-looking man, about ten years younger than she was, and I had always noticed that they got on very well together. Whenever he was there on one of the days she had made bouillabaisse, she always gave him some, even though he was on his own. The *patronne* gave no warning of her departure. One morning

when I came down to the kitchen as usual to turn on the cooker and start work, she was just not there. She had left a letter for her husband, however, but though she told him she was leaving, she did not say where she was going. All his friends came to see him in his bar, and everybody gave advice. At last he set off in search of the offending couple. It took him three weeks before he finally located them living together in a hotel in Limoges. During that time I was alone in the kitchen, and to all intents and purposes I was in full charge of the restaurant. It was an odd position to be in, though it was a useful experience. Eventually the *patron* returned but his wife was not with him. She never came back to La Ciotat; and I heard that in the end there was a divorce, that she married her lover, and that they opened a restaurant in Limoges.

My next job, which I started in the spring of 1970, was in Switzerland, in the Pays de Vaud, at a health clinic about twenty-five miles to the north of Lausanne. The clinic occupied a beautiful eighteenth-century château with a wide terrace and fine views southwards over a rolling landscape of vines, villages and farms. The popularity of the establishment rested on its somewhat unusual variety of slimming cure. Indeed the director of the clinic was himself unusual, to start with, since he was ungainly, grossly overweight and an obvious gourmand. When I first went to see him for a preliminary interview, he told me he always enjoyed talking to cooks because he was fascinated by food and he loved eating. For half an hour we talked about recipes, and then he told me how his own patent slimming cure was supposed to

overleaf: *Making Bouillabaisse (recipe p. 124)*

work. Instead of being put on an immediate diet of dry biscuits and lemon juice, new patients were first asked to name their favourite food, then were told that they could eat as much of it as they wanted whenever they wanted, on the sole condition that they were not allowed to ask for anything else. Whatever you chose (it could be sole, turbot, steak, kidneys, roast pigeon, grilled salmon or anything else you might think of), you had to have for every single meal until you got heartily sick of it and were incapable of facing any more. At that point, the theory ran, you would start to beg for dry biscuits and lemon juice, and your cure could begin in earnest. I have no idea whether these cures were successful or not, but they certainly made for some very curious cooking programmes in the kitchen. It sometimes took people as long as six or seven days to learn to detest their favourite dish. In the meantime we had to prepare large quantities of the dish in question, and keep on sending it up to the dining room until more and more of it started to find its way back to the kitchen. The *partie* system had to be very flexible. Sometimes we were all fish cooks, preparing generous amounts of salmon or sole; sometimes half of us would be *rôtisseurs*, producing dozens of chateaubriands, and the other half *entremettiers*, responsible for gallons of some particular soup or stew; and then we would suddenly all have to go back to being fish cooks again to produce innumerable *raies au beurre noir* or *homards à l'américaine*. The clinic was expensive, the clients were rich, and no one worried about the cost of procuring immediately whatever ingredient somebody had unexpectedly asked for. I remember there was one patient, the wife of an important German newspaper proprietor, who found it quite impossible to choose between roast beef and oysters. This meant that the start of her cure would be held up indefinitely, and the anxious director came down to consult us in the kitchen. I managed to find a solution to the problem by suggesting a dish which combined both items, a recipe which, incidentally, I still do sometimes at La Tante Claire.

MIGNON DE BOEUF AUX HUÎTRES

FILLET STEAK WITH OYSTERS

4 × 100 g / 3½ oz fillet steaks
12 large oysters, shelled, juices reserved
75 g / 3 oz butter
1 tablespoon finely chopped shallots
30 ml / 1 fl oz white wine vinegar
150 ml / 5 fl oz Chicken stock (page 49)
100 ml / 4 fl oz double cream
1 teaspoon snipped chives
salt and freshly ground pepper

Melt 50 g / 2 oz butter in a frying pan and season the fillet steaks. Cook them on both sides until done to your liking. Transfer to a dish and keep in a warm place.

Discard the fat from the frying pan and put in the shallots. Sweat for 1 minute, then add the vinegar and reduce completely. Add the stock and the oyster juices and reduce by three-quarters. Add the cream and reduce until the sauce coats the back of a spoon. Put the oysters in the sauce to heat through, but do not boil. Check the seasoning, going easy on the salt.

Place the steaks on warm plates, put 3 oysters on top of each and coat with the sauce. Sprinkle the chives on top and serve immediately. (Photograph p. 130)

I only stayed at the clinic for about two months. The job of producing large amounts of deliciously cooked food with the principal aim of putting one's customer off eating, and of judging one's success as a chef by the quantity of food which was left on the plate, did not appeal to me at all. As soon as I could, I managed to get a place as commis chef at a restaurant at Ouchy, right on the shore of the Lake of Geneva. The restaurant was in the upper part of a big modern concrete building which stood next to the jetty used by the tall-funnelled, white and gold passenger boats which sailed round the lake. I shall always remember the regular splish-splash of their paddle-wheels as they left Ouchy on their way to Evian or Geneva; and in my mind's eye I shall always retain a picture of the jagged masses of the Savoy Alps on the other side of the lake, touched here and there with snow, and reminding me of the Pyrenees I used to see from Tarbes. The kitchen was in the centre of the building, and the restaurant extended outwards all round it, mostly on wide, open-air terraces looking out over the splendid scenery of the lake. The *chef de cuisine* was small and fat, almost a caricature of everybody's idea of a typical cook; but the kitchen was quite a large one, and it employed nearly thirty people. It was my biggest kitchen after that of the Aubette in Strasbourg. I quite liked the atmosphere, and I worked well and happily there, being promoted to the rank of sauce chef after only two months. The general character of the food we cooked was rather monotonous, however, since it was largely a restaurant for tourists, and the multilingual menus were printed on thick, glossy cards illustrated by coloured photographs of the various dishes. These were exactly the same as those served by almost every other similar restaurant on the shores of the lake, so the menu was not terribly original. The most interesting items were probably the lake fish. Besides perch and the little fish like minnows and gudgeon which were served as *petite friture*, the two best were dace, known as *féra* in French, and char, a trout-like fish which we call *omble chevalier.*

After a while I began to tire of working in this standardised, unvarying way; so once more I began hunting among the job pages in *L'Hôtellerie* and other trade papers. One day my eye fell upon an advertisement for a commis cook in a French restaurant in London, and I decided to apply for the job. I had been interested in England ever since one of the *entremettiers* at Strasbourg had told me how many French cooks, past and present, had done well there; but in my mind England was chiefly connected with Twickenham and rugby, and I could easily imagine myself, once established in London, spending happy afternoons watching all sorts of exciting matches. The first answer to my letter was to the effect that the present vacancy was filled but, as soon as another one occurred, I would be informed. In a few weeks I got the offer of a second job which I immediately accepted.

My journey to London, which, looking back, I now see as a turning point in my life, took place in the early autumn of 1970. I was quite on my own; my knowledge of English was virtually non-existent; but I felt no great anxiety about my immediate future. A cook must be prepared to travel in order to learn and to get on. As I settled back comfortably in the train taking me from the Gare du Nord to Calais, I had the instinctive feeling that I was making the right move at the right moment, and that I had nothing to worry about. I was quite shaken, nevertheless, by my very first contact with the British railway system. After the easy efficiency of French trains, the one into which I climbed at Dover seemed like some battered relic left over from the nineteenth century. It was dirty, slow, uncomfortable, and over half an hour late in leaving. All through the journey it kept on stopping and starting, stopping and starting. Darkness fell as we rumbled past the interminable rows of slate roofs which announced the suburbs of London. By the time we finally reached Victoria, the journey had taken so long that I was hopelessly late for my appointment.

It was nearly eleven at night when I reached my destination – Le Gavroche in Lower Sloane Street, the restaurant which Albert and Michel Roux had opened about three years before. Part of the deal was that a room would be found for me, so I would not have to worry about accommodation, but when I presented myself, this particular detail had either been entirely forgotten or simply ignored. It seemed for a time that there was nowhere at all for me to sleep, and that I would have to bed down that first night on one of the banquettes in the restaurant. I felt suddenly worn out and longed

Mignon de Boeuf aux Huîtres (recipe p. 128)

to get to bed and to sleep at once, so the prospect of having to wait until the last customer had left before I could lie down did not appeal to me in the least. The situation was saved, however, by one of the waiters, who had an extra bed in his room and offered to put me up for the night. The next day I was able to find a room for myself in a large, red-brick house in one of the streets near Sloane Square. It is a house I shall never forget, for not only was it my first London address, but, by a curious coincidence, it was in another house almost exactly opposite, that my small daughter first went to school. Waiting outside to collect her at the end of the afternoon, I have often looked across at the window of my old room and thought again about those first important months at Le Gavroche.

The two Roux brothers had started Le Gavroche in 1967, and it was already successful and well-known. The restaurant was only open for dinner, but each evening we served between fifty and sixty covers. There were only five of us in the kitchen but we worked well together, and there was that feeling of exhilarating excitement when we were hard pressed, which has always stimulated me. In Guy Mouilleron, who later opened his own London restaurant, Ma Cuisine in Walton Street, we had an excellent *chef de cuisine*. The traditional *partie* system was adhered to but reduced to its most basic form, since each one of us constituted an entire *partie* all on his own. We organised ourselves as *entremettier*, *poissonnier*, *rôtisseur*, *légumier*, and a *pâtissier* who was responsible for all the desserts. We had no *plongeur*, at least not of our own. The washer-up from the Brasserie Benoît, the Roux restaurant in the City, used to come in for an hour every evening between 5 and 6 o'clock to do all the really heavy washing-up involving such items as casseroles, saucepans and the larger kitchen utensils; but once he had gone, we had to do all the other washing-up ourselves. During the *service* the dirty plates and cutlery brought back to the kitchen by the waiters piled up relentlessly, and whoever had a moment's pause in his work rushed over to the sink to wash and dry what he could, then hurried back to his work table or his corner of the cooker. Our hours of work were from one o'clock in the afternoon until about one in the morning. Our first job on arrival was to store away the supplies which had been delivered to the restaurant during the morning (at first Albert employed a special buyer who went round all the markets, but later on the dealers used to call in to see the chef personally); then we had to prepare all the sauce bases and the right cuts of meat; then we would clean and fillet the fish and make the fish stock from the heads and bones; and we would also make any necessary mousses.

Albert and Michel Roux did not spend much time with us in the kitchen. They knew that things were being well run, and they had confidence in us. Albert would look in for about an hour most afternoons, but he never interfered with the cooking, though he was always interested in seeing how a new chef (such as myself) worked, what his particular style was, what new skills he had, and so on. Like all good cooks, Albert was always on the look-out for new knowledge; he was always ready to learn. For my own part, the most important thing I learned from Albert was always to respect the customer. At Le Gavroche the customer is always king. It was one of Albert's maxims that if a dish appeared on the menu, it must always be available if a customer ordered it, even though it was late at night and a particular dish was finished. If necessary it was the chef's job to prepare some more. It was a good approach, a good discipline, and I have always followed it at La Tante Claire.

The cooking at Le Gavroche at that time was completely classical, with no hint of *la nouvelle cuisine*. In fact the sauces were richer and heavier even than those I had learned to make at Reffye, and were the closest I have ever met to those of the *grande cuisine* of the nineteenth century. The customers delighted in them. To give some idea of the quality of the cooking, I remember that we used a good twenty litres of double cream a day to cook the food for about fifty customers. That meant that each customer, on average, must have been consuming almost half a litre of cream with his meal!

We revived quite a number of the more famous nineteenth-century dishes. One, I remember, was a *selle de veau Orloff*. This is an entire saddle of veal which has been sliced, mixed with ham, truffles and a cream sauce, then finally reconstituted to look once more like a complete saddle. It is a celebrated dish which was invented by Léonor Cheval, the chef of the Tortoni restaurant in Paris in the 1830s, and was first served to the Prince Orlov who was Nicholas I's ambassador to the court of France. On another famous occasion, in July 1913, it appeared on the menu which Auguste Escoffier prepared for the Kaiser on board the Imperator, the newly completed German liner for which the great French chef had designed and and organised the kitchens. But despite these historical associations, and the fact that the dish was very popular at Le Gavroche, I was never myself very impressed by it. It was not excessively rich, indeed it was no richer then most of the other dishes we served, but it always struck me as being slightly ridiculous and over-elaborate. One Gavroche recipe which I did keep on at La Tante Claire with slight alterations or variations of my own was fish terrine, made with bream and asparagus tips, served with a *beurre blanc*, and named after the great fourteenth-century cook who was *chef de cuisine* to Charles VI of France.

TERRINE DE POISSON À LA GUILLAUME TYREL

— • —

FISH TERRINE GUILLAUME TYREL

— • —

1 kg / 2¼ lb hake or John Dory, cut into chunks
1 L / 1¾ pt whipping cream
1 egg white, lightly beaten
15 g / ½ oz tarragon, chopped
4 tablespoons finely chopped parsley
1 tablespoon snipped chives
1 egg white
4 John Dory fillets (total weight about 250 g / 9 oz), flattened between 2 pieces of clingfilm with a heavy knife or cutlet bat.
12 asparagus tips, lightly cooked
salt, pepper and cayenne

— • —

Preheat the oven to 180°C / 350°F / gas 4.
Lightly dampen a 27 × 11 cm / 11 × 4 in cast iron terrine dish and line it with a large piece of clingfilm. Set aside.

Prepare a fish mousse by processing the chunks of fish in a food processor until smooth. Pass through a fine sieve and refrigerate until well chilled. When the fish is very cold, return it to the food processor and mix, adding the whipping cream little by little, until homogeneous. Season to taste with salt and pepper.

In a bowl, mix 500 g / 1 lb 2 oz fish mousse with the tarragon, parsley and chives. Set aside. Spread half the plain fish mousse over the bottom of the lined terrine dish. Brush with a little lightly beaten egg white, lay 2 John Dory fillets on top and brush again with a little egg white. Spread the herb-flavoured fish mousse evenly over the fillets, then arrange the last two John Dory fillets on top. Brush with a little egg white and lay the asparagus tips dipped in egg white on top. Finish the terrine with a layer of the plain fish mousse. Tap the dish on the work surface to settle the mousse and fold over the overhanging clingfilm.

Place the terrine in a deep roasting pan. Pour in boiling water to come halfway up the sides of the terrine, and cook in the oven for 1½ hours. Serve hot.

BEURRE BLANC

WHITE BUTTER SAUCE

250 g / 9 oz butter, diced, at room temperature
65 g / 2½ oz shallots, finely chopped
100 ml / 4 fl oz white wine
50 ml / 2 fl oz white wine vinegar
1 bay leaf
10 black peppercorns, crushed
salt

Put the shallots, white wine and vinegar into a small saucepan. Add the bay leaf and peppercorns, bring to the boil and reduce to 50 ml / 2 fl oz liquid.

Season and pass through a fine conical sieve back into the pan. Over low heat, whisk in the butter, a little at a time, until the sauce is completely homogeneous. Serve warm.

Everyone who worked at Le Gavroche was French. We ate most of our meals together in a corner of the restaurant; our rooms were often in the same boarding house, or at least in houses which were quite near to each other; we spent a good deal of our time in each other's company, and as a result we did not have much contact with the outside world of London. I myself only got to know it very gradually. On two mornings a week I attended English classes in South Kensington, but even there the other students were mostly French and we never spoke English together. We only knew English food by the bad reputation it had in France, and we never set foot in an English restaurant. We lived happily in a little group of our own which included cooks and waiters from other French restaurants or hotels, and we were really quite cut off from our surroundings. The silent, empty streets of London on a Sunday morning were at first as strange and foreign to me as had been the run-down railway carriage at Dover. In the end it was through my love of rugby (which, after all, had been the main reason for my coming to England in the first place), and through enjoying the matches and mingling with excited crowds of fellow-enthusiasts that I was able to put down my first very tentative roots into English soil.

I think it all began with the smell of badly-fried onions coming from a hamburger stall at Twickenham very late one chilly winter afternoon. I was frozen with cold; the match had been disappointing; I had had nothing to eat all day, and was ravenously hungry. The lean stallkeeper looked undernourished and thoroughly miserable. He was even colder than I was and probably even hungrier. The crowd flowing past ignored him completely. The smell of his onions grew worse the nearer I got to his stall, but nevertheless, half in hunger and half in sheer pity, I bought a hamburger, crushed with its onions between the two halves of a sad, soggy bun, and ate it. The man's icy cheeks broke into an amazed little cockney smile as he watched me. My stopping had taken him completely by surprise; but what he did not know was that because I actually found the hamburger quite good, I was far more surprised even than he was. It was a special moment, because for the very first time I felt I had made a genuine contact with England. Some sort of inner reluctance melted away as I ate the hamburger, and afterwards London seemed less strange, and I started to feel at home there.

In the early part of 1971, after I had been working at Le Gavroche for about six months, Albert Roux asked me to become *chef de cuisine* at his other restaurant, the Brasserie Benoît in the City of London. It was an important promotion for me. The Brasserie was an extremely busy lunchtime restaurant, full every weekday with office workers; and on the first floor, above the dining room, there was quite a large snack bar where you could eat quickly. In the kitchen (we did about a hundred covers a day) I was in charge of four cooks and a *plongeur*, the one who used to come to help out at Le Gavroche. Later on I was to find the experience of running a kitchen which specialised in lunches very useful when I decided to introduce short three-course lunch menus at La Tante Claire.

SOUPE DE PRINTEMPS

SPRING VEGETABLE SOUP

1.5 L /2½pt Chicken stock (page 49)
100 g / 3½ oz lean smoked ham
1 kg / 2¼ lb broad beans, shelled
100 g / 3½ oz potatoes, cut into 1 cm / ½in dice
450 g / 1 lb fresh peas, shelled
100 g / 3½ oz onions, cut into
1 cm / ½ in dice
1 garlic clove, finely chopped
4 slices good country bread, toasted and buttered
salt and freshly ground pepper

Garnish
finely chopped mint leaves
finely chopped basil leaves
4 tomatoes, blanched, skinned, deseeded and diced
4 teaspoons extra virgin olive oil

Bring the stock to the boil. Put in the ham and all the vegetables. Bring back to the boil, skim and simmer for 20 minutes, or until all the vegetables are tender. Check the seasoning. Put a slice of buttered toasted bread in the bottom of 4 soup bowls. Pour over the soup and garnish with plenty of diced tomato, the fresh herbs and a trickle of olive oil.

RIS DE VEAU AUX AMANDES

VEAL SWEETBREADS WITH ALMONDS

4 × 150 g / 5 oz veal sweetbreads, soaked in cold water for 2 hours
50 ml / 2 fl oz vegetable oil
50 g / 2 oz butter
1 onion, finely chopped
200 ml / 7 fl oz port
200 ml / 7 fl oz Chicken stock (page 49)
250 ml / 9 fl oz whipping cream
juice of ½ lemon
100 g / 3½ oz slivered almonds, lightly toasted
salt and freshly ground pepper

Preheat the oven to 200°C / 425°F / gas 7.

Blanch the sweetbreads in boiling water for 5 minutes, drain and carefully peel off the outside membrane without damaging the sweetbreads.

In a large frying pan, heat the oil until sizzling. Season the sweetbreads and seal both sides. Cover lightly with foil and transfer to the oven. Cook for 10 minutes.

Put the sweetbreads on a warm plate and cover with the foil to keep them warm. Tip off the fat from the frying pan, add the butter and sweat the chopped onion. Deglaze with the port and reduce by half. Add the chicken stock and reduce by three-quarters. Then add the cream and lemon juice and cook until the sauce coats the back of a spoon. Pass the sauce through a fine sieve over the sweetbreads and sprinkle on the almonds.

Glace aux Pruneaux à l'Armagnac (recipe p. 136)

GLACE AUX PRUNEAUX À L'ARMAGNAC

PRUNE AND ARMAGNAC ICE CREAM

500 ml / 18 fl oz vanilla-flavoured *Crème Anglaise*, chilled (page 41)
100 ml / 4 fl oz double cream
50 ml / 2 fl oz armagnac
6 Prunes in armagnac, diced (recipe below)
3 tablespoons syrup from the prunes

Pour the chilled vanilla custard into an ice cream maker and churn until thick but still just soft. At this point add the double cream, the armagnac, diced prunes and their syrup. Continue to churn until thick, then transfer to a container and freeze until ready to use (Photograph p. 135)

PRUNEAUX À L'ARMAGNAC

PRUNES IN ARMAGNAC

1 kg / 2 lb prunes
4 tea bags
350 g / 12 oz sugar
500 ml / 18 fl oz armagnac

Boil 1.7 L / 3 pt water in a saucepan. Take off the heat and add the tea bags. Leave to infuse for 2 minutes, then add the prunes. Cover the pan. Make a syrup with the sugar and 100 ml / 4 fl oz water; bring to the boil, leave to cool and refrigerate.

The following day, strain the prunes and put them in a large glass jar, pouring the armagnac over. Add the cold syrup. Leave to macerate for a month in a cool place.

It was at the Brasserie Benoît that I first met Annie Barraud, the girl whom I was to marry the following year, and without whose support and encouragement La Tante Claire could never have flourished as it has. The occasion was therefore a most important one, but oddly enough, we each remember it quite differently. For my part I merely recall that one morning the manageress came down to the kitchen with a small, slim, blonde French girl who had just arrived in London and was going to be in charge of the upstairs snack bar. I was told that she had been working in Geneva, and that she had decided to take a job in London to improve her English. We were introduced, and I noticed at once that she was rather attractive, but, apart from that, I cannot remember very much more.

The cooks at the Brasserie Benoît started work at 7 o'clock, and every morning, at about nine, Annie came down to the kitchen to collect the dishes and bowls she needed for her snack bar. At first I watched her in silence as she stood on tiptoe to get her dishes from the high shelf in front of the table where I worked; then, one day, we got talking, and gradually, from that moment on, we came to know each other better and better.

We discovered that we had been born in the same year, 1948; that we had both trained at a catering college, and that neither of our fathers' families had been French; but in other ways our two childhoods were very different. Annie was born in Bellegarde, an old frontier town lying deep in the valley of the Rhone between Lyons and Geneva and surrounded by mountains, and she always remembers how sad the place was. It was a complete contrast to the Gascon village of Saint Puy and the fields and vines of my grandparents' farm. Bellegarde was a small industrial town with grim factories and smoking chimneys, and a long main street which always seemed mournful because of the grey, unpainted walls of the houses and the hundreds of slate roofs which were cheerless even when they glistened on a wet day.

Annie and I soon discovered that we both enjoyed talking about food. At her Bellegarde college she had specialised in restaurant management, cooking being only a subsidiary subject, and, as a result, she felt that she was no cook, and has never really liked working in a kitchen. She feels she has no innate sense of taste or imagination when it comes to food, although she knows far more about it than she realises. As a boy I had grown up with the local cooking of Gascony, but Annie had known that of Savoy, and both her mother and father were good cooks.

Her father had a small garden where he grew vegetables and kept rabbits. Once a month, for Sunday lunch, Annie's mother cooked one of these rabbits in a *civet de lapin* which she served with polenta, an old Savoyard dish dating back to the eighteenth century when present-day French Savoie formed part of the kingdom of Savoy, governed from Turin, and when maize was already cultivated extensively in the wide plains of Piedmont. Madame Barraud did not cook the polenta until it was firm, as the Italians do, but made it instead more like a purée of potatoes, and she added a lot of milk and cream to soften it. For Annie it was one of those magic, childhood dishes which she has never forgotten, just as I have never forgotten my own mother's *brandade de morue*. Annie remembers how she and her sister used to make little wells in the middle of their polenta and wait for their mother to pour in the *civet* sauce, and how special this moment of pouring always was. Even now, when I offer her one of my sophisticated rabbit dishes from La Tante Claire, I still feel that secretly she would rather have her mother's *civet*. There was something about it, some vital detail which made all the difference. To find out what it was, you would have had to watch Madame Barraud very carefully while she cooked her rabbit, and, by watching, you would have learned her secret.

CIVET DE LAPIN

•

RABBIT STEW

•

1 × 1.2 kg / 2½ lb rabbit, cut into serving pieces
100 g / 3½ oz seasoned flour
50 ml / 2 fl oz vegetable oil
150 g / 5 oz carrots, cut into large dice
150 g / 5 oz onions, thinly sliced
4 garlic cloves, chopped
1 Bouquet garni (page 11)
1.1 L / 2 pt good quality dry white wine
1 tablespoon finely chopped parsley
salt and freshly ground pepper

•

Preheat the oven to 200°C / 400°F / gas 6.
Roll the rabbit pieces in the seasoned flour. Heat the vegetable oil in a large, heavy ovenproof casserole. When very hot, brown the pieces of rabbit quickly and evenly. Add the carrots and onions and sweat gently for 5 minutes. Hold the lid over the casserole and pour away all the cooking fat. Deglaze with the white wine and bring to the boil. Put in the chopped garlic and bouquet garni and season.

Cover the casserole and cook in the oven for about 1 hour. Stir the stew regularly during cooking, adding a little water if too much evaporates. When the rabbit is very tender, take it out of the casserole with a slotted spoon and put into another pan. Pass the sauce through a fine sieve over the meat. Discard the vegetables and bouquet garni. Simmer the stew for 10 more minutes on the hob. Serve on warm plates and sprinkle with parsley.

This stew is delicious served with lightly-buttered fine french beans and sautéed button mushrooms.

LAPEREAU FARCI AU FOIE GRAS, AUX ARTICHAUTS ET TRUFFE

—— • ——

RABBIT STUFFED WITH FOIE GRAS, ARTICHOKES AND TRUFFLE

—— • ——

1 large or 2 small rabbits, skinned and cleaned, rib bones removed
225 g / 8 oz fresh foie gras
1 truffle, scrubbed
2 artichoke bottoms (see *Pavé de loup Barigoule*, page 110), cooked
2 tablespoons vegetable oil
25 ml / 1 fl oz armagnac
200 ml / 7 fl oz Chicken stock (page 49)
a knob of butter
salt and freshly ground pepper

—————— • ——————

Preheat the oven to 220°C / 425°F / gas 7.

Cut the foie gras, truffle and artichoke bottoms into cubes and mix. Stuff the inside of the rabbit with the mixture. Sew up the belly and place the rabbit in a roasting pan with the oil. Season and roast in the oven for 20-30 minutes.

Remove the cooked rabbit from the pan and keep warm. Pour off the fat from the pan and add the armagnac and chicken stock. Reduce the liquid until it coats the back of a spoon, then stir in the butter. Slice the rabbit, arrange on a serving plate and pour over the sauce.

DOS DE LAPEREAU AUX LANGOUSTINES

—— • ——

SADDLES OF YOUNG RABBIT STUFFED WITH LANGOUSTINES

—— • ——

saddles of 4 young rabbits, boned, with their kidneys
8 large langoustines
50 ml / 2 fl oz extra virgin olive oil
75 g / 3 oz shallots finely chopped
1 tablespoon tomato purée
100 ml / 4 fl oz French dry vermouth
300 ml / ½ pt Chicken stock (page 49)
1 Bouquet garni (page 11)
1 clove garlic, chopped
30 g / 1 oz butter
100 g / 3½ oz spinach, cooked
4 tablespoons vegetable oil
200 ml / 7 fl oz double cream
1 tablespoon chives, finely snipped
salt and freshly ground pepper
300 g / 11 oz Home-made noodles (page 196), for serving

—————— • ——————

Preheat the oven to 220°C / 425°F / gas 7.
Bring a large pan of salted water to the boil. Pull off the langoustine tails and plunge them in the boiling water for 30 seconds. Drain and remove the shells. Refrigerate the langoustines.

With a heavy knife, roughly chop the claws, head and body (with the intestines removed) and the tail shells. Make a stock by cooking these for 5 minutes in the very hot olive oil, stirring from time to time. Add 50 g / 2 oz chopped shallot and cook for 1 minute. Add the tomato purée, stirring well while it cooks for another minute. Deglaze with the dry vermouth and chicken stock.

Add the bouquet garni and garlic, bring to the boil and simmer for 20 minutes. Pass through a fine conical sieve, pushing hard with a small ladle, to extract as much stock as possible. Set aside. Discard the crushed shells left in the sieve.

Over low heat, melt the butter in a saucepan. Sweat the remaining shallot until soft, then add the rabbit kidneys and brown them quickly. Put in the spinach, stirring with a fork to mix it thoroughly with the kidneys and shallots. Season with salt and pepper, place on a plate and allow to cool.

Open out the 4 rabbit saddles, skin-side down, on the work surface. Take half the spinach mixture and spread one-quarter between the fillets of each rabbit saddle. Top with 2 langoustines for each saddle and spread over the rest of the spinach. Pull the overhanging skin over the stuffing and tie up with 3 pieces of string, one at each end, and one in the middle. Season well with salt and pepper.

Heat the vegetable oil in a roasting pan. When very hot, quickly brown the rabbit saddles on both sides. Transfer to the oven and cook for 12 minutes, turning the saddles over halfway through so that they brown evenly. Discard the cooking fat and keep the saddles warm. Deglaze the roasting pan with the prepared langoustine stock. Whisk in the cream and reduce until the sauce just begins to coat the back of a wooden spoon. Pass through a fine sieve and keep warm.

Remove the string and cut each saddle into 3 equal slices. Place on warm serving plates and pour the sauce around, sprinkling over the chopped chives. Serve with lightly-buttered noodles.

When Annie was about twelve, her mother died. Almost at once she had to become the housekeeper of the family, looking after her brother and sister, doing most of the shopping, and helping and supporting her father. Outwardly she was still the small, quiet, rather old-fashioned child, who was only just getting used to wearing her first pair of glasses, and whose straight hair was cut in a fringe across her forehead (a style she hated, and which won her the nickname of Mademoiselle Rue de la République, after the long, straight main street of Bellegarde), but inwardly she felt older and more responsible. 'I was no longer a little girl,' she once told me, 'I was suddenly a little woman. I had to do things.'

It was now her father who cooked the Sunday lunches. The meals were different but they were still good. Annie can remember how well he made *bugnes*, the fried, sweet fritters which are the Savoyard version of the Gascon *merveilles* my grandmother cooked for me at Saint Puy, and which were one of the traditional cakes eaten by children at Mardi Gras. She recalls, too, her father's patient, respectful love for cardoons. The cardoon, a sort of cross between a thistle and an artichoke, is Savoy's most prized winter vegetable, and is always eaten at Christmas time. Annie's father grew them in his little garden, taking immense pains to protect them from the frost by covering them with a heterogeneous variety of paper bags, and devoting hours of his time to getting them ready for cooking once he had brought them home. Cleaning them, avoiding the thorns, cutting up the green, delicate flesh, and dropping the pieces into a bowl of vinegar and water before they have time to blacken is an incredibly tedious task. Even the tiniest scrap of skin or peel left on the edible part of a cardoon will give it a horrible, bitter taste and make it uneatable. Armand Barraud was a small, upright, self-contained man, and he would sit interminably at the kitchen table, looking very dignified, as he carefully and laboriously peeled his cardoons.

CARDONS À LA MOELLE

•

CARDOONS WITH BEEF MARROW

•

1 cardoon, cleaned and cut into 3 cm / 1¼ in pieces
150 g / 5 oz marrow bones
15 g / ½ oz butter
40 g / 1½ oz flour
80 g / 3 oz grated gruyère
juice of 1 lemon
500 ml / 18 fl oz Chicken stock (page 49)
salt and freshly ground pepper

•

Cook the cardoon in a large saucepan of water mixed with 20 g / ¾ oz flour, the lemon juice and 20 g / ¾ oz salt until tender. Heat the butter in a shallow pan, add the remaining flour and cook for 3 minutes, stirring continuously with a whisk. Add the chicken stock, still stirring, then simmer gently for 20 minutes. Season.

When the cardoon is cooked, drain, mix with the sauce and transfer to a gratin dish. Scoop out the marrow from the bones and poach in a little simmering water for 10 minutes. Drain, slice and place on the top of the cardoon. Sprinkle with gruyère, brown and serve.

BUGNES

•

ORANGE FLOWER FRITTERS

•

(Makes about 10)
250 g / 9 oz plain flour, sifted
¼ teaspoon salt
15 g / ½ oz caster sugar
2 eggs, lightly beaten
50 g / 2 oz butter, softened
15 g / ½ oz fresh yeast
2 tablespoons tepid water
1 teaspoon orange flower water
2 L / 3½pt fresh vegetable oil, for deep-frying
100 g / 3½ oz icing sugar

•

Put the flour in a large bowl and make a well in the centre. Dissolve the yeast in the tepid water and pour it into the well along with the salt, sugar, eggs and the softened butter.

Add the orange flower water drop by drop at the beginning of the kneading; you may need a little more depending on the moisture content of the flour. Knead until the dough is rather firm. Dust the dough with a little flour, wrap in a tea towel and leave to rest for about 30 minutes in a cool place. Divide the dough into four. Take one piece, roll it out to a thickness of no more than 3 mm / ⅛ in and cut into 2 × 8 cm / 1 × 3½ in rectangles. Heat the oil to 180°C / 350°F and cook the first batch of bugnes. They are cooked when they rise to the surface. Lift them out of the oil with a slotted spoon and drain on absorbent paper. Repeat the operation with the 3 remaining pieces of dough. Sift icing sugar over the bugnes and serve them with a rosé wine.

As a boy at Saint Puy I had enjoyed many helpings of my grandmother's *magret de canard* and foie gras, and it was good to discover that Annie as a young girl had enjoyed the same things when she went to visit her paternal uncle's farm near Bordeaux. She could only go there occasionally; but she was fascinated by the vines and the wine-making and the work in the fields, and by the big, open fireplace in the farmhouse kitchen, which must have been very much like that at the Oratoire, where great pieces of beef could be roasted over a wood fire. These glimpses of real country life were a wonderful change from daily routine in the drab little flat in Bellegarde.

At the age of about sixteen, Annie decided to go into the restaurant business, and started her course at the catering college at Bellegarde. She now felt more than ever that she was no longer a child. My own childhood died away far more gradually. My visits to Saint Puy and my contacts with my grandparents continued for a long time, and I was often in touch with them even while I was doing my cookery course, so that the spirit of my school holidays extended itself into my early working life. Where Annie and I did, at this stage, share a common experience was in the quality of our professional training. We were both taught to respect and follow the same high, demanding, perhaps even rather old-fashioned standards of work; and this was one of the things which brought us together while we were working at the Brasserie Benoît, and which marked us off from some of the other cooks and waiters whose methods were often more easy-going than ours. It must also have caught the attention of Albert and Michel Roux. Early in 1972 they had bought the Waterside Inn, a delapidated pub right on the banks of the Thames at Bray in Berkshire, which they wanted to restore and convert into a very good French restaurant where everything from the cooking to the setting would be of outstanding quality. Very soon after acquiring it, Albert asked Annie and me if we would like the job of getting the place into order and then managing it. It was a wonderful offer, and we knew at once that accepting it would mean a turning point in our lives.

Albert has always been a man full of life and energy who never slackens for a moment, and who is interested by everything and everybody. Annie had at once felt stimulated by his enthusiasm, and soon got into the swing of running the snack bar. At the height of the lunch hour, when the serving of terrines and salads and cold chicken was at its busiest, she had help from a talkative Algerian waiter called Said, whose rapid dexterity in filling up empty bowls with fresh salad, carving hams, making sandwiches, and doing the washing-up was astonishing; but otherwise she was completely on her own and responsible for everything. She really liked the work, enjoyed seeing the same customers every day, and, of course, her English improved dramatically. Albert noticed all this, and saw that Annie was always willing to put in extra hours if there was still work to be done at the end of the day. As far as I was concerned, both the Roux brothers had got to know me very well by then; they knew my

style, the way I ran the kitchen, and what my professional standards were, so that when they knew that Annie and I were going out together, they must have thought that we would make a good couple to run the new restaurant.

It did not take us long to make up our minds to accept the offer. Albert was very excited about the inn; he said it was absolutely right for what he had in mind, and one day he took us to see it. Neither of us had been to Bray before, but as soon as we saw the place we were charmed by it. Bray must be every Frenchman's idea of the typical English village. We drove past the almshouses built in 1627 'for the poor for ever', and found ourselves near a village green where Georgian houses and earlier half-timbered gables mingled harmoniously together.

When Albert led us inside the Waterside Inn, we found builders already at work and everything in chaos. It was hard to imagine what it would all be like in the end. The place had been used as an ordinary pub, and, as you entered, the bar was on your left, in the room where now customers sit in comfortable chairs to sip aperitifs before starting their meal. What astonished us the most was the sight of the big room facing the Thames which Albert was going to turn into his restaurant. It was in a terrible state of dilapidation, and the floor was bare, beaten earth like that of a peasant's barn in one of the French villages I knew as a boy. I had never imagined that I could ever see a floor like that in England! About a month later, in July 1972, Albert took us to Bray for a second visit so that, amongst other things, we could discuss the lay-out of the kitchen. The work was getting on well; the decorators were now painting and wallpapering, but it was still not easy to see it all as a completed, working restaurant.

Annie and I had by now definitely decided to get married, but we did not feel in any great hurry to do so. Albert Roux, on the other hand, was adamant that he wanted to open the Waterside in November, and we knew that he would very much like us to take on the job, right from the start, as a formally married couple. We were going to be the bosses, he said, and we would have more weight and authority if we were husband and wife. We were young, full of admiration for Albert, and very excited about the new job, so we agreed to marry as soon as we reasonably could. It was a quick decision, but we have never regretted it because, even without Albert, we would certainly have got married sooner or later. Annie had only visited Tarbes and Saint Puy once, in May, when she had met my family for the first time. When we told them a couple of months later that we were going to marry, the family felt it was a little hurried, though nobody knew that it was all to do with the Waterside! To smooth things over, we decided to have the wedding in Gascony, in the village of Saint Puy, near my grandparents' farm, where my uncle was the mayor and would conduct the civil ceremony which in France precedes the wedding in church. When the marriage finally took place towards the end of September, everyone enjoyed themselves and had a good time, and forgot any concerns they may have had!

Once back in England, we were able to devote ourselves whole-heartedly to the Waterside. Annie spent almost the whole of October at Bray, organising all the things which would have to be in perfect order for the arrival of the first customers: decorations, curtains, furniture, cutlery, tablecloths, and so on. She was so determined to make a real success of the restaurant that she must have worked twelve hours a day at that time. Though I was still working as chef at the Brasserie Benoît, I too spent quite a lot of time at Bray that October, checking the new equipment in the kitchen and devising menus. At last, in November 1972, exactly as planned, the Waterside Inn was ready to open.

We ran it for two years, and they were the two best years of my life. Albert and Michel gave me complete freedom to manage the kitchen as I liked, and to cook whatever dishes I wanted. They looked in from time to time, and I always showed them the menus I was thinking of doing, but they never interfered with my plans or my system. They felt they could rely on me and knew that I would only cook and serve dishes which I myself enjoyed eating and which I knew to be good. Albert selected and interviewed the staff who worked under us, both in the kitchen and in the restaurant, and as they were trained in the same way and to the same standards as we were ourselves, our relationship with them was always good. Otherwise we felt as free as if we were managing our own business. There were usually four or five of us in the kitchen which I organized on the lines of the Gavroche kitchen. We were each responsible for the work of a particular *partie*, but we had a permanent *plongeur*, which made things a lot easier. We had no trouble with managing ninety to a hundred covers at a busy weekend lunchtime, though when there were more than that, as sometimes happened in the summer, we had to arrange menus with a larger proportion of cold dishes, which we could prepare in advance and have ready on hand for serving quickly.

ESCALOPE DE SAUMON CRU AU CORIANDRE

•

MARINATED RAW SALMON WITH CORIANDER

•

300 g / 11 oz salmon fillet, skinned and very thinly sliced
50 ml / 2 fl oz virgin olive oil
10 soft green peppercorns
20 coriander seeds
20 fresh coriander leaves
salt

•

Gently crush the pepper and coriander and mix them with the oil and salt to taste. Put in the salmon and marinate for 30 minutes. Brush some of the marinade on a dish. Place the salmon on top and brush over some more marinade. Arrange the fresh coriander leaves on top. Serve with Melba toast.

TERRINE DE LOTTE EN GELÉE AUX GOUSSES D'AIL

JELLIED MONKFISH TERRINE WITH GARLIC

(Serves 8)

750 g / 1 lb 10 oz monkfish, boned weight
200 ml / 7 fl oz vegetable oil
100 g / 3½ oz garlic cloves, peeled and blanched 3 times
750 ml / 1¼ pt Fish stock (page 49)
100 ml / 4 fl oz French dry vermouth
100 ml / 4 fl oz dry white wine
1 pinch of saffron threads
2 egg whites
10 gelatine leaves
300 g / 11 oz long thin courgettes sliced lengthways with a mandoline into 18 cm / 7 in ribbons, cooked in boiling salted water and drained
75 g / 3 oz carrots, cut into 5 cm / ¼ in dice, cooked in salted boiling water and drained
75 g / 3 oz fine French beans, cut into 5 cm / ¼ in lengths, cooked in salted boiling water and drained
2 tablespoons chopped mixed herbs (chervil, fennel, parsley, chives)
salt

Heat the vegetable oil to 90°C / 194°F and cook the blanched garlic until soft and golden. Drain on absorbent paper.

In a shallow pan, heat the fish stock with the vermouth, white wine and saffron, and season with salt. Bring to a simmer and poach the monkfish in this barely-simmering stock for about 15 minutes, depending on the size of the tail. As soon as you can insert a larding needle into the thickest part easily and without resistance, take the fish out and allow to cool. Leave the cooking stock to cool.

Measure out 1.1 L / 2 pt of the stock. Whisk the egg whites until just frothy and pour over the cold stock.

Bring to a simmer, whisking continuously, and cook for 5 minutes to clarify the stock.

Meanwhile, soak the gelatine leaves in cold water. Pass the stock gently through a fine conical sieve, lined with a piece of muslin. It should be very clear. Reheat and whisk in the softened gelatine leaves until dissolved. Leave to cool, then transfer to the fridge until syrupy and thick but not set. Lightly dampen a 25 × 10 × 7½ cm / 10 × 4 × 3 in terrine dish and line with 2 layers of overhanging clingfilm. Line the bottom and sides of the dish with the courgette ribbons, laying them end to end so that the ends of the ribbons join in the middle of the dish and overhang the clingfilm.

Stir the diced carrots, French beans, chopped herbs and cooked garlic cloves into the half-set jelly and pour half the jelly into the lined terrine dish. Put in the fish and cover with the rest of the jelly. Fold over the overhanging courgette ribbons and clingfilm and refrigerate for 12 hours.

Cut the terrine into 1 cm / ½ in slices. Place a slice on each plate and drizzle a few drops of lemon juice and extra virgin olive oil over each portion. The terrine can be garnished with fresh dill sprigs and a small tomato and lamb's lettuce salad.

I have always cooked in my own way. Right from the start, at the Waterside, I knew exactly what I wanted to do in the kitchen and where to find my inspiration. My food has always had a rather rustic character, because it is based on the country dishes of south-west France, the *cuisine du terroir* I knew and enjoyed as a boy, and which was exemplified for me in my mother's cooking at Tarbes or my grandmother's at Saint Puy. It was the traditional family cooking of the French provinces. Today, when most housewives spend far less time in their kitchens than they used to, it has largely disappeared, and I am lucky to have belonged to what is probably the very last generation to have known it naturally and genuinely through ordinary, everyday experience. It was based on the dozen or so great local dishes of France; on the *pot-au-feu*, and on dishes like *daubes*, *civets*, *blanquettes*, *bouillabaisses*, *choucroutes*, *garbures* and *poule-au-pot*, which would simmer away for hours in iron pots hung on hooks over wood fires or on the top of ornate, brass-decked, cast-iron stoves. Every ingredient was fresh and full of flavour because it was the local produce of the area. It was a *cuisine* of affection and respect in which the mother of the family prepared the food she liked for the people she loved and who she knew also appreciated her food. In the old days a family meal was almost a sort of family communion, and I have been very much influenced by that both at the Waterside and at La Tante Claire. I am never happier than when a customer comes to the kitchen to tell me he has taken as much pleasure in eating a meal as I have taken in cooking it. Even if it were to prove commercially profitable, I would never put a dish I disliked on the Tante Claire menu.

In those days family cooking was known as *la cuisine de femme*, because, obviously, it was done by women; by wives, mothers, and grandmothers who devoted a great deal of their time to it and were usually excellent cooks. Cooking was a highly important part of their traditional social role in town and village life, and, of course, it was an essential acquisition for any young girl who was hoping to find a good husband. These housewives may not have aspired to very elaborate sauces, but I can remember many who could make a far better *boeuf bourgignon* than most *chefs de cuisine*. My grandmother, for example, used to make such a good *civet de lièvre* that whenever anybody for several miles around shot a hare, they always brought it to her to be cooked. Secret skills were passed on from generation to generation, from mother to daughter; and any child who grew up with this cooking, and really got to know its tastes and methods and ingredients, served a very good apprenticeship as a cook without even realising it.

It was certainly so in my own case. When I started my first year at Reffye, I was already competent at cooking local and regional dishes, but I had no knowledge at all of French classical cooking. This therefore, was what I had to learn at my catering college, and it meant restaurant cooking, *la cuisine d'homme*. This differs from *la cuisine de femme* in two main respects – kitchen organisation and ingredients. The restaurant kitchen works in *parties*, and this enables it to carry out many simultaneous activities which would be far beyond the physical capacity of a single housewife working alone at the family cooker. As regards ingredients, a restaurant can usually afford to purchase a far wider variety of items which it can store, and which free it from the seasonal or geographical limitations of the old *cuisine du terroir*. Another important difference is that a chef can take on the labour of making large amounts of stock or *fonds de cuisine* which, in the past, were never part of family cooking but which contribute so much to the taste and character of *la cuisine d'homme*.

These were the two traditions I wanted to bring together in my cooking at the Waterside Inn. The principal emphasis was to be on the country nature of *la cuisine du terroir*, but it was to be enhanced, though not completely transformed by the extra skills and resources of *la cuisine de restaurant*. I decided to use ingredients such as truffles and sole and scallops which certainly my grandparents would never have had in their village; and that the sauces would contain stocks and essences which would have been equally unknown to them. I am sure my grandmother would have enjoyed the gastronomic alliance of the old and the new.

SOLE GRATINÉE À LA GASCONNE

•

SOLE GASCON-STYLE

•

4 small Dover sole, each about 350 g / 12 oz,
skinned and heads removed
100 g / 3½ oz butter
10 g / ⅓ oz chopped shallots
2 tablespoons tarragon vinegar
100 ml / 4 fl oz white wine
1 teaspoon tomato purée
200 ml / 7 fl oz Fish stock (page 49)
50 ml / 2 fl oz double cream
1 egg yolk
1 teaspoon parsley
1 tablespoon breadcrumbs
salt

•

*In a shallow gratin dish, melt 20 g / ¾ oz butter. Add
the shallot and sweat for 1 minute. Add the vinegar
and reduce completely. Add the wine, boil for 1 minute,
then add the tomato purée, fish stock to taste and salt.
Bring to the boil. Place the sole in the dish, cover with
foil and simmer for 5 minutes. Turn the fish over and
cook for a further 3 minutes. Drain the cooking juices
into a small pan, and keep the sole warm in the dish.*

*Add the cream to the cooking juices, boil quickly and
reduce to about 200 ml / 7 fl oz. Take the pan off the
heat and leave the sauce to cool for 2 minutes. Add the
egg yolk, whisking very quickly. Stir in the parsley and
check the seasoning. Pour the sauce over the fish and
sprinkle the breadcrumbs on top. Place the dish under
a hot grill until the breadcrumbs are golden, and serve
at once.*

TERRINE DE CASSOULET

•

JELLIED TERRINE OF CASSOULET

•

500 g / 1 lb 2 oz dried haricot beans, soaked
overnight
3 Preserved duck thighs (page 181, boned and
coarsely chopped
1.5 L / 2½ pt Chicken stock (page 49)
1 Bouquet garni (page 11)
100 g / 3½ oz smoked bacon, in 1 piece
2 gelatine leaves, soaked in cold water for 10
minutes before using
400 g / 14 oz carrots, 18 cm / 7 in long, peeled and
sliced lengthways with a mandoline into ribbons
1 tablespoon finely chopped parsley
salt and freshly ground pepper

•

*Drain the beans and put them in a large saucepan
with the chicken stock, bouquet garni, smoked bacon
and pepper to taste. Bring to the boil and simmer for
about 2½ hours, adding more water if necessary, until
the beans are tender. Once the beans are cooked,
discard the bacon and bouquet garni. Add the soaked
gelatine leaves and stir until completely dissolved. Cool
and refrigerate until thick but not set.*

*In a pan of boiling salt water, lightly cook the carrot
ribbons, drain and cool. Meanwhile, line a 27 × 10 ×
9 cm / 10½ × 4 × 3½ in loaf tin with a double layer
of overhanging clingfilm. When the carrot ribbons are
cold, use them to line the bottom and sides of the tin,
laying them end to end so that the ends join in the
middle of the tin and overhang the clingfilm.*

*When the bean and gelatine mixture is cold and thick,
mix in the parsley and the chopped preserved duck.
Pour into the carrot-lined tin and fold over the carrot
ribbons and clingfilm. Refrigerate for 12 hours.*

*Serve with a Vinaigrette (page 25) with added finely
chopped herbs. (Photograph p. 146)*

Terrine de Cassoulet (recipe p. 145)

Of course, my idea of combining *la cuisine du terroir* with *haute cuisine* is by no means original. All through the history of French cooking, people have been trying to freshen up a classical tradition grown stale by introducing into it the stimulation of new tastes drawn from fresh, natural ingredients which nearly always means a return, in one way or another, to country food. 'Let a cabbage soup taste entirely of cabbage,' wrote Nicolas de Bonnefons in *Les Délices de la Campagne* of 1654, 'a leek soup of leeks, a turnip soup of turnips.' About a century later, cookery writers interested in the idea of creating simpler and purer tastes were already talking about '*la cuisine nouvelle*'. Curnonsky, the great discoverer of French country cooking in the 1930s, wrote frequently in support of fresh ingredients of good quality, and praised food which tasted of what it was in contrast to the uniform, standardised flavours he found in the restaurants of the big palace hotels. In October 1973, when I had been cooking at the Waterside for just about a year, Henri Gault published his famous article '*Vivre la Nouvelle Cuisine Française*' which hit the catering world like a manifesto, and started off the *nouvelle cuisine* fashion of the 1970s and 1980s. I have never been a fashionable cook and never will be; I have certainly never been an adept of *nouvelle cuisine*, even though, when I combined country and classical cooking, the results I aimed at were not unlike some of the ones envisaged by Gault and Millau and their followers. My own approach was much less extravagant, however, and far more eclectic. I may have followed *nouvelle cuisine* methods for cooking fish and vegetables, but I would never think of doing so for meat or game; I suppose that most restaurant chefs now have been influenced by the 'new' style of colourfully grouping and arranging the food on customers' plates. The great attack on flour is excessive, in my opinion, nor am I particularly excited by the craze for a *cuisine minceur*, the origins of which are more social than gastronomic. In any case, the increased use of cream to thicken sauces does not make the 'new' food very much less rich than the old!

Whenever you see the start of a new fashion in cooking, you seem to get at the same time the seeds of a counter-fashion. The enthusiasm for *nouvelle cuisine* is being superseded by an enthusiasm for *la cuisine du terroir*, but even this will only last for a short time. Cooks of my generation knew country food like the backs of their hands because they ate it every day at home and at little local restaurants where the cooking was still genuine and traditional. Today's young cooks, however, have usually never eaten a real cassoulet or bouillabaisse; they only know them out of tins or packets. How then can they possibly tell what the old home-made dishes actually tasted like? I sometimes wonder what the next fashion will be after *la cuisine du terroir*. Perhaps simplicity will be rejected altogether, and there will be a return to elaboration and transformation, to the *grande cuisine* of former days. There is nothing we can do to stop tastes evolving and changing, but I find it interesting to speculate about them.

In 1973, in the Waterside kitchen, I was singularly untouched by culinary doubts and uncertainties, fashionable or otherwise. Both Annie and I felt attracted by the old English inn with its white windows and its warm, red bricks and tiles, so completely unlike anything to be found in France; and we loved the immense willow tree whose long branches trailed down towards the water's edge and whose top was higher than the roof of the house. I was doing the work I knew and liked, cooking as I wanted, and I was confident and happy at feeling that I had really found myself professionally. Annie, on the other hand, who was now in charge of the dining room and indeed of running the whole establishment, was not as lucky as I was, and at first she found it all quite hard.

At Bray the official opening came right on the heels of the strenuous month during which Annie had pushed and pulled the whole place out of builders' and painters' chaos into something like order. Straightaway she found herself in charge of the waiters, the bar, the buying of supplies, the laundry, basic book-keeping, and hundreds of other things. We were inundated with telephone calls which we hardly knew how to answer, though we had to give the impression that we did, and we had to sound efficient about it too! Did we cater for large (and probably noisy) parties? Did we cook specially requested dishes which were not on the menu? Did we do formal banquets? Did we allow live music to be played in the restaurant? Did we permit credit accounts? We did not always know the Roux company policy on many of these matters; we did not want to make mistakes, nor did we want to disturb Albert constantly by telephoning him to ask him what we should do or say. Sometimes we ordered the wrong brand of some product, or we had no idea where to buy some item which we desperately needed. If ever anything had gone really seriously wrong, then, of course, Albert would have driven out from London and helped us, but we were very anxious not to bother him unless it was absolutely necessary. As far as general management was concerned, we had been thrown in at the deep end and we just had to learn how to swim.

We were busy right from the start. We were certainly helped by the wide publicity organized by Albert Roux, but very often people who came once returned a second and a third time, so they must have enjoyed my cooking, and, of course, the setting and the view from the big front window of the restaurant were unique. You could sit at a table and look straight out at the Thames flowing past you at the end of the lawn. During the summer there were boats of all kinds and sizes using the river, and at night these included long, brightly-lit pleasure craft which emerged dramatically from the darkness like small liners and then disappeared into it, leaving behind only a faint sound of music and voices. The bank opposite the inn consisted of a wide, open field which came right down to the water's edge and made you think of Rat and Mole in 'The Wind in the Willows.' Before lunch or dinner, as you sat in the Waterside summer-house, enjoying an aperitif, or moored your boat at the little landing stage, everything seemed to build up a perfect, enchanted

epitome of river life.

Annie, however, had no time for gazing at the scenery. Officially she was the manageress; but unofficially she was also mother, counsellor and nurse to the waiters and cooks, who were often only seventeen or eighteen years old, away from their homes and families in France for the first time in their lives, and now inconsolably homesick in a foreign country. In her capacity as *maître d'hôtel* she had to welcome customers at the door, serve them with aperitifs, show them to their tables, explain the menu, take their orders, and then, at the end of their meal, act as cashier and prepare their bills. She was doing the work of at least three different people, and she had to be prepared to change jobs instantly as the occasion demanded. At first it was taking the orders which alarmed her most, especially if the customers were difficult or if she did not know them; it reminded her of the panic she felt when she had to serve in the restaurant of the catering college. Everything had seemed very easy while she was just sitting in a classroom, taking notes and listening to a teacher telling her how to fill up an order slip or pour a glass of claret; but the day she had to walk up to her first real customers sitting at a real table, she became paralysed with stage-fright, and could hardly remember what she was supposed to say to them.

There are all sorts of pitfalls waiting for you when you take customers' orders for the first time, especially if you serve them as well. Hurried handwriting can turn out to be an illegible scrawl when you get to the kitchen. You can omit one order completely because, at the precise moment you were going to write it down, somebody asked you an unexpected question, and for a split second you failed to concentrate on what you were doing. Then, when you bring the starters to the table, you find yourself facing six customers with only five plates. As you gain experience, of course, you learn how to avoid this sort of thing; and if you do miss a dish, you just have to apologise and look foolish and unprofessional. Though these are quite elementary mistakes, lots of students make them when they start serving in a restaurant. With experienced waiters they should never happen at all; but at La Tante Claire we have a way of making absolutely sure. We use a system of combined letters and numbers to designate each place at each table; as the *maître d'hôtel* takes an order, he marks the slip of paper with the appropriate symbols so that the serving waiter will know that every order has been noted, and exactly which customer has ordered which dish. It may seem quite a small matter, but from the customer's point of view it can be very important. There is nothing more annoying, when you are deep in an interesting conversation, than to be interrupted by a waiter with a plate saying, 'Excuse me, sir, but is the lamb for you?' or, more peremptorily, 'Whose is the lobster?' The food should come smoothly and almost magically to each customer without a word more being spoken after the initial giving of the order to the head waiter. That is service at its most professional, which you should always expect to find in any first class establishment.

CHARTREUSE D'AGNEAU AU PERSIL

•

LAMB FILLETS WITH PARSLEY DARIOLES

•

4 lamb fillets, 200 g / 7 oz each
2 tablespoons vegetable oil
2 courgettes, trimmed
2 carrots, trimmed
200 g / 7 oz flat-leafed parsley leaves
100 ml / 4 fl oz double cream
2 shallots, finely chopped
2 teaspoons wine vinegar
200 ml / 7 fl oz Chicken stock (page 49)
salt and freshly ground pepper

•

Preheat the oven to 220°C / 425°F / Gas mark 7.
Using a mandoline, cut the carrots and courgettes into

long thin ribbons. Cook them separately in boiling salted water until just tender. Refresh in cold water, drain and set aside. Cook the parsley leaves in salted boiling water, drain and squeeze between your hands to extract as much water as possible.

Heat the oil in an ovenproof dish. When very hot, brown the meat quickly all over. Transfer to the preheated oven and cook for about 12 minutes, or until done to your liking.

In the meantime, line 4 buttered dariole moulds with the carrot and courgette ribbons. Place the middle of a courgette ribbon at the bottom of the mould, bringing the ends up the sides. Lay a carrot ribbon at right angles to make a cross, then alternate more ribbons of courgette and carrots to make a star shape. Continue until the whole mould is lined with vegetables.

Bring the double cream to the boil, add the squeezed parsley and cook until quite thick. Season and keep warm.

When the lamb is cooked, put it on a plate and keep warm. Discard the cooking fat and sweat the shallots in the roasting dish. Deglaze with vinegar, and reduce until you are left with a shallot purée. Reduce this by one-quarter. Whisk in the butter and keep warm.

Slice the lamb fillets thinly. Fill the vegetable-lined moulds with the parsley cream. Press down with the back of a spoon and fold the vegetable strips over the top. Turn out the moulds onto the middle of the serving plates and arrange the slices of lamb fillet around them. Pour the sauce over the meat and serve immediately.

HOMARD ECOSSAIS AU GEWÜRZTRAMINER

—— • ——

LOBSTER WITH GEWÜRZTRAMINER SAUCE

—— • ——

4 × 500 g / 1 lb 2 oz female lobsters, with their eggs
50 ml / 2 fl oz olive oil
80 g / 3 oz shallots, sliced thinly
1 garlic clove, peeled
50 ml / 2 oz fl oz marc de Gewürztraminer
1 L / 1¾ pt Gewürztraminer
80 g / 3 oz butter
salt and freshly ground pepper
Home-made noodles (page 196), for serving

—— • ——

Boil 3 L / 5½ pt water in a large saucepan. Break the lobster tails, claws and body and reserve the eggs. Cook the tails for 1 minute, then place in cold water. Chop the heads into small pieces.

Heat the oil in a frying pan. Add the lobster heads and cook over medium heat until red. Add the shallots and garlic and sweat for 5 minutes. Flame with the marc, then add the wine and cook slowly for 10 minutes. Season. Whizz in a blender, then pass the stock through a sieve into a small pan. Add the lobster eggs and boil for 1 minute. Place in the blender with 60 g / 2 oz butter and process until smooth. Return the sauce to the pan and keep hot.

Shell the lobster tails. Heat the remaining butter in a sauté pan. Season the lobster flesh with salt and pepper and cook for 5 minutes. Place the lobsters in a serving dish and pour the sauce around. Serve with fresh noodles.

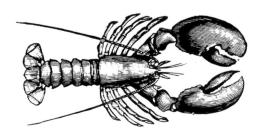

Very soon the Waterside was averaging about forty covers at both lunch and dinner on weekdays, but at weekends we were feeding well over twice that number and for Sunday lunch, we regularly served ninety to a hundred people and sometimes even more. It meant a lot of work in the kitchen, but I never minded that. I had a good team with me, and I always work best when under pressure. There is a wonderful feeling of excitement about a really busy kitchen when everything is going well, and I often imagine at such moments that I am soaring triumphantly like an eagle over hundreds of petty problems and difficulties. I am no longer afraid of mistakes or crises because I sense that if anything happened I would always know how to react quickly and save the situation. Everything seems to be rushing and moving; each process or action is linked perfectly with another; and above all the noise and the rattling you hear the orders being called out and the answering cries of *'Oui, chef! Oui, chef!'* from the different *parties*. There is something splendid about work at times like this, and it is then that you give the very best of yourself. At La Tante Claire I sometimes find I have to push the cooks hard to make them realise that they too are capable of excellence. Sometimes they do not understand this; they are not interested enough. *'Il nous emmerde!'* they mutter to each other, 'He's a pain in the neck!' Perhaps I do not always express myself as clearly as I might, and I know I often push them right to their limit; but I am trying to make them feel proud of themselves and their work. It is the difficult things which are exciting, not the *tralala* of everyday routine, and that is what we used to feel in the Waterside kitchen when we suddenly had to cook for a hundred people instead of forty.

But whereas at our ovens we cooks felt confident we could cope, those hectic weekends were far harder for the people working in the restaurant itself. When you are starting a completely new establishment, you have no idea how it is going to develop. One day it may do well, and the next day less well, therefore you take on the minimum number of waiters until you know for certain that you can afford more. This meant that on Saturdays and Sundays the dining room really was under-staffed, and everyone had to work extra hours, extra hard, and extra fast. It was to the immense credit of the people who worked for us that never once in the whole of the two years that we were at Bray did we have to ask anyone to work harder or to make a greater effort. Their energy and their enthusiasm were automatic; getting them to take on extra work was as easy as changing gears in a car; they always rose to the occasion. Our wine waiter, Jean-Claude Barthélemy, was one of the most amazing workers I have ever known. Nothing daunted him, nothing stopped him. At that time we had to keep on the previous pub bar in order to have a liquor licence, so Jean-Claude was at one and the same time barman in the pub and wine waiter in the restaurant. I have never seen anyone who could move about so fast. At one moment he would be drawing a couple of pints of bitter in the pub, then he would rush into the restaurant with the wine list to discuss with some heavily indecisive customer the respective merits of a Puligny Montrachet and a Chablis *grand cru*. In an instant he would be back in the pub to draw another bitter and to mix a quick Manhattan; then, once more, he would reappear in the restaurant to advise a table of six as to what wine they could drink with their *pigeon en cocotte* and would stay to produce a satisfactory bottle and ceremoniously pour it out before getting back to the bar to mix four more cocktails. He was everywhere at once, he was indefatigable. Without Jean-Claude it would have been impossible to run the Waterside dining room in the way we did; and later on he was to give us the same wonderful quality of service at La Tante Claire.

PIGEON FERMIER EN COCOTTE, FEUILLES DE CHOUX AU FOIE GRAS

———— • ————

YOUNG PIGEONS BRAISED WITH CABBAGE LEAVES STUFFED WITH FOIE GRAS

———— • ————

4 young pigeons
50 ml / 2 fl oz vegetable oil
8 small unpeeled garlic cloves
12 small shallots or baby onions
80 g / 3 oz bacon, diced
1 bay leaf
1 sprig of thyme
12 baby button mushrooms
100 ml / 4 fl oz dry white wine
30 g / 1 oz butter
4 slices of foie gras, 30 g / 1 oz each
4 small savoy cabbage leaves, blanched
salt and freshly ground pepper

———— • ————

Preheat the oven to 220°C / 425°F / gas 8.

Season the pigeons. Heat the oil in a cocotte dish or flameproof casserole, and seal the pigeons on both sides. Add the garlic, shallots or onions, bacon, bay leaf, thyme and mushrooms and cover. Put the dish in the hot oven and cook for about 12 minutes if you like your pigeon pink, longer if not.

Transfer the pigeons to a dish, breast down, cover with foil and keep warm. Pour off the fat from the cocotte and pour in the wine. Reduce until syrupy, then add 200 ml / 7 fl oz hot water, reduce by half, then whisk in the butter. Check the seasoning and keep warm.

Season the foie gras and pan-fry it without any fat for about 1 minute on each side. Wrap it in the cabbage leaves. Place a pigeon on each warm plate, spoon the vegetables, bacon and sauce around and put a cabbage parcel on each plate. Serve hot.

Annie's English was still far from perfect, and she had to summon up a good deal of courage to greet customers, make conversation and explain the recipes to them. She felt more at ease with customers whom she knew well because they came regularly; and she was much more fluent when explaining a familiar dish or a recipe which she herself liked than one she did not know or did not like so much. She managed well during the week, but on Saturdays and Sundays, when we were full, it really was a difficult job. Problems in the restaurant ranged from customers' grumbles to invasions by wandering swans. The birds waddled in from the river, and strode menacingly among the tables, their eyes and beaks on a level with the tablecloths, and everybody was terrified of them. Sometimes they even got into the bar. Waiters, weighed down with plates and dishes, went in fear of attack as they edged their way past them, so proud and powerful did the birds look once they were out of the water. Eventually they would just walk away, and the problem was solved.

Once we found a swan with an injured wing sheltering under the willow tree near the river. I had always wanted to know how the roast swans of mediaeval banquets tasted, and this seemed a wonderful opportunity to find out. I was all ready and prepared to cook my first swan when everyone became rather alarmed and told me that I would be committing a very serious offence if I killed it, and that I would get myself and the Waterside into a lot of trouble. In the end I allowed myself to be dissuaded, and we informed the Thames authorities who sent someone to take the bird away.

Customers' complaints turned out to be much more difficult than dealing with marauding swans, though really it was not so much the complaints themselves which worried us but the way in which they were made. Our English customers could never make a complaint directly, which we would have preferred. We had just opened the place, and were still at the stage when we found every criticism helpful, and when we really did want to know what we

had done wrong so that we could put it right. While still at the table, people would tell Annie that every aspect of the meal had been very good, and when she said goodbye to them at the door they would tell her again what a wonderful time they had had and how they had enjoyed themselves. We thought no more about it until, a few days later, Albert Roux would telephone to tell us that he had had a long letter of complaint from that particular customer, and would like to know what had happened. That would be our very first intimation that anything could possibly have been wrong. Perhaps the English (unlike the French who are born thinking they are all food experts, irrespective of whether they actually are or not) feel that they are not knowledgeable enough about food to be able to complain intelligently about it; perhaps they dislike the prospect of a direct confrontation; or perhaps they want to go away quietly and think twice about what they wish to say. But whatever the reason, we found this particular English characteristic difficult to get used to; and Annie felt very strongly that she would much prefer a customer to come straight out with 'No, it was disappointing today. The steak was so tough it was inedible!' We would know where we were; we could find out why the meat was tough; and we could make sure that it did not happen again.

With most of our customers, however, we got on very well indeed. There was one elderly man who came every day for lunch, bringing his dog with him, a wire-haired dachshund called Percy. On Percy's birthday, we prepared him a special lunch, and for a present we gave him a bone specially gift-wrapped in coloured paper and tied up with a bright, shiny ribbon. I have no idea what the dog thought of it all, but his owner was overjoyed. We also got to know well some of the people who came for dinner every Saturday night. At the very beginning of the Waterside, part of the old pub was still being used as a sort of disco with music and dancing, and it was one of Annie's numerous extra jobs to be in charge of this. We got so used to the pulsing din of the music while we were dashing about working that it was not until one of the restaurant customers complained about it, very directly for once, that we realised how awful the noise was for people trying to enjoy their dinner. Very soon after we were able to get rid of the disco altogether.

It was things like the music which caused a lot of friction with local residents. Bray, after all, was a quiet, very beautiful English village, and the home of a number of wealthy, retired people who had lived there for a long time with nothing happening to disturb them; then, all of a sudden, this 'French place' opens, and everything changes. Our cooks and waiters, all aged about eighteen or twenty, did tend to be noisy when they came back late at night on their day off, despite our efforts to keep them quiet. The same sort of annoyance was caused by customers going out to their cars after a good dinner, talking and laughing, slamming car doors and starting their engines; as we were at the very end of Ferry Road, all cars had to turn round before they could drive away, which only made everything worse. One Wednesday night, when we were in the middle of serving dinner, a customer, who had just left, came back into the restaurant, and said to Annie 'Mrs. Koffmann, would you come and look at my car?' It was a superb, brand-new, white Porsche; but someone had thrown a large can of red paint right over it. I was horrified. At weekends, people came in to the bar just to make jokes about the French and to call us 'frogs' and other insults. It was very unpleasant to have to work feeling you were surrounded by people who hated you so much; but, looking back, I consider that we should not have been so surprised, and that certainly we should have taken much more care over our public relations. There was no denying that we had made a disruptive impact on the village. Now, twenty years later, Albert and Michel Roux have made the Waterside even more attractive than it used to be; there is a proper car park nearby, and the restaurant is fully accepted and appreciated by the local community who by now may even have discovered that frogs can actually be rather good.

FRITURE DE CUISSES DE GRENOUILLES EN PERSILLADE

---•---

DEEP-FRIED FROGS' LEGS

---•---

24 pairs of frogs' legs
juice of ½ lemon
1 tablespoon vegetable oil
1 tablespoon chopped parsley
2 garlic cloves, chopped
oil for deep-frying
salt and freshly ground pepper
100 g / 3½ oz Snail butter (page 24), melted

---•---

Marinate the frogs' legs with the lemon juice, oil, parsley, garlic and salt and pepper to taste for 1 hour in the fridge. Heat the frying oil until very hot. Dip the legs into the snail butter and deep-fry them until golden. Drain on absorbent kitchen paper and serve.

It was during our time at the Waterside that Annie and I had to learn to work together as well as live together. At first it was not easy, and there was quite a lot of tension between us during the *service*. We suffered, I think, from our own private version of the conflict between kitchen and dining room which I had met for the first time at Strasbourg. At the height of what we call the *coup de feu*, when work in the kitchen is at its most frantic, Annie, in the restaurant, might be being pressed by two or three impatient tables for dishes which were slow in coming, so she would rush into the kitchen to find out what had happened to them. I might answer her brusquely, she would tell me to get a move on, and in no time at all we would each be accusing the other of shouting!

Another difficulty used to arise when I cooked one of my regular recipes in a new way (often on the spur of the moment) and I had not had time to tell Annie about this. She had described it to a customer in its original form, and he would then grumble if the food on his plate did not match the description he had been given. Annie would then get annoyed with me for not having warned her about the alteration, and for making her appear unjustifiably inefficient. It is true that I do not always like to be told what to do by other people, especially in my own kitchen, and this, too, upset Annie. I found out later that it made it hard for her to talk to me about things that might, perhaps, be starting to go wrong or which should be changed. I always prefer to say what I think in an open and straightforward way so that people can see at once where they stand with me; but Annie is more sensitive and more afraid of hurting people. It was a difference of personality which we had to work out between ourselves, just as we had to understand that the tensions and strains of the *service* affected both of us in much the same way. At first we were utterly exhausted and bad-tempered as we crept up to our flat after a really busy Sunday lunch, but, as time went on, we became stronger and more mature, and found we could take things more in our stride.

The catering trade is one of the hardest and most demanding that there is, and you have to have the strength to surrender yourself totally to it if you want to succeed.

By the end of our second year at Bray I was ready for another move, a move this time in search of what really would be our own place, a restaurant we would own and run as sole proprietors. My cooking had won the Waterside two Michelin stars in the two years I had been there, and during that time Annie and I had put everything we could into making the restaurant a success. I think we felt that we had reached the limit of what we could achieve there. We arranged to leave Bray towards the end of 1974, and planned to try to buy a restaurant in France, probably in the south-west which I knew so well. The very last thing we did at the Waterside was to give a great farewell lunch for all our friends and those people who had helped us and encouraged us. It was a big party. We sat at two long tables in the big window looking out on to the river, and I cooked a genuine Gascon *poule-au-pot* which contained enough chickens to feed everyone. It virtually provided the entire meal. First we ate the soup; then we had the stuffed chicken and the herb-flavoured *boudins*; then there were the brioches; and finally there were delicious stuffed cabbages which are enough to make a complete course just by themselves. It was a warm, happy example of *la cuisine de l'amitié*, country cooking at its very best, and it was one more step in the direction of La Tante Claire.

Poulet de Bresse Façon Poule au Pot (recipe p. 156)

POULET DE BRESSE FAÇON POULE AU POT

CHICKEN IN THE POT

(Serves 8)

1 × 1.5 kg / 3¼ lb Bresse chicken
500 g / 1 lb 2 oz foie gras
30 g / 1 oz fresh truffles, thinly sliced
5 L / 8¾ pt clear Chicken stock (page 49)
1 onion
3 carrots
2 leeks
2 celery stalks
1 clove
2 garlic cloves
5 peppercorns
salt

Clean the chicken. Season the foie gras. Insert the truffles under the chicken skin and put the foie gras inside the chicken. Sew up the neck and body opening with a needle and thread. Put the chicken in a large pot with the chicken stock and bring to the boil. Simmer for 10 minutes, skimming the surface carefully, then add the vegetables and seasonings. Simmer, uncovered, for 1¼ hours. Meanwhile, prepare the garnishes.

Brioche:
20 g / ¾ oz fresh yeast
100 ml / 4 fl oz lukewarm water
700 g / 1½ lb plain flour
100 g / 3½ oz duck fat
3 eggs
a pinch of salt and sugar

Dilute the yeast in the water, then add all the other ingredients and mix well to make a smooth dough. Shape into a ball, cover with a light cloth and leave to rise for 1 hour. An hour before eating the chicken, put the brioche in the pot with the chicken, cover and cook for 30 minutes, then turn it over and cook for another 30 minutes. Remove the brioche from the pot with a slotted spoon and serve it instead of bread.

Stuffed cabbage:
1 savoy cabbage
500 g / 1 lb 2 oz All-purpose stuffing (see next recipe)

Blanch the 8 largest cabbage leaves in boiling water. Lay a clean muslin cloth on the table and arrange the cabbage leaves overlapping like a rosette. Put the stuffing in the middle and wrap it in the leaves like a ball. Enclose it all in the muslin, tie up the top and cook with the chicken for 1 hour.

Farce à Tout Faire (All-purpose stuffing)

600 g / 1¼ lb pork fat
600 g / 1¼ lb lean pork
100 g / 3½ oz chicken livers
1 garlic clove, peeled and left whole
1 tablespoon chopped parsley
75 g / 3 oz fresh white breadcrumbs
100 ml / 4 fl oz dry white wine
25 ml / 1 fl oz armagnac
salt and freshly ground pepper

Mince the meats, garlic and parsley in a mincer. Place in a food processor and process at low speed until smooth. Add the breadcrumbs, season to taste and process for 3 minutes. Pour in the wine and the armagnac and process for another 5 minutes, until the stuffing is very smooth.

Milhas (Cornmeal porridge)

750 ml / 1¼ pt milk
100 g / 3½ oz cornmeal
15 g / ½ oz duck fat

Bring the milk to the boil in a saucepan, then sprinkle the cornmeal like rain and stir with a wooden spoon. Add the duck fat, season to taste and cook over low heat for 5 minutes.

Boudins verts (green sausages)

50 g / 2 oz plain flour
4 eggs
150 ml / 5 fl oz milk
1 onion, finely chopped
20 g / ¾ oz duck fat
25 g / 1 oz Bayonne ham, diced
2 garlic cloves, chopped
1 tablespoon chopped parsley
100 g / 3½ oz spinach, cooked and chopped
1 teaspoon chopped tarragon
1 tablespoon snipped chives
80 cm / 32 in sausage casing

Mix the flour, eggs and milk and leave to rest for 15 minutes. Meanwhile, sweat the chopped onion in the duck fat for 5 minutes. Mix together the ham, garlic, parsley, spinach, tarragon and chives. Add the cooked onion and mix into the milk mixture. Season to taste. Spoon the mixture into the sausage casing and tie at 10 cm / 4 in intervals to make about 8 sausages. Heat a saucepan of water to 90°C / 194°F, put in the sausages and poach for 15 minutes.

Pour the broth into a tureen. Serve the chicken on a large dish with all the garnishes beside it, and leave the broth on the table at the same time, so that everyone can help themselves. (Photograph p. 155)

CHAPTER 5

LA TANTE CLAIRE
THE QUEST BEGINS

There was never a precise moment at which I first consciously decided to open a restaurant of my own. In the catering business it almost goes without saying that anyone who has reached the position of *chef de cuisine* wants one day to set up as a *chef propriétaire*. Becoming my own master was a normal progression in my career; it was part of life, it was all in the order of things. By the end of 1974 Annie and I had had a very successful two years at the Waterside, and before that I had been *chef de cuisine* at the Brasserie Benoît. In addition to my knowing how to run a kitchen, we both now knew how to run a restaurant as well. Albert Roux had promised us financial backing, and Jean-Pierre Durantet, who was then manager of Le Gavroche and is now our *maître d'hôtel* at La Tante Claire, was ready to join us. Everything seemed to point propitiously to a change, but, in the event, the road from the Waterside to La Tante Claire was not as easy as we had imagined.

My first idea was to return to France and open a restaurant somewhere in the Gers, in the country I had known so well as a boy. For most of 1975 Annie and I rented a flat in Tarbes and spent our time looking for premises which could be turned into an attractive restaurant. We must have seen over a hundred places; remote farmhouses built on the slopes of long Gascon hillsides which could only be reached by tortuous tracks of beaten earth, abandoned mills at the bottom of valleys, and roofless barns and derelict shops in towns and villages. One of the mills still had its wheel and some of the old gearing. The water ran right beneath it, and, near what might have been the steps leading up to a restaurant dining-room, you could lean over a parapet and look down into the stream and see plump, dark-backed trout quivering and darting about in the current. The availability of *truite au cresson* would have depended rather heavily on my cooks' fishing skills!

In another place we found a big seventeeth-century house which had a fine, stone staircase with magnificent ironwork. At the end of a long passage leading to an overgrown garden, which might have provided a summer extension to a dining-room, there was the old kitchen which still had its charcoal-burning *potager* over which, in the past, pigeons and veal tongues would have simmered for hours. Next to this was the great open fireplace where all the roasting would have been done. There were the rusty remains of a clockwork jack for turning the spit; and when we peered up the throat of the chimney, blackened with the smoke of three hundred years, we could see all sorts of chains and bars embedded in the masonry for the hanging of pots and the smoking of hams. I was tempted to retain some of these features and to design a modern kitchen around them, but the idea never came to fruition. We discovered that an adjoining building housed the workshop of a very active carpenter, and the noise of saws and drills would have been more than enough to ruin anybody's enjoyment of a good meal.

It was just one disappointment among many; indeed that year taken as a whole was not a happy one for us, especially as it came so quickly after our success at the Waterside. Apart from members of my immediate family we knew nobody in the area; our flat in Tarbes was small and cramped; we made no new friends; but above all we soon realised that the whole purpose of our stay in France, the opening of a restaurant, was going to prove an impossibility. Although Albert Roux had promised to finance us, the amount of money he could lend us in France would not be enough for the whole project and the rest we would have to raise ourselves. The French banks did not know me, had no appreciation of my work at the Waterside, and refused to lend us anything except through a mortgage on property in France, which, of course, we did not have. The cost of converting any of the places we had seen seemed, in these circumstances, hopelessly expensive. There was nothing to show for all the time we had spent trekking from estate agents to banks, from banks to old buildings, and from old buildings back to other estate agents.

In the meantime we both had to take what

jobs we could get in order to earn enough money to live on. At first I cooked in the kitchen of a local restaurant and Annie worked at a Tarbes café. It was a bad time. Later Annie got a better job as a hotel receptionist, but when the restaurant where I worked closed for the annual holidays, I could not get another job anywhere. In the end, a friend who had a plumbing business employing about a dozen workmen, and who had just secured a contract to lay the drainpipes on a new housing estate, offered me some work on the building site. It was a trade in which I was totally unskilled, so I could only do the very simplest things. I worked five days a week with pick and shovel, digging trenches and laying drainpipes, and at first I found it terribly hard. In a kitchen you are standing all day on your feet and working in the heat of the stove, but once you have got used to that, the rest is physically quite easy. Digging trenches was another story altogether. First you had to hack away the earth with the pick, then you had to toss it up on to the side with the shovel. For the first week or two my hands blistered and every single muscle in my body ached appallingly. I was soon longing to get back into a kitchen, even if it was somebody else's, for it was quite clear to us by the end of the year that it was going to be extremely hard to start an independent career in France.

So in 1976 we found ourselves back in London. Albert was still ready to help us with finance, and through him we could find additional backers; and, of course, the English banks were readier to take an interest in us and to lend us money than the French had been. Nevertheless, although I now felt far more confident about the financial aspect of the venture, I was determined not to be too hasty over any decision about premises, and to take my time over finding the right place. I took up again my old job as *chef de cuisine* at the Brasserie Benoît in the mornings, and in the evenings, to make some extra money, I worked in the kitchen of a French restaurant in the Fulham Road. The chef was one of the liveliest characters I have ever come across. He was very small, brimful of energy, a good worker, and

professionally very skilful, but at the same time he had a passion for enjoying himself and for having a good time. He would never refuse a glass of champagne and he adored every woman he met. We soon lost all count of his girlfriends, though the only thing they seemed to have in common was the fact that they were always about a foot taller than he was. He had an extraordinary gift for laughter and for making others laugh, and he always made the best of any bad situation. Like me, he was a great rugby enthusiast, and once, when there was some important match at Cardiff, he arranged that a whole party of us should travel to Wales together by train and that a magnificent champagne breakfast would be served during the journey. About twenty minutes after leaving London, an attendant came along with the news that the eggs and bacon for our breakfast had all been left behind at Paddington. We were disappointed and furious, but as soon as the chef discovered that the champagne was safely on board, he made the whole thing seem like a hilarious joke. By the time we stepped on to the platform at Cardiff, we had enjoyed the journey even more than if we had had our eggs and bacon.

In the restaurant kitchen there was only, besides the chef, a *sous-chef* and one commis cook. When the chef saw how I worked and what I could do, he quickly realised that the kitchen could get on very well without him in the evenings, and that there was nothing to stop him going out to enjoy himself in more interesting company than ours, though he had to be careful how he did this. The customers might have felt rather uneasy if they had seen the chef saying good-night at the very start of the *service* and walking out through the restaurant and apparently leaving for home, so he devised a rather less obvious method of escape. The kitchen was in the basement, and there was the usual delivery hatch set into the pavement above, consisting of two strong wooden trap doors. As soon as he had checked that we were all working well and things were running smoothly, the chef would slip a pot of caviar into his pocket, tuck a bottle of champagne under one arm, ascend the ladder to the trap door, clamber out mysteriously into the night, and disappear. Sometimes he came back the same way an hour or two later, and sometimes we did not see him until the next day. His professional speciality was French regional cooking. Each week he selected a different region, and every dish on the menu would come from that particular part of France. During the Alsace week, for example, we would do a *choucroute* and black pudding; for Burgundy we would do a *queue de boeuf bourgignon* or a *jambon braisé au chablis*; or for my own part of France, Gascony, we might serve calf's tongue with capers and a special Basque cake. There were always the right local wines to go with the food, and the menus were interesting and well thought out.

LA SALADE DE BOUDIN

BLACK PUDDING SALAD

1 boned pig's head, with the tongue, cut into 10 big chunks
200 g / 7 oz bacon rind, cut into 2 pieces
pig's lungs
pig's heart
4 carrots, coarsely chopped
2 onions, coarsely chopped
1 Bouquet garni (page 11)
1 head of garlic, cloves peeled and left whole
3 shallots, coarsely chopped
3 tablespoons vegetable oil
200 g / 7 oz onion, finely chopped
2 leeks, white part only, finely chopped
1 pinch each cinnamon, ginger, nutmeg
1 L / 1¾ pt fresh pig's blood
20 g / ¾ oz coarse salt for each 1 kg / 2 lb 3 oz meat
⅛ teaspoon ground pepper for each 1 kg / 2 lb 3 oz meat

Put the pig's head, bacon rind, pig's lungs and heart, carrots, onions, bouquet garni, the cloves and chopped shallots in a large saucepan. Cover with cold water, bring to the boil and simmer for 2 hours. Discard the vegetables and chop the meat finely.

Heat the oil in a large saucepan, add the finely chopped onion and leek and sweat for 5 minutes. Put the vegetables over the chopped meat and add the spices. As soon as the mixture has cooled down, pour the blood over and mix thoroughly with a large spoon. Weigh the mixture, then add salt and pepper in the proportions given in the ingredients. Pour into sterilized straight-sided preserving jars and put on the disc and screw top. Stand the jars in a big pan and cover with cold water. Bring to the boil and simmer for 30 minutes. Allow to cool in the water, then keep in a cold larder and wait for a few days before eating.

Remove the boudin from the preserving jar by running a long, thin knife blade around the edge of the jar. When ready to serve, heat a little vegetable oil in a saucepan. Cut the boudin into 2 cm / 1 in thick slices and sauté in the oil over medium-high heat for 1 minute on each side.

Serve over a mixed salad of batavia, lollo rosso and frisée tossed with a little olive oil, lemon juice and salt.

Andouilletes de la Mer aux Graines de Cassis (recipe p. 168)

GAZPACHO AUX ECREVISSES

CHILLED GAZPACHO WITH CRAYFISH

32 freshwater crayfish, cleaned and cooked
100 g / 3½ oz cucumber
5 tomatoes
75 g / 3 oz onion, coarsely chopped
1 red pepper
1 green pepper
3 garlic cloves, peeled
300 ml / ½ pt wine vinegar
100 ml / 4 fl oz extra virgin olive oil
1 tablespoon tomato purée
1 tablespoon snipped chives
salt and freshly ground pepper

Blanch and skin the tomatoes, halve and deseed them. Peel the cucumber and scoop out the seeds. Skin the peppers, halve and remove the seeds and white membrane. Put all the ingredients except the crayfish and chives in a blender with 0.5 L / 1 pt cold water and process until smooth. Season and chill.

Pour the soup into serving bowls and top with the crayfish. Sprinkle over the chives and serve immediately.

LANGUE DE VEAU AUX CÂPRES

CALF'S TONGUE WITH CAPER SAUCE

1 calf's tongue
1 small Bouquet garni (page 11)
350 g / 12 oz carrots, halved
350 g / 12 oz onions, halved
900 g / 2 lb leeks, split lengthways and washed thoroughly

Sauce
15 g / ½ oz butter
15 g / ½ oz flour
250 ml / 9 fl oz cooking stock from the tongue
100 g/ 3½ oz butter, cut into small dice
2 tablespoons capers
salt and freshly ground pepper

Pour 7 L / 12 pt water into a huge pot, put in the tongue and boil for 20 minutes, skimming very thoroughly until the stock is quite clear. Add the bouquet garni, season and simmer gently for 1½ hours. Add the vegetables and cook for another 45 minutes. Strain and reserve 250 ml / 9 fl oz stock.

Meanwhile, prepare the sauce: Melt the butter in a saucepan stir in the flour and cook gently for 2 minutes. Whisk in the 250 ml / 9 fl oz cooking stock. Over low heat, add the diced butter, a little at a time, stirring continuously. Season the sauce, pass through a fine sieve and finish by adding the capers. Keep warm.

Remove the tongue and peel it, then slice and arrange on a warm serving dish. Pour the sauce over and around the tongue. Purée the remaining vegetables and stock in a blender to make a soup, or serve the vegetables with butter or vinaigrette and use the cooking liquid for stock.

GÂTEAU BASQUE

•

BASQUE CAKE

•

(Serves 8)

300 g / 11 oz plain flour, plus extra for dusting
200 g / 7 oz caster sugar
200 g / 7 oz butter, diced and softened
1 egg, lightly beaten at room temperature
2 egg yolks, lightly beaten, at room temperature
40 ml / 1½ fl oz dark rum
grated zest of 1 lemon
grated zest of 1 orange
1 egg yolk whisked with 1 teaspoon of water, for
eggwash
225 g / 8 oz fresh ripe cherries, stoned

Almond cream:
65 g / 2½ oz butter, at room temperature
65 g / 2½ oz sugar
1 egg, lightly beaten
65 g / 2½ oz ground almonds
1 teaspoon almond essence

•

Preheat the oven to 190°C / 375°F / gas 5.

*Sift the flour into a large bowl and mix in the sugar.
Make a well in the centre. Put the softened butter, the
whole egg, and the egg yolks in the middle. Mix in the
flour little by little, starting from the inside to avoid
getting lumps in the dough. Add the rum, lemon and
orange zests and mix well until homogeneous and firm.
The dough should not be sticky. Dust with flour, wrap
in clingfilm and refrigerate for 1½ hours.*

*Meanwhile, prepare the almond cream: Whisk the
butter and sugar together until fluffy. Whisk in the
egg, little by little, then mix in the ground almonds,
then the cherries. Cover and keep at room temperature.*

*Divide the dough into 2 pieces of equal weight. Roll
them out on a lightly floured surface into thick 28 cm /
11 in circles. Grease a 28 cm / 11 in round cake tin*
*and line it with a piece of dough. Spread the almond
cream over and cover with the other piece of dough.
Pinch the edges together. Make a small hole in the
middle and brush with the eggwash.*

*Bake in the oven for 50 minutes. Leave the cake to cool
and eat at room temperature.*

===

I did not start my evening job until about six. I therefore had every afternoon to myself, and I used the time to visit estate agents and look at any premises which sounded even remotely suitable. Annie at that time had a full-time job as a translator in the accounts department of an engineering firm at Morden, and we were living in a dark and rather damp basement flat not far from World's End. Every night, when I came home from the restaurant, she would ask me if I had seen anywhere good. Usually there was nowhere worth bothering about. The only thing to do was to be patient, especially as I realised that I was concentrating more and more on the Chelsea area and had stopped considering other parts of London.

In the early spring of 1977, an estate agent sent me details of a medium-sized restaurant called Le Sans Souci. It was in a street I had never heard of, not far from the Royal Chelsea Hospital, and when I saw it, I felt at once that it was right for us. By a curious chance the road led in one direction towards Lower Sloane Street and Le Gavroche, where my English cooking career started, and in the other to the Thames, the river beside which, at Bray, it had come to its maturity. I remember my feeling of excitement when I got home that night and called out as I opened the door 'Annie! I think I've got something!'

We bought the Sans Souci lease for £40,000 at an annual rent of £1,400. Nowadays, this seems incredibly little, especially when you compare the figure to the rent we have to pay at the present moment, and even in 1977 it was not too expensive. We also reaped the benefit of the former owner's obsession with house-work. Everything was immaculate and dazzlingly bright both in the dining room and in the kitchen. The cooker was gas-fired, of English make, and both it and the refrigerator were in excellent working order. In the dining room, the chairs, tables, banquettes, pictures and decorations were all in perfect order, so we had nothing more to spend and nothing to change, except that we had to give the restaurant a new name. We wanted to call it something which evoked French cooking and *la cuisine de femme* even though may own menus were to be slightly more elaborate than that. After a lot of thought we chose the name of an aunt of a French friend of mine whom I had never actually met, but her name sounded right and seemed to convey the idea of a busy cook in an attractive provincial kitchen. She was called Claire, so the restaurant was duly christend La Tante Claire.

We formally opened for dinner one Wednesday evening in the autumn of 1977. It was a very important day for me, but I do not remember feeling nervous or anxious. That would not be my way. Friends looked in during the course of the afternoon, and were amazed by the disorder which reigned everywhere; they could not imagine that the restaurant would be ready to open at half past seven. Food was still being delivered to the kitchen; the cooker had only just been lit; benches, tables and chairs were all piled on top of each other; six dozen bottles of wine had been temporarily lost; tablecloths were being counted; and people were working and pushing and rushing in every direction. The sublime professional calm which distinguishes a first class restaurant seemed centuries away, but I was not worried. I knew exactly what had to be done, and how long it would all take, and I knew that in the end everything would be ready at the right time. The years I had spent with Albert and Michel Roux had given me a very good training, and there was no difference between what I was doing now and what I had always done for them except, of course, that the setting had changed and I was now working for myself.

I was excited but confident. My favourite memory of that first evening is of my grandmother. She had written to me from Saint Puy to remind me of a promise she had made years ago that if ever I opened a restaurant of my own, she would send me twelve of her best chickens to serve on the opening night. She now offered to do this for La Tante Claire. To her a restaurant meant a small village café, like the one in the little market square in Saint Puy, or the simple restaurant at Fleurance where she used to have lunch on market days. She had absolutely no conception of somewhere like La Tante Claire. To the cook at the sort of establishment my grandmother imagined I owned, a dozen free chickens would have been a welcome present, but at La Tante Claire they would not really have made much difference to me, and in any case I cannot imagine how she could possibly have sent the birds all the way from Gascony to Chelsea without their deteriorating. To me the important thing was that she had remembered her promise; even if it was impracticable, it was still her way of showing her love and good wishes, and that alone meant a very great deal to me.

We were full from the outset. That night we fed about thirty people, some of whom were friends, while others had known me at the Waterside or were local people who had come out of curiosity or because they had read about us in the papers. There were both French and English there, and in my menu I had tried to combine English associations with a reference to my own part of France. The first course was a *pannequet* of oysters wrapped round with smoked salmon. The French word *pannequet* is quite simply a disguised form of the English word 'pancake'; a *pannequet* is normally a little *crêpe* which encloses a filling and is then glazed in the oven, but in my Tante Claire version I make the 'pancake' out of smoked salmon. Gascony is famous for its ducks, so the main course of the meal was a duck dish. The dessert was a *crème brûlée*, another dish with English associations, since the English claim it was invented at Cambridge. My own version is flavoured with raspberries and the caramel on top of the custard is not 'burnt' very hard, so perhaps it is more French than English.

Pannequets de Saumon Fumé et d'Huîtres (recipe p. 168)

Pannequets de Saumon Fumé et d'Huîtres

•

OYSTERS WRAPPED IN SMOKED SALMON

•

16 oysters
400 g / 14 oz smoked salmon, cut into sixteen
5 cm / 2 in squares
20 g / ¾ oz shallots, finely chopped
1 tablespoon wine vinegar
100 g / 3½ oz butter, at room temperature
1 tablespoon finely snipped chives
1 large tomato, blanched, skinned, deseeded and
diced
fresh dill fronds, to garnish

•

Open the oysters into a fine muslin-lined strainer set over a bowl to catch the sea water.

The sauce: Put the shallots and vinegar in a pan and reduce until no liquid is left. Add three-quarters of the sea water from the oysters, bring to the boil and whisk in the butter, a little at a time. Check the seasoning and add the chives and diced tomato. Keep in a warm place.

Heat the oysters very gently in the remaining sea water to 60°C / 140°F. Roll a piece of smoked salmon around each one. Serve on warm plates, pour on the sauce and garnish with the dill fronds. (Photograph p. 167)

Andouillettes de la Mer aux Graines de Cassis

•

TURBOT AND SMOKED SALMON SAUSAGES WITH BLACKCURRANT SAUCE

•

4 turbot fillets, 125 g / 4 oz each
300 ml / ½ pt whipping cream
1 tablespoon butter
120 g / 4 oz thinly-sliced smoked salmon, cut into
thin strips
30 g / 1 oz shallots, very finely sliced
2 teaspoons wine vinegar
50 ml / 2 fl oz good quality dry white wine
20 blackcurrants
salt and white pepper

•

Chop one of the turbot fillets and purée in the food processor until smooth. Push through a fine sieve and refrigerate until thoroughly chilled. Gradually whisk in 125 ml / 4 fl oz whipping cream, season with salt and white pepper to taste and refrigerate.

Cut one turbot fillet into long, thin strips and season. Heat the butter in a frying pan and sauté the strips of turbot very quickly. Set aside to cool. When cold, add them to the prepared fish mousse, together with the smoked salmon strips. Mix well and return to the fridge.

Place the last two turbot fillets between two layers of clingfilm and pound them into thinner and larger pieces. Cut into four 10 cm / 4 in squares. Spread the fish mousse over each square, dividing it equally. Roll them up into a "sausage" and wrap each one in a piece of buttered foil, twisting the ends. Cook in a steamer for 12 minutes.

Meanwhile, prepare the sauce: Put the shallot, wine vinegar and white wine in a small saucepan, bring to the boil and reduce until nearly dry. Pour in the remaining whipping cream and add the blackcurrants. Bring to the boil, season and keep warm. To serve, pour the sauce onto warm serving plates and place the andouillettes in the middle. (Photograph p. 163)

CANARD AU VIN ROUGE

•

BRAISED DUCK IN RED WINE SAUCE

•

1 × 1.8 kg / 4 lb duck, cut into 4 pieces
50 ml / 2 fl oz vegetable oil
120 g / 4 oz smoked bacon, de-rinded and cut into
2 cm / 1 in cubes
100 g / 3½ oz seasoned flour
150 g / 5 oz carrots, cut into large dice
150 g / 5 oz onions, cut into large dice
1.1 L / 2 pt good quality red wine
4 garlic cloves, chopped
1 Bouquet garni (page 11)
salt and freshly ground pepper
Armottes (next recipe), for serving

•

Preheat the oven to 200°C / 400°F / gas 6.

Put the bacon cubes in a small pan and cover with cold water. Bring quickly to the boil and drain. Heat the vegetable oil in a large, heavy casserole. When very hot, fry the bacon until golden brown and crisp. Using a slotted spoon, remove the bacon and drain on several layers of kitchen towel.

Roll the pieces of duck in the seasoned flour and brown them quickly and evenly in the oil in which the bacon was cooked. Add the carrots and onions and sweat gently for 10 minutes. Hold the lid over the pan and pour off all the cooking fat. Deglaze the pan with the red wine and bring to the boil. Put in the chopped garlic and bouquet garni and season.

Replace the lid and cook the duck in the oven for about 2½ hours. Stir regularly during cooking, adding a little water if too much evaporates. When the duck is tender,

transfer the pieces to a saucepan. Pass the sauce through a fine sieve over the duck. Discard the vegetables and bouquet garni, and simmer the dish for 10 more minutes on the hob. Serve on warm plates with Armottes and sprinke the bacon over the meat. (Photograph p. 170).

ARMOTTES

•

CREAMED POLENTA

•

160 g / 5½ oz instant polenta
50 g / 2 oz butter
salt and freshly ground pepper

•

In a large saucepan boil 1 L / 1¾ pt water with 1 teaspoon salt. Scatter in the polenta like rain. With a wooden spoon, stir continuously for about 5 minutes over medium heat until thick and creamy. Mix in the butter, check the seasoning and serve piping hot, like mashed potatoes.

Canard au Vin Rouge (recipe p. 169)

CRÈME BRÛLÉE AUX FRAMBOISES

•

RASPBERRY CRÈME BRÛLÉE

•

125 ml / 4½ fl oz whipping cream
125 ml / 4½ fl oz double cream
half a vanilla pod, split lengthways
5 egg yolks
50 g / 2 oz sugar
1 small punnet of raspberries
4 heaped teaspoons caster sugar, for the caramel

•

Preheat the oven to 150°C / 300°F / gas mark 2.

Combine the whipping and double creams and scrape out all the seeds from the vanilla pod into the creams. Bring to the boil, together with the vanilla pod and seeds. Set aside. Whisk the egg yolks with the sugar until thick and ribbon-like. Pour the creams over, whisking continuously, and pour back into the pan. Cook over very low heat, stirring with a wooden spoon. As soon as the cream custard thickens lightly and coats the back of the spoon, it is ready. Pass through a fine conical strainer and set aside.

Divide the raspberries between 4 ramekins and pour the cream custard over them. Put the ramekins side by side on a deep ovenproof dish and pour in not more than 2 cm / 1 in boiling water, being careful not to spill any on the creams. Cook in the preheated oven for about 45 minutes, or until set. The recipe can be made 24 hours in advance up to this point. Keep the creams in the fridge until needed.

Before serving, sprinkle each portion with a teaspoon of caster sugar and caramelise under a hot grill. Serve with a small crisp biscuit, if you like.

Royal Hospital Road runs from the bottom of Lower Sloane Street to the river which it meets near Cheyne Walk and the Albert Bridge. La Tante Claire is on the same side of the street as Wren's Chelsea Hospital, built in the reign of Charles II as a home for veteran soldiers, and we soon got used to the sight of Chelsea pensioners in their scarlet or blue uniforms walking past our door, just as later we got used to the annual excitement of the Chelsea Flower Show. The restaurant was part of a little group of buildings which had suffered from a German V2 rocket during the war, and had subsequently been rebuilt, though the eighteenth-century house immediately next to us had come through unscathed. We shared the ground floor with a local building firm; their offices were on the left and we were on the right. The restaurant was not large, but it was just the right size for Annie and me to manage. The dining room was long and narrow, like the inside of a railway carriage, and there were about ten tables parallel with the walls at which we could seat some thirty-six people. The walls were covered in a russet and green striped fabric, and were adorned with reproductions of well known but somewhat unappetising paintings by Egon Schiele – they were the only thing we took over from the Sans Souci about which we had had doubts! At the far end of the room, there was a small opening through which you could get a glimpse of what was going on in the kitchen. From here a door led out into a little yard which I turned into an open-air larder with cupboards protected by wire gauze and an outside freezer with a sheet of marble which doubled as a pivoting lid and as a cool working-top for pastry-making. The kitchen was on the small side and we needed all the extra space we could get. Beyond the wall of the little yard was a much larger yard (recently replaced by a fashionable neo-Georgian housing scheme) which served as a car park, and was patrolled during the day by a particularly lugubrious-looking security officer who spent his time staring menacingly at the cooks. When we started, there were only ten of us to do absolutely everything so we were pretty active and interesting to watch, I suppose. In the dining room Annie was *maître d'hôtel* as she had been at the Waterside, and the heroic Jean-Claude continued to be our wine waiter. There were three commis waiters to do all the ordinary serving. In the kitchen I had three cooks, a *plongeur*, and that was all. Everyone had plenty to do, but we worked well together, we were a closely-knit little group, and the staff were as enthusiastic as Annie and myself.

Gradually I began to learn about the history of that particular part of Chelsea. In the eighteenth century our street was called Paradise Row, a lovely name which I wish it still had, and the surrounding land was all open country and consisted of market gardens which grew vegetables for London. The yard where the security officer patrolled belonged to a timber merchant who sold wood which had been brought to Chelsea in Thames barges. I discovered all this from one of our customers, an elderly, bookish man who used to come regularly to the restaurant with his lively French wife. He told me he was writing a book about Chelsea, and we called him 'the historian'. The waiters had to be very careful when serving him because he had a habit of sitting very still, deep in thought, and then suddenly flinging his arms in the air and bursting into animated talk. The unexpected gesture could easily have spelt disaster for a waiter walking past him with a plate of soup in one hand and a ragout of duck in the other. The 'historian' often came to see me in the kitchen after he had finished his meal, and it was then that he regaled me with interesting bits of local history, especially when they had some connection with cooking or food. He told me about the immense breakfasts which Dante Gabriel Rossetti used to eat at Cheyne Row when he amazed his friends by devouring a whole mountain of grilled bacon together with a surrounding garland of about a dozen overlapping fried eggs.

At the bottom of Swan Walk, which runs between La Tante Claire and the Thames, is the house where Osbert and Sacheverell Sitwell lived between 1917 and 1919; one can still see the basement windows of the kitchen where their eccentric housekeeper, Mrs Powell, once cooked a dinner for important literary guests at which she made culinary history by starting the meal with fish and serving soup as the second course. On the other side of La Tante Claire, near the delightful Rogers de Rin antique shop, you can turn down Tite Street, pass Oscar Wilde's blue plaque, and find yourself near the site of Whistler's White House where the painter lived for a few months in 1879. He was then on the verge of bankruptcy, but the 'historian' told me that he still went on giving the famous lunch parties known as 'Sunday breakfasts' despite the fact that the deferential, dark-suited waiters who served them so adroitly were none other than the bailiffs sent to detain his belongings, whom Whistler's charm had seduced into lending a helping hand. The food was always good and frequently included smoked salmon and turbot, two of Whistler's favourite fish, and which I combine in one of my favourite recipes at La Tante Claire.

The Society of Apothecaries founded the Chelsea Physic Garden in 1673. It is a stone's throw away from La Tante Claire, and I always enjoy visiting it. Since the seventeenth century it has been a centre for the preservation and study of all sorts of medicinal and culinary plants, and it possesses the largest olive tree in the country which in 1976 produced seven pounds of edible olives. As a cook, I love to walk round the herb garden, identifying herbs I know, and always discovering others I have never heard of. I am fascinated by the wonderful old English names of many of the plants, names like lovage, angelica, lemon balm, sweet cicely, tansy and dill. Most of these are herbs which French cooks never use. The English are familiar with a much wider variety of plants than we are, and have a longer, more continuous tradition of using them in their cooking. When I was learning French classical cooking at Tarbes, the only herbs our teachers mentioned were tarragon, parsley, chervil, chives, thyme and rosemary. Basil was only used in Provence, never anywhere else. We never cooked with sage, for example, or borage or marjoram, and we never used mint, except for an infusion. The French are horrified at the thought of eating mint sauce with their lamb, and they never even cook potatoes with mint. The English like food to have a rather neutral taste which can be made sharper by the addition of herbs or spices or a strong sauce; but the French prefer the desired taste to be inherent in the food right from the start. Each herb has a different character and a different use, though this depends very much on the ideals and preferences of the cook. I myself like to use cumin seeds with red mullet and basil with lobster; sea bass is brilliant with a sweet and sour sauce and I love to combine a dish of roast pigeon with oriental spices. Incidentally, the idea of the pigeon 'gigolette' suddenly occurred to me one day, when I thought it would be fun to make a pigeon leg look like a miniature leg of lamb. The result is most effective.

CHINOISERIE DE BAR, POIREAUX ET PETITS OIGNONS

— • —

SWEET AND SOUR SEA BASS WITH LEEKS AND BUTTON ONIONS

— • —

4 sea bass steaks, 150 g / 5 oz each
15 g / ½ oz sugar
50 ml / 2 fl oz vinegar
50 ml / 2 fl oz port
300 ml / ½ pt strong red wine
80 g / 3 oz butter
4 leeks
50 ml / 2 fl oz double cream
100 g / 3½ oz button onions
salt and freshly ground pepper

— • —

Season the bass and wrap each steak individually in clingfilm. Prepare the sauce: Mix the sugar and vinegar in a pan and cook until caramelised to a light golden colour. Add the port and wine and reduce by half. Whisk in 50 g / 2 oz butter, check the seasoning and if the sauce seems too sour add a pinch of sugar. Keep hot.

Poach the leeks in salted water until tender. When cooked, cut into 1 cm / ½ in pieces and mix with the cream. Check the seasoning. Melt the remaining butter in a frying pan, add the onions and cook slowly until golden. If necessary add some water during cooking to prevent them from burning. Check the seasoning and keep warm.

Put the unwrapped fish in a steamer set over boiling water and steam for about 10 minutes, depending on the thickness of the fish. To check if the fish is cooked, pierce it with a needle. If it goes through easily, the fish is ready. Place the fish steaks in the middle of the plates. Put the sauce around and arrange the vegetables attractively. Serve immediately.

GIGOLETTE DE PIGEONNEAU AUX EPICES

•

YOUNG PIGEON WITH ORIENTAL SPICES

4 young pigeons
80 g / 3 oz butter
20 g / ¾ oz shallots, sliced
50 ml / 2 oz port
25 ml / 1 fl oz madeira
25 ml / 1 fl oz brandy
1 garlic clove, chopped
1 star anise
1 pinch of cinnamon
1 pinch of curry powder
200 ml / 7 fl oz Veal stock (page 49)
salt and freshly ground pepper

•

Preheat the oven to 230°C / 450°F / gas 8.

Bone the pigeons and cut them in two to leave a breast and a leg together. Pull the breat out of the skin and fold it down against the leg so that it looks like a miniature leg of lamb. Tie up with string and season.

Heat 30 g / 1 oz butter in a frying pan and fry the pigeon 'legs' on all sides until browned. Cook in the hot oven for 5 minutes, then leave in a warm place. Add the shallots to the pan and sweat for 2 minutes. Pour off the fat and add the port, madeira and brandy and all the spices. Reduce by half. Add the veal stock and reduce by one-third. Incorporate the rest of the butter and pass through a sieve. Check the seasoning. Place the meat on a serving dish and pour the sauce around. Serve immediately.

In the early 1980s, largely due to the widespread influence of *nouvelle cuisine*, French cooking became more open to the use of certain herbs and spices which were either new, such as those imported from south-east Asia, or which had existed for a long time but had fallen out of fashion. Ginger and coriander were rediscovered, and saffron, which had once been so important but now, like basil, only survived in the cooking of Provence, was employed in all sorts of new and unexpected combinations. The special crocus from the pistils of which saffron is made, is one of the plants I found growing in the Chelsea Physic Garden, not far from the beds alloted to what, in the old days, the English called pot-herbs and which for us are now, quite simply, vegetables. Indeed I was truly surprised to find that pot-herbs included leeks, onions, carrots, peas, beans, spinach and fennel! Vegetables, too, were accorded a much more important place on the menu during the reign of *nouvelle cuisine* than they enjoyed in the time of the old *cuisine classique*. When I first started cooking, they were taken for granted as routine accompaniments to a main course, but as soon as the search for natural, untransformed tastes began to dominate the culinary scene, vegetables became important dishes in their own right.

LAITUES BRAISÉES

•

BRAISED LETTUCES

800 g / 1¾ lb round lettuces
50 g / 2 oz butter
120 g / 4 oz carrots, thinly sliced
150 g / 5 oz onions, thinly sliced
a large piece of bacon rind
3 tablespoons Chicken stock (page 49)
coarse salt
1 Bouquet garni (page 11)
salt and freshly ground pepper

•

Preheat the oven to 180°C / 350°F / gas 4.
Discard the wilted outer leaves and keep the lettuces
whole. Fill the sink with cold water and gently plunge
in the lettuces. Agitate them gently to get rid of the
earth. Empty the sink and repeat the operation twice.
Place the lettuces on a tray. Again, fill the sink.

Bring a large saucepan of salted water to the boil and
gently put in the lettuces. Bring just to boiling point,
then put the lettuces into the cold water in the sink and
agitate gently to get rid of any remaining earth. Take
the lettuces out and squeeze them gently but
thoroughly.

In an ovenproof pan, melt the butter over medium heat.
Add the carrots, cook for 5 minutes, then add the
onions and sweat gently. Arrange the lettuces on top,
pour on enough chicken stock to come three-quarters of
the way up the lettuces, then add the bouquet garni,
some coarse salt and freshly milled pepper.

To protect the lettuces from drying out, cover them
with the piece of bacon rind, fat-side down. Cover the
bacon with buttered greaseproof paper. Bring back to
the boil, then cook in the preheated oven for about 1
hour. When cooked, drain the lettuces gently, reserving
the cooking juices. Halve lengthways and trim the
cores. Reduce the cooking juices by half and pass
through a fine strainer. Pour over the lettuces.

PETITS FLANS AUX CAROTTES

•

LITTLE CARROT FLANS

200 g/ 7 oz carrots, sliced
15 g / ½ oz butter
50 ml / 2 fl oz milk
50 ml 2 fl oz double cream
1 egg
salt
4 sprigs of parsley or chervil, to garnish

•

Preheat the oven to 200°C / 400°F / gas 6.
Melt the butter over gentle heat. Add the carrots, cover
the pan and cook until soft, stirring occasionally.

Mash the carrots with a potato masher to make a
coarse purée, leaving some largish carrot pieces in.
Bring the milk and cream to the boil, pour over the
carrots and mix well. Stir in the egg and salt. Check
the seasoning as it is difficult to improve once the flans
are cooked.

Spoon the mixture into 4 buttered dariole moulds and
place in an ovenproof dish. Half-fill the dish with hot
water, cover with buttered greaseproof paper and bake
in the oven for 20 minutes or until just set. Unmould
the flans on to individual plates and garnish each with
a sprig of parsley or chervil.

These flans make an excellent accompaniment to the
beef stew, and also a pleasant light starter.

Aubergines Braisées aux Oignons

—— • ——

Braised aubergines with onions

—— • ——

2 aubergines, 250 g / 9 oz each
4 tablespoons salt
6 onions, 100 g / 4 oz each, sliced into thin rings
500 g / 1 lb 2 oz tomatoes, blanched, skinned, deseeded and diced
4 garlic cloves, peeled, crushed and very finely chopped
6 tablespoons extra virgin olive oil
2 tablespoons flat-leaved parsley leaves, finely chopped
butter, for greasing
salt and freshly ground pepper

—— • ——

Preheat the oven to 180°C / 350°F / gas mark 4. Trim the aubergines and halve lengthways. Using a small knife, make 3 long shallow incisions in the fleshy side of each aubergine half. Sprinkle with 2 tablespoons salt and leave to rest at room temperature for at least 30 minutes. Rinse well under cold water, squeeze gently and pat dry with a cloth.

In the meantime, put the onions in a colander and sprinkle them with 2 tablespoons salt, mixing well with your hands. Leave to rest at room temperature for at least 30 minutes. Rinse under cold water and gently squeeze out the excess water. Mix in the tomatoes, garlic, salt, pepper and 2 tablespoons olive oil. Smear the bottom of a large ovenproof dish with 2 tablespoons olive oil and put in the aubergines skin-side down. Stuff the incisions with as much of the tomato and onion filling as possible. Sprinkle the rest over and between the aubergines and add the remaining olive oil. Cover with a piece of buttered foil and bake in the preheated oven for 1½ hours. Sprinkle with the parsley.

This makes a good vegetarian dish; just add 400 g / 14 oz cooked chick peas 15 minutes before the end of the cooking. Serve over steaming basmati rice.

Barigoule

—— • ——

Artichokes, carrots and onions cooked in white wine

2 large artichoke bottoms (see *Pavé de Loup Barigoule*, page 110) cut into 8
100 g / 3½ oz carrots, thinly sliced
75 g / 3 oz onions, thinly sliced
1 small Bouquet garni (page 11)
50 ml / 2 fl oz extra virgin olive oil
100 ml / 4 fl oz good quality dry white wine
1 garlic clove, finely chopped
salt and freshly ground pepper

—— • ——

Heat the olive oil in a large shallow pan. Sweat the artichoke pieces for 5 minutes, then add the carrots and mix well. Add the onions and garlic, and sweat for 3 minutes. Pour the white wine over and reduce by half.

Add 200 ml / 7 fl oz water and the bouquet garni. Bring to the boil, season and simmer until all the vegetables are tender and all the liquid has evaporated.

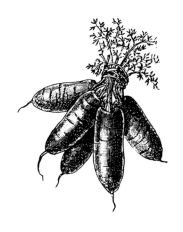

We were lucky at La Tante Claire. We were really busy right from the start, and we never had an evening when we were not full. Annie says that it had a good deal to do with the quality of my cooking, and this may well be so, but I still think we had a lot of good luck. It was simply amazing. We never found ourselves sitting anxiously at the back table of a half-empty restaurant, wondering if we were going to be full tomorrow or not. Of course, Albert and Michel gave us wonderful publicity; between their three restaurants, they saw many more customers than we ever could, and they told them about us. We also had many local residents who came out of curiosity and returned the following week to become regular customers. We had made an agreement with our shareholders that each had the right to £250 worth of free meals a year; this was quite a good deal, since a meal at that time cost about £20. The only condition was that they brought with them at least three other friends or acquaintances (a husband or wife did not count) with the idea that the friends would like the restaurant and come back to it. They usually did.

We were lucky, too, in getting good reviews, though as a rule I have certain reservations about food critics. They are often too harsh when judging a restaurant which has only been open for a short time. The first month is the hardest for a chef with a new restaurant; he has to get used to and adapt to all sorts of new elements: premises, equipment, suppliers, and even new members of his staff. He is at his most vulnerable and financially insecure; and it is indeed quite probable that there will be a night when things go wrong and the kitchen will not be at its best. If a food critic comes on that particular night and gives the chef a poor review, its effect can be catastrophic and the bad reputation he gets may be out of all proportion to the quality of his food sampled over a longer period of time. In cases like that, I think critics should visit a restaurant a number of times before writing about it. I am also annoyed by the fact that some food critics have had absolutely no professional kitchen training. Several times during my first two years at La Tante Claire, critics described in great detail how I had prepared certain dishes, but not a single detail was correct. These critics had no conception of what I had done in the kitchen, and yet they set themselves up as expert commentators on my recipes. The best informed and most discerning judges of food that I can think of are the Michelin inspectors, each one of whom must be professionally trained and has to have actually worked with distinction in the hotel or restaurant business.

CHAPTER 6

LA TANTE CLAIRE
SUCCESS

I was awarded my first Michelin star at La Tante Claire in 1978, a year after opening, and the second two years later in 1980. During that time Annie did all the bills and acted as cashier besides being *maître d'hôtel*, just as she had done at the Waterside, and Jean-Claude darted about as actively as ever with bottles and wine lists. The passageway between the two lines of tables and chairs was very narrow, and of course it was always busy with the coming and going of customers besides being the only route for waiters hastening backwards and forwards with plates of food. Usually they managed very well and became skilled at passing each other and manipulating trays and dishes so that they did not collide. One day, however, two waiters were simultaneously serving two separate tables on opposite sides of the restaurant, when one of them suddenly turned round and slightly jogged the elbow of the other. The result was disastrous. A whole plate of lobster *pot-au-feu* went straight over the shoulders and down the back of one of the customers. Everyone was aghast, and all Annie could do was to apologise profusely and take full responsibility for cleaning the jacket; luckily the man was very nice about the whole thing. When the news of the accident was brought to me in the kitchen, and I had to prepare another portion of lobster, I was a little taken aback because it was a new recipe I was trying out that night for the first time, and I hoped the incident was not a bad omen! As it happened, the dish became very popular and I sometimes have it on the menu even now. It is a modern, not a traditional *pot-au-feu*, though the *confit de canard* does give it a bit of the atmosphere of south-west France.

POT AU FEU DE HOMARD ET CONFIT DE CANARD

—— • ——

LOBSTER AND PRESERVED DUCK GIZZARDS IN SAVOURY BROTH

—— • ——

4 lobsters, 500 g / 1 lb 2 oz each
4 Preserved duck gizzards, thinly sliced (see opposite)
200 g / 7 oz carrots, turned
200 g / 7 oz leeks, white part only
200 g / 7 oz courgettes, turned
2 tomatoes, blanched, peeled, deseeded and diced
500 ml / 18 fl oz *Petite marmite* (page 20), clarified as in *Consommé de canard aux betteraves* (page 27)
4 savoy cabbage leaves
8 tarragon leaves finely chopped
12 chervil leaves
30 g / 1 oz coarse sea salt
salt and freshly ground pepper

—— • ——

Separately cook the carrots, leeks and courgettes in boiling salted water. Drain, slice the leeks diagonally and keep all the vegetables warm. Lightly cook the cabbage leaves in boiling salted water, drain and keep warm.

Bring a saucepan of water to the boil, large enough to contain the 4 lobsters. Add the sea salt. Plunge the lobsters into the boiling water, for 2 minutes, then remove immediately. Break open the shells and remove all the flesh. Cut each tail into 4 thick slices and keep warm.

Make sure the consommé is well-seasoned. If necessary, reduce it slowly, without boiling and season again. Cook the pieces of lobster in the very hot but not boiling consommé for 3 minutes, then add the thinly sliced gizzards.

Lay a cabbage leaf in each warm soup plate and top with the vegetables. Ladle the consommé over, dividing the lobster pieces equally. Sprinkle the chopped tarragon and the chevril leaves on top and serve immediately. (Photograph p. 182)

CONFIT DE CANARD

PRESERVED DUCK

1 duck, complete with head, feet etc., plucked and drawn
300 g / 11 oz coarse sea salt

Cut the duck into pieces: thighs, breasts, wings and neck. Keep the feet, head, heart and neck. Clean the gizzard under cold running water and pat it dry with kitchen paper. Skin the neck, being careful not to tear the skin that can be stuffed (recipe page 28). Trim off the skin and any excess fat from the duck pieces and reserve it. Put all the duck pieces in a large bowl with the feet, head, heart, neck and gizzard. Using your hands mix in the coarse salt thoroughly. Cover with clingfilm and refrigerate overnight.

Chop the reserved fat and skin into small dice. Put 3 tablespoons water in a saucepan, bring to the boil and quickly add the fat and skin. Cook very gently for 1½ hours. Strain the liquid fat through a fine sieve and keep in a cool place until ready to use.

Remove the duck pieces from the coarse salt, rinse under cold running water and pat dry with a tea towel. In a large saucepan, melt the duck fat over a very low heat until it reaches 90 °C / 194°F. First put in the small pieces (feet, head, heart, neck, wings and gizzard) and cook for about 1 hour, skimming the surface if necessary. The temperature of the fat should be kept constant; under no circumstances let it boil. The meat is ready when you can insert a larding needle without resistance. Using a slotted spoon, remove the meat from the fat and cover it with a lid or a plate to

prevent it from drying out. Cook the thighs and breasts in the same way for about 1½ hours. When these are ready, put the small pieces of duck (feet, head, heart, neck, wings and gizzard) back into the fat with the larger pieces and leave to cool completly.

Using a slotted spoon, put the small pieces of duck into a very clean preserving jar (or any large jar with a good lid) and the breasts and thighs into another. Every piece must be well coated with fat, so do not pack the pieces too tightly into the jars. Pour in the fat, being careful not to add the cooking juices, as these are perishable. Leave the confit to cool completely before screwing on the lids, then refrigerate. It will keep for a year.

One of our early Tante Claire customers, whom I am sure we shall never forget, was the man who managed to eat an extra plate of turbot without paying for it. The fish was his main course; he had finished it, and the waiter had duly removed his empty plate together with his knife and fork, so that the customer was now ready for his dessert. Another waiter, with a second plate of turbot intended for a different table, made a mistake and put it down in front of the customer who was expecting his dessert. Instead of calling the waiter back and pointing out this error, the man said nothing and surreptitiously and very quickly ate the second turbot – using his spoon!

Generally speaking, however, the narrowness of the restaurant made serving easier in some ways than in a larger area, and untoward incidents were rare. Storage of ingredients and cleaning were more difficult; and having only one cloakroom meant that an early customer would often bump into a late waiter hurriedly changing his trousers. It was really the cooks who were the most incommoded by cramped conditions and by having to spill out whenever possible into the little yard, but at the back of my mind I always hoped that one day we would be able to improve the premises.

By the end of 1984 La Tante Claire had worked very well indeed for a period of seven

Pot au Feu de Homard et Confit de Canard (recipe p. 180)

years. We had repaid all the capital we had borrowed to start the business, and we felt we were free now to embark on a further stage in our career. We thought about selling the Chelsea premises and buying a larger restaurant somewhere else, and we looked at several possibilities in Mayfair and the West End, but somehow none of them seemed quite right. They only made us realise the advantages we had gained from becoming well established in Royal Hospital Road: an attractive area, regular local customers, comparatively easy parking and so on. Then in 1985 the builder next door to us on the ground floor decided to sell his offices, and we immediately made up our minds to buy them. We were now the sole owners of the entire ground floor area of the building, and could re-plan both the dining room and the kitchen on more generous lines. Our private arrangement was that Annie would have freedom to do what she wanted in the dining room, while I would have the same sort of freedom in the kitchen. We found an architect, David Collings, through one of our customers; in the dining room Annie asked him to design something that was elegant but at the same time quite simple, and I, in the kitchen, wanted the most efficient and up-to-date equipment I could get.

The alteration work started in early spring and went on for five traumatic months. It seemed that the banging and the hammering and the dust would never come to an end, and that the wreckage and the rubble would never assume the shape of a viable restaurant. One thing I gained from it all was an interesting insight into the English workman's attitude towards restaurants and food. When I offered some of the men a free meal at La Tante Claire to celebrate the end of the work, I was really surprised when they all refused it on the grounds that they would feel uncomfortable and out of place in an expensive restaurant. How different a French workman's reaction would have been! He would have accepted the offer at once with enthusiasm, and would never for a moment have allowed social diffidence to get in the way of his enjoyment of *haute cuisine*.

At last the impossible happened, and everything was finished. To launch the new Tante Claire, we gave a big party, spread over three evenings, to which we invited all our friends and customers, and the following week the restaurant was formally open. The dining room was now larger and smarter and more brightly lit, but this was not to everyone's taste. At the party a Frenchman, who had been a regular customer for a very long time, came to Annie and said 'It's wonderful what you've done here, Mrs Koffmann, but you do realize, don't you, that it will be quite impossible for me to eat here any more?' For a moment Annie was nonplussed, but then she understood what he meant. The Frenchman had always had the same table in the old restaurant, right at the end of the room, in a dark and secluded corner where other customers never bothered to look, and he always brought a girlfriend with him. I think he was married, so the combination of good food, intimacy and complete discretion had been ideal. Neither he nor his girlfriend was ever noticed. Now, of course, the new lighting and the more open table arrangement would make concealment impossible.

The old table arrangement had not allowed for any variation, but in the new big square restaurant, it was possible to be much more adaptable. Tables could be extended, shortened or moved about as necessary. Whereas before we could only serve a maximum of thirty-six people, we now regularly did between thirty and forty-five covers at lunch and fifty to sixty in the evening. This naturally depended on some tables becoming vacant during the period of *service*, since the extension had given us only seven or eight extra places. Despite the considerable amount of capital we had had to raise to do the building work, we were still a long way from being a large restaurant, that is to say one where there is so much space between the tables that they rarely have to be moved, even for cleaning purposes. At La Tante Claire we cannot afford that luxury, and our tables have to be folded and moved each morning when the waiters sweep and hoover the restaurant, which means that after a while they tend to become rather worn and unsteady. It is all a question of space and money, and space is the besetting problem of most restaurants. At first we thought the new Tante Claire was very spacious, but after two or three months we found ourselves grumbling about being almost as cramped as we had been in the old dining area. We were trying to push in as many places as possible, until in the end there was hardly any room between the tables for waiters to pass each other or to manoeuvre the liqueur trolley. However much space you have, you always seem to want more!

I often ask myself if we did the right thing in enlarging La Tante Claire in the way we did. It was certainly right to make our premises bigger, but perhaps it was wrong to opt for such an obvious Art-Deco style of decoration. The interior details are so much part of the architectural design of the room that it is impossible to change them or even to combine them with some other decorative scheme, should we ever want to give the restaurant a different look. The decoration we inherited from the old Sans Souci was far less obtrusive and perhaps more comfortable. I sometimes rather miss it. One thing we very definitely lost with the change was the close-knit, friendly relationship we had with our original staff; but this was inevitable when we increased the number of employees from eight to nineteen.

In 1983, when our daughter Camille was born, Annie gave up her work at La Tante Claire, and her place was taken by Jean-Pierre Durantet, with whom we had planned to open a restaurant in France in 1975, and who now became our *maître d'hôtel*. Patrice Jegat, who had worked for us before and who had an encyclopaedic knowledge of wine, became our wine waiter when Jean-Claude left to take up a job in Paris. In addition to them, we now employed five waiters instead of three. In the kitchen, besides myself as chef, we now employed nine cooks instead of three, and two *plongeurs* instead of one. We also took on two cashiers to do the bills in place of Annie. The extra cooks in the kitchen were essential, not only because the restaurant was bigger, but also because I wanted to improve the quality of the work, and working more carefully usually means working more slowly, so you need more people to do it. The increase in employees meant that everything became more formal, and we found that cooks and waiters tended to treat us with the awed respect due to beings from another world. Annie and I felt much more remote from them than we had been from our earlier staff; we realised we had turned into figures of authority – we were the bosses. Every dish on the menu and how it was served was now entirely our responsibility.

RAVIOLIS DE RIS DE VEAU AUX TRUFFES

•

RAVIOLI OF VEAL SWEETBREADS WITH TRUFFLES

•

200 g / 7 oz veal sweetbreads
150 g / 5 oz Home-made pasta dough (page 196)
rolled out very thinly
40 g / 1½ oz truffles, slivered

•

Braise the sweetbreads as in Pithiviers de ris de veau et de morilles *(page 209) taking care, for this recipe, to divide the quantity of sweetbreads given here into 4 equal portions. Prepare the same sauce, adding the slivered truffle at the end of the cooking. Keep warm.*

Cut the fresh pasta dough into four 15 cm / 6 in squares. Put a piece of sweetbread on each square and fold the pasta over, pressing well between the palms of your hands. A little water may be needed to seal the edges together. Make sure there are no holes.

Cook in 3 L / 5 pt salted boiling water for 3 minutes. Drain well and serve with the sauce on warm plates.

FILETS DE LIÈVRE AU POIVRE, SAUCE AU CÂPRES

———— • ————

PEPPERED HARE FILLETS WITH A CAPER SAUCE

———— • ————

4 hare fillets, about 120 g / 4 oz each
3 tablespoons vegetable oil
30 g / 1 oz coarsely ground black pepper
30 g / 1 oz capers
2 shallots, finely chopped
500 ml / 18 fl oz red wine
200 ml / 7 fl oz Veal stock (page 49)
50 g / 2 oz butter
salt and freshly ground pepper

———— • ————

Roll the hare fillets in the coarsely ground pepper and sprinkle salt over them. Heat the oil in a frying pan. When very hot, cook the fillets for 3-4 minutes, until done to your liking. Set aside and keep warm while you prepare the sauce.

Pour off the fat from the pan, then put in the shallots and sweat until soft. Deglaze with red wine, and reduce to 125 ml / 4½ fl oz. Add the veal stock and reduce by half. Whisk in the butter and check the seasoning. Pass the sauce through a fine sieve. Add the capers and pour the sauce over the hare fillets.
(Photograph p. 186)

GRATIN DE POMMES

———— • ————

APPLE GRATIN

———— • ————

425 g / 15 oz sweetened apple purée
4 large dessert apples, peeled, cored and cut into eight
175 g / 6 oz butter, softened
120 g / 4 oz caster sugar
2 size 3 eggs, lightly beaten
120 g / 4 oz ground almonds

———— • ————

Preheat the oven to 180°C / 350°F / gas 4.
Spread the apple purée in a shallow ovenproof dish. Fry the apple pieces lightly in 50 g / 2 oz butter until golden and arrange them on the sauce. In a small bowl, cream the remaining butter and sugar together until fluffy. Whisk in the eggs, little by little, then mix in the ground almonds. Cover the apples with this almond cream.

Bake the apple gratin in the oven for 15 minutes, then place under a hot grill until golden brown. This gratin should be served just warm.

The improvements we made to the kitchen were probably the most successful part of the whole project. A side wall was rebuilt to take in what had formerly been the outside yard, thus making the kitchen a great deal larger. It allowed me to install better refrigerators and sinks, to have a small office area for myself, and to plan a better space for the *passe-plat*, the table near the entrance where the waiters bring their orders and collect their food. I was also able to fit in a smoke box for smoking fish and hams. Now I can smoke halibut as a replacement for cod in a *brandade*, and even smoke my own salmon. In the very centre of the kitchen I placed its crowning glory, a large cooking stove built by the French firm of Rorgue, the Rolls Royce of kitchen equipment. The model I bought for La Tante Claire was the very latest, and I was the first person in

Filets de Lièvre au Poivre, Sauce au Câpres (recipe p. 185)

England to buy one. The thought that I was a pioneer in owning such a superb piece of machinery gave me an enormous amount of pleasure, as did the fact that when others made enquiries about this particular model, the Paris headquarters of Rorgue suggested that they should visit La Tante Claire and see for themselves how it worked. The first two purchasers to install one after looking at ours were the Claridges and Connaught hotels.

The Rorgue is magnificent, of simple, classical appearance, very robust, and I have nothing but praise for it. It is gas-fired and it heats superbly. When we first used it, we found we were burning everything because we simply refused to believe that it could attain such a high temperature so rapidly. I was used to the old cooker of the Sans Souci, an English model which heated very slowly indeed. If you wanted to boil a saucepan, you had to leave it on the hob for minutes before it even simmered. With the Rorgue, on the other hand, you only have to put a saucepan on to a burner for two seconds for it to be boiling really hard.

My new kitchen has given me a great deal of satisfaction. I really enjoy working in it, and every morning I am the first person there. Annie and I live now in Battersea, so my day starts with walking my two dogs in the park, a labrador and a tough, irrepressible beagle (he once ate the Christmas cassoulet for seven people and nearly died), then I drive or, in summer, cycle over Chelsea Bridge to La Tante Claire. I open the blue front door about eight o'clock, and like to sit down with a cup of tea or coffee and a slice of the country bread we bake ourselves, and let my thoughts run freely over anything that happens to come into my head. It is a good time; there is nobody there and I can do what I want. The cooker is not yet lit; the restaurant tables are still folded against the wall with the chairs piled on top of them, and I can be sure of a good half hour in which to go over new ideas for menus or recipes before the cooks start to arrive for work at a quarter to nine. At half past eight I light the cooker. It remains on until half past two, when it is turned off for the

afternoon, and then it is lit again at half past five and finally turned off for the night at about eleven. In the morning it is most important that all the ovens are ready at the right temperature when work starts at nine.

The first cook to arrive is always the baker, since bread-making has to be started well in advance of any other kitchen activity. The process has always fascinated me. Whenever I smell new, hot bread in the oven, my thoughts go back to the little bread shop I knew as a boy in Tarbes. It was in a narrow street near our flat, and it had golden letters above the door and two wonderful wheatsheaves painted on panels on either side of the window. It was always brightly lit and busy, and the magic perfume of fresh bread which wafted out of it almost redeemed the drab sadness of the surrounding houses. I must have been seven or eight years old at the time, but even now I still think that bread is special, and that its function in connection with food is of fundamental importance. Eating a piece of bread is the ideal way to begin a meal. Quite apart from the enjoyment you get from the flavour of a good bread (and the danger is that if it is too good, you eat too much of it!), the action of chewing wakes up the taste-buds, excites the saliva and generally heightens your gastronomic awareness. When you eat something soft, like a purée or a mousse, you tend not to taste it immediately, and it often slips down your throat unappreciated. But if you eat it with some bread, your taste-buds become more active, and you know at once what it is you are eating. It is the same with sauces. If you just swallow a spoonful of sauce, it goes straight down to the stomach and you only get the briefest taste. Whenever I eat a dish with a sauce, I always dip a bit of bread into it first and savour that on its own, to get the full taste of the sauce, before continuing to eat the complete dish in the usual way. You will find you appreciate the relationship of the sauce to the main ingredient of the dish much better like that.

The first time I worked in a kitchen which made its own bread was at Le Gavroche. My pleasure in eating bread now became merged with an interest in the technique of making it, and that was why I made bread at the Waterside and why I went on making it at La Tante Claire. Nevertheless the baker I have at the moment is a comparatively new addition to my staff, and it is the first time I have ever employed a cook whose sole job is to make bread. I decided on this quite recently, when I acquired two outstanding items of bakery equipment which I thought would complement the Rorgue cooker. The first was the newest, most efficient and easy-to-run model of steam-heated, electronically-controlled bread oven, which produces steam at the push of a button. The other purchase was a kneading-machine made in Switzerland. It is remarkable for having jointed, articulated levers which imitate exactly the motions and positions of the hands of the old-fashioned baker as he laboriously kneaded his dough in a traditional, wooden kneading trough. There were on the market quite a number of mechanical kneaders, but their dough was never as good as dough made by hand. Here, at last, was the ultimate answer to the problem – a real robot baker!

PAIN DE MIE

SOFT WHITE BREAD

(Makes 3 Loaves)
500 g / 1 lb 2 oz superfine pastry
500 g / 1 lb 2 oz strong plain flour
30 g / 1 oz sugar
30 g / 1 oz fresh yeast, or 15 g / ½ oz dried yeast
20 g / ¾ oz powdered milk
30 g / 1 oz butter, melted
900 ml / 1½ pt tepid water
20 g / ¾ salt

Combine all the ingredients except the salt in an electric mixer and mix for 6 minutes. Add the salt and mix for 2 more minutes. Put the dough in a bowl and place it in a plastic bag. Seal tightly and leave to rise for 45 minutes.

Cut the dough into three 400 g / 14 oz pieces and place them in loaf tins. Leave to rise for 1-1½ hours.

Preheat the oven to 240°C / 475°F / gas 9. Place a dish of hot water at the bottom of the hot oven to create steam (this will make the bread crustier), and bake the loaves for 30 minutes.

PAIN BAGUETTE

600 ml / 1 pt tepid water
1 kg / 2¾ lb strong plain flour
20 g / ¾ oz sugar
100 g / 3½ oz butter, melted
30 g / 1 oz fresh yeast, or 15 g / 1½ oz dried yeast
30 g / 1 oz salt

Combine all the ingredients except the salt in an electric mixer and mix for 6 minutes. Add the salt and mix for another 2 minutes. Roll the dough into a ball, put it in a bowl, then place in a plastic bag and seal tightly. Leave to rise for 25 minutes.

Preheat the oven to 220°C / 450°F / gas 8. Cut the dough in 4 and roll each piece into a sausage shape. Place on a baking tray, cover with a light cloth and leave to rest for 30 minutes. With a razor blade, make 4 slashes on the top of each loaf, then bake for 15 minutes in the very hot oven. Place a small dish filled with hot water inside the oven in order to produce steam to make the bread crustier.

At La Tante Claire we make ten different sorts of bread every day. First we make typical French loaves – white, country and rye and nut breads with walnuts or almonds; then we make a raisin bread and others which are flavoured with cumin or cinnamon. The baker worked for a long time in Switzerland, and developed the Swiss taste for bread made with flower seeds, such as sunflower and poppy seeds. These are not really French breads, but I let him do them because they add variety to our selection, and the customers seem to like them. The bread baskets which the waiters take round the tables are a source of pride to me. They are piled high with little breads and loaves of all different shapes and colours: white, brown, golden, honey-coloured; long, round and square. I am sometimes quite puzzled as to why I offer so many kinds of bread. Am I just trying to make life more complicated, or is it all part of my genuine interest in the subject?

After the baker, the next person to arrive at La Tante Claire is often my fishmonger, William Black. He has his own van and travels regularly backwards and forwards between London and the big Paris food markets at Rungis. He calls two or three times a week, at half past eight or a quarter to nine, to show me fish bought about two or three o'clock the same morning on the other side of the Channel. William is an excellent fishmonger; he has a real eye for fish and the quality of his stock is always outstanding. All La Tante Claire's fish come from France, as does all its poultry. I order my chickens and ducks, and, when required, geese, turkeys and guinea fowl directly from my dealer at Rungis, and William brings them over in his van when he comes with the fish. The French produce the best poultry in the world, and all the top restaurants in London buy their birds directly from France. I must admit than I am not always satisfied with Bresse chickens, even though they bear a famous name, and the conditions under which they are reared are strictly controlled by law. They have very white flesh but their breasts and legs are usually rather small so that one bird can really only feed two people. All the Tante Claire chickens, therefore, are plumper birds which come from French 'factory' farms similar to one I visited recently in the Landes. Here the birds are allowed to run completely freely and even to fly about; they are not kept penned up in narrow cages where they can

hardly move. The farms are called 'factories' because they produce about ten thousand birds a week which, since they are free-range, are almost of the same quality as the old, genuine *poulets fermier* that I knew at my grandparents' farm at Saint Puy. In France, a housewife can buy very good chickens at a local market or from a farmer, but a restaurant, which depends each week on a fixed quantity of birds always of the same size and quality, cannot make do with a source subject to the sort of fluctuations experienced by the small supplier, who might sometimes produce fifty good birds a week and sometimes hardly any.

Our ducks, too, all come from France. Every Friday morning I ring Rungis and order, say, twenty-four ducks for the following week. The birds will be killed on Sunday or Monday, and William collects them early on Tuesday, brings them across the Channel with the fish, and they are in the refrigerator at La Tante Claire by nine o'clock. We pack them in special bags, and, as they are fresh, they can easily be kept for a week if necessary. To be edible, poultry must have been dead for two days, so this means that we can use them as from the Wednesday morning. I insist on French ducks because I am always disappointed with English ones. An Aylesbury duck looks a large bird but this is because it is full of fat, and, in comparison with a French bird, such as a Challans duck, it has a very small breast. Ultimately, the English duck is much more expensive than the French and more troublesome to cook. When it comes to meat, however, I buy all my beef and my lamb from dealers in London. English meat is outstanding, and it is very hard to get anything comparable in France. Fruit and vegetables I buy in person at Covent Garden, and I always buy my game in England. My pheasants, partridges, grouse, woodcock and snipe all come from the country, and are the only naturally-reared birds we have on the menu. I sometimes wonder where they all come from. It is astonishing to think of the thousands of birds which have to be shot each season just to maintain a decent supply for London restaurants! Some years the market has been so saturated with pheasants that dealers were reduced to selling them at sixty pence a bird, and even to burning them.

Once the deliveries from William's van have been checked and stored, the serious part of the day's work starts at nine, with each section in the kitchen doing the things that are going to take the most time. The baker is now well advanced with the early stages of bread making; the cooks in the meat section are starting to cut up and bone the meat and, if necessary, to make veal or chicken stock in one of the very efficient Rorgue boilers I bought when I acquired the cooker; the fish cooks clean and fillet the newly-arrived fish and will then start to make the fish *fumet* for the day, and the fish terrines and other entrées which will eventually be served cold at lunch; another group is washing and dicing the vegetables; and the *pâtissiers* are starting to make sorbets and tarts and the basic creams and pastries. Each *partie* has a different programme to follow, including a certain amount of preparation for the evening's dinner menu; but at midday, everyone is doing the things which take less time, like preparing garnishes or herbs. By one o'clock, we are all hectically busy with the *coup de feu* and the final combination and serving of some forty three-course lunches in the space of about an hour.

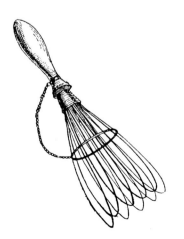

Le Ragoût de Coquilles St Jacques et Huîtres

—— • ——

Ragout of scallops and oysters

—— • ——

12 scallops, thoroughly cleaned
8 oysters, in the shell
4 large spinach leaves
175 g / 6 oz butter
1 shallot, chopped
1 small bunch of chives, snipped
2 tomatoes, blanched, skinned, deseeded and diced
salt and freshly ground pepper

—— • ——

Remove the spinach stalks, wash the leaves in plenty of water and blanch for 1 minute in slightly salted boiling water. Refresh under cold water to keep the colour and drain thoroughly. Open the oysters over a bowl to catch the juices, then pass the juices through a piece of muslin into a small pan. Shell the oysters and add them to the juices, then bring to a simmer over low heat. Place 2 oysters on each spinach leaf and wrap the spinach around them.

Preheat the oven to 100°C / 200°F / gas ½. Halve the scallops lengthways and pan-fry them with a knob of butter for about 1 minute. Place the spinach-wrapped oysters in the middle of lightly-buttered plates and arrange the scallops around them. Heat the plates in the oven for no longer than 2 minutes.

To make the sauce:
Sweat the shallot in 1 tablespoon butter in a saucepan. Add the oyster juices and reduce by one-third. Add the the remaining butter, chives and diced tomatoes. Check the seasoning.

Remove the plates from the oven and pour the sauce around the scallops and oysters. Serve immediately.

BAR AUX OLIVES NOIRES ET SALSIFIS

SEA BASS WITH BLACK OLIVES AND SALSIFY

4 fillets of sea bass, 150 g / 5 oz each
12 black olives, stoned and coarsely chopped
300 g / 11 oz salsify, peeled and cut into thin rounds
100 ml / 4 fl oz extra virgin olive oil
75 g / 3 oz butter
200 g / 7 oz spinach, cooked
100 ml / 4 lf oz Fish stock (page 49)
30 g / 1 oz shallots, very finely chopped
juice of 1 lemon, strained
2 tomatoes, blanched, skinned, deseeded and diced
1 tablespoon chives, finely snipped
salt and freshly ground pepper

Fill a medium saucepan with water, add half the lemon juice and ½ teaspoon salt and bring to the boil. Cook the salsify until tender, drain and set aside.

Heat 50 ml / 2 fl oz olive oil in a large shallow pan until very hot. Season the fish on both sides and cook in the hot oil, skin-side down, for about 4 minutes, until the skin is golden and crisp. Lower the heat and cook the fish slowly on the other side for about 4 more minutes. The precise cooking time depends on the thickness of the fillets. When you can slide a larding needle into the flesh without resistance, the fish is ready.

While the fish is cooking, melt 50 g / 2 oz butter in a frying pan and heat the spinach. Season with salt and keep warm. Over medium heat, melt 25 g / 1 oz butter in another saucepan and lightly and quickly brown the salsify rounds in it. Season with salt and keep warm.

When the fish is cooked, transfer to a plate and keep warm. Skim off the fat and sweat the shallots in the cooking juices from the fish. Deglaze with the fish stock, add the remaining olive oil and bring to the boil.

Pour into a blender and liquidize for 1 minute, until emulsified. Add lemon juice to taste and season with salt and pepper. Place the spinach in the middle of warm plates and arrange the fish on top. Pour the sauce around and scatter on the chopped olives and salsify. Sprinkle with the diced tomatoes and chives.

MOUSSE AU FROMAGE BLANC ET MELON CHARENTAIS

FRESH WHITE CHEESE MOUSSE WITH CHARENTAIS MELON

400 g / 14 oz *fromage blanc* or *fromage frais*
4 gelatine leaves
3 tablespoons milk
100 g / 3½ oz caster sugar
200 ml / 7 fl oz double cream, lightly whipped
2 ripe charentais melons, deseeded and peeled
1 ripe charentais melon, for garnish
mint leaves, for garnish

To make the mousse: Soak the gelatine in cold water, then dissolve it in the milk over gentle heat. Whisk the cheese and sugar together until very smooth. Whisk in the dissolved gelatine and fold in the double cream. Refrigerate.

To make the coulis: Cut the two melons, into chunks and purée in a blender until liquid. Pass through a fine conical sieve. Pushing the fruit pulp with a small ladle. Add sugar to taste.

With the third melon, scoop out little balls over a bowl so as not to waste any of the fragrant juice. Pass the juice through a fine sieve and add it to the coulis. Thoroughly chill the melon balls and coulis. Pour some of the coulis into deep chilled plates and, using a large serving spoon or 2 smaller spoons, shape the mousse into oval quenelles and arrange them gently on the coulis. Garnish with melon balls and fresh mint leaves.

I organise the work in the kitchen after my own special fashion. Some people might think that there is no organisation at all, simply because I keep my system to myself and do not tell the cooks what to do until I consider that the right moment has come for them to know. Sometimes I plan my menus a week in advance, sometimes I do them day by day. This works well as long as I am there in person to direct things, but if I am absent it can be difficult. It might be better to have a regular work scheme which everyone would follow irrespective of whether I was there or not. I can certainly leave La Tante Claire for a couple of days, but it would be risky to trust the cooks on their own for longer. I hate routine if it goes on for too long, and I like to cut down monotony by always introducing new ideas into my cooking. Sometimes these come to me so unexpectedly that there is no time to warn people.

A dish may be basically the same from one day to another, but some little change can give it a more interesting taste or make it more attractive to the eye or renew the life of an over-familiar recipe. These spur-of-the-moment changes are important because they are what make cooking exciting.

For the cooks to work well, the atmosphere in the kitchen must be one of quiet concentration on the job in hand. There must be order and there should be silence. I know that as soon as my back is turned, everyone starts to chatter, but while I am there nobody talks, unless they want to ask me something or I have something to say to them. Annie always makes out that the cooks are frightened of me and that I intimidate them, but that is not quite true. I certainly have no desire to operate a reign of terror at La Tante Claire, though I am the chef and there must be respect for authority in a kitchen if it is to be well-run. For that reason I would never have a kitchen which is so big that I could not see or be aware of everything that is going on in it at any given moment. It is the only way a chef can be sure of giving a personal touch to each dish which is set before a customer. This means I am always watching the cooks, and can intervene at once with a quick comment or a useful demonstration if I notice that something may be going wrong. I can only do this by concentrating intensely on everyone's work; but to the cooks, I suppose, it must seem as though the eye of God were watching them perpetually. It is not very often that a mistake passes unobserved.

Many young French cooks come to ask me for a job at La Tante Claire, but I refuse most of them. Sometimes I have no vacancies, but usually they are simply not good enough. If out of ten cooks you have two who show any real talent, you are doing well. The majority of them have left their catering colleges without any of the good basic training in classical cooking which was still given to students of my own generation, nor have their mothers had the time or the desire to spend very much time in the kitchen, so that they have grown up, in many cases, equally ignorant of French family cooking. Even after three years training, they are still astonishingly insensitive towards the ingredients they use. When they are doing a roast, for example, they will put carrots and onions into the juices at the same time, completely unaware that these vegetables require totally different cooking times; or they will put white wine into a meat juice and never bother to reduce it, which means that the acidity will remain in the sauce and give it an unpleasant flavour; or they will see fat on the top of the veal stock and never think of skimming it off. A true cook, who is aware of food, should sense these simple things almost instinctively. Nor do young cooks taste their food as carefully as they should. They seem to judge dishes by their looks rather than by their flavour. When they do remember to sample something, they do it much too superficially. They will taste a sauce just once, quickly, with the very tip of their finger, then completely forget to taste it again. There is no depth of concentration in their tasting, and I often wonder what they think about while they are doing it. I am amazed, too, at the way they cook the food they eat themselves. At La Tante Claire the staff eat at about half past eleven in the morning and then again at six in the evening. We never eat the restaurant food; we have something simple like a steak with sautéed potatoes, a salad, or some rice, and we eat to feed ourselves, not for a gastronomic treat. Nevertheless even simple food can be cooked well. The other day I found all my cooks, French as well as English, eating chips covered with mounds of tomato ketchup. I was really shocked. That the English cooks were eating it hardly surprised me, but that the French were doing it as well, really did! I make certain that at least half my cooks are French to try to keep up standards and to ensure that French remains the principal language spoken in the kitchen, but on this occasion they seem to have let me down.

Perhaps I am sometimes too hard on my cooks, and perhaps I have not always appreciated them as fully as I should have done. In the kitchen I demand the same standards from everyone, be they eighteen or twenty nine, whether they have been with me two years or it is their very first morning. Whatever a cook does, I like him to do it to the very best of his ability or not at all. A friend once told me that he had never met anyone who was less tolerant of mediocrity than I, and maybe he was right. I always tell my cooks to achieve the desired end by the quickest and most efficacious means. If I see someone laboriously trying to empty a large pan of soup with an ordinary ladle, I just pass him a small saucepan without a word. The gesture alone should be enough to show the cook a more practical way of performing a straightforward task. When a new person joins the kitchen I give him ordinary things to do, and watch him carefully in order to assess his ability and his capacity for work. Then I allot him a place in one of the *parties*, and from time to time I go and work with him and stand near him. After about two months I move him to another *partie*. He may be nervous at first, but I move him to stop him getting into a rut and to make him realise that it is quite easy to do different things. Then in another month or two I move him again, so that by the end of a year he will have worked in every *partie* in the kitchen, and as a result will know a great deal

more about cooking than he did when he first came. I try to coax the most I can out of my cooks, though one of them told me I made him feel like an orange which had been squeezed so hard that even the pips had nothing more to give. Nobody can be a great cook at the age of twenty, but I like mine to feel that they could eventually become great if they wanted. I try to give them the will to persevere, to carry on. When they talk to me about some elaborate recipe which frightens them, I tell them not to think of it as difficult, but as a once simple method which has subsequently become complicated by being embellished and added to. Once you understand the basic theme, there is much less need to get alarmed about the variations.

Another advantage of the new kitchen was that there was now enough room for me to give the *pâtissiers* a whole corner to themselves. *Pâtissiers* are specialists, their work is quite different from that of the cooks, and they constitute a separate group. I would never ask a *pâtissier* to work in one of the other *parties*, though if I found that one of the cooks had a marked aptitude in their direction, I would always let him work with the *pâtissiers*. As a student I was trained in all the basic skills of *pâtisserie* by Monsieur Hèche, but nowadays a lot of the young cooks we get have virtually no knowledge of the craft. They regard it as a trade apart, and indeed I have long been aware of a profound difference between my own temperament as a cook and that of the typical *pâtissier*. When I am cooking, I like to improvise as I go along; but the *pâtissier* has none of that freedom, he is a perpetual prisoner of the laws of chemistry, of precisely-calculated temperatures and quantities and times, which he must obey with undeviating accuracy. If he gets one thing wrong, everything goes wrong, and the only way to get the cream or the pastry right is to throw it away and start again from scratch. In large kitchens, such as that of the Aubette at Strasbourg, the *pâtissiers* had a large, cool, quiet room all to themselves, remote from the hurly-burly of the kitchen, where they could work with dedicated, undisturbed concentration as though in a library or a scientific laboratory.

Apart, of course, from fruit and chocolate and various flavourings, the *pâtissier* has only four basic ingredients to work with, flour, sugar, eggs, and milk, and with these he makes everything. It is really quite amazing. He never touches meat, and this is what, in the eyes of the more sanguine cooks, gives him the reputation of being rather a cold, pedantic character. A *pâtissier* can learn to be a cook, but I think it would be very hard indeed for a cook to learn to be a *pâtissier*. In the *grande cuisine* of the last century *pâtissiers* enjoyed far greater prestige than they do now. In those days their trade included that of the modern *charcutier*. Their imposing *pièces montées* and their *pâtés en croûte*, containing meat or game, were responsible for much of the visual splendour of the banquets and dinner tables of the time. When I first began working as a cook in the late 1960s, the *pâtissier's* job was simply to produce a dull and rather standardised range of desserts consisting of endless *millefeuilles* and *religieuses* and *babas*. You could go from one restaurant to another in those days and the puddings would always be the same. Now there is much more variety, but the *pâtissiers* still have to work with all the meticulous accuracy of a chemical technician.

CLAFOUTIS AUX PÊCHES

•

PEACH CLAFOUTIS

•

3 large ripe peaches
250 g / 9 oz sugar, for the syrup
4 eggs, at room temperature
150 g / 5 oz caster sugar
300 ml / ½ pint double cream
1 tablespoon flour, sifted
2 tablespoons raspberry liqueur
Raspberry coulis (optional), for serving (page 44)

•

Preheat the oven to 180°C / 350°F / gas 4.

Prepare a syrup with the water and 250 g / 9 oz sugar. Bring to the boil and plunge in the peaches. Cook for no more than 3 minutes after the syrup has come back to the boil. Take the peaches out with a slotted spoon, peel, halve and stone. Set aside.

Whisk the eggs and sugar together until frothy. Mix in the flour, add the cream and whisk until homogeneous. Add the raspberry liqueur, stirring well. Butter an ovenproof dish and put in the halved poached peaches, cut-side down. Pour the batter over and cook in the preheated oven for about 30 minutes or until set. Eat at room temperature, accompanied by a Raspberry coulis, if you like.

Clafoutis aux Pêches (recipe p. 194)

SOUFFLÉ AU CHOCOLAT

•

CHOCOLATE SOUFFLÉS

•

250 ml / 9 fl oz milk
20 g / ¾ oz bitter chocolate, finely grated
50 g / 2 oz caster sugar
40 g / 1½ oz flour, sifted
20 g / ¾ oz cocoa powder
8 large egg whites
a handful of caster sugar
50 g / 2 oz butter, softened
50 g / 2 oz bitter chocolate, finely grated, for the
soufflé dishes
icing sugar, for dusting

———— • ————

Preheat the oven to 240°C / 475°F / gas 9.

Heat the milk gently in a small saucepan with 20 g / ¾ oz grated chocolate and the sugar until dissolved. Cool until tepid.

Sift the flour and cocoa into a bowl. Pour the tepid milk mixture over, little by little, mixing with a whisk until smooth. Pour back into the pan and cook over medium heat, whisking continuously, until thick. Boil for 2 minutes, then pour into a bowl and leave to cool.

Generously butter 4 individual soufflé dishes. Put the grated chocolate inside and rotate the moulds so that the chocolate completely covers the inside, sticking to the soft butter.

Beat the egg whites until soft peaks form, then add a handful of sugar, a little at a time, and whisk until stiff. Add a small quantity of the whites to the chocolate mixture to soften it, mixing gently with a whisk, then fold in the rest of the whites and pour into the soufflé dishes. Bake in the hot oven for about 15 minutes, or until well risen. Immediately, dust the tops with icing sugar and serve.

All the pasta I serve at La Tante Claire I make myself in the kitchen. When I was a boy, the only pasta we knew at home was the macaroni we bought in packets or the monotonous, ribbony, French *nouilles*; so when I first saw a cook actually making her own pasta dough, rolling it and cutting it out into different shapes, I was spellbound. To dry her pasta she hung it all over the house, and I remember how chairs, tables, shelves, beds and even the staircase were festooned with dough.

At La Tante Claire I love making green, sage-flavoured noodles, and I often do light, delicate ravioli which I sometime stuff with sweetbreads and sometimes with crayfish or crab. When I fill them with crayfish, I change the sauce from time to time, but the basic idea is always the same. Sometimes the mousse is made with olive oil and herbs from China or south-east Asia, and on other occasions I use asparagus tips and truffles. My ravioli have always been very popular, but if I altered them too drastically, the demand might cease!

PÂTE À RAVIOLI

•

HOME-MADE PASTA DOUGH

———— • ————

1 kg / 2¼ lb strong bread flour, plus extra for
dusting
9 size 3 eggs

———— • ————

Put the flour in a large bowl, make a well in the centre and put in the eggs. Whisk with a fork, drawing in the flour gradually until it is all incorporated. On a lightly floured surface, knead the dough until smooth. Divide it into five or six pieces, and cover with a damp cloth. Put one piece of dough through the thickest setting of the pasta machine, dusting it well with flour; fold it, roll again and repeat the operation six times for each piece of dough. Finally, put the piece of dough through the thinnest setting of the pasta machine. Cut into squares or ribbons and keep in a cool place between sheets of greaseproof paper.

To cook the pasta, bring a large pan of salted water to the boil, then put in the pasta. The exact cooking time for filled pasta depends on the filling, and is given in the individual recipes. Unfilled pasta (eg: noodles or spaghetti) is ready as soon as it rises to the surface of the boiling water. Drain the pasta, refresh under cold water and reheat gently in hot butter. Season with salt before serving.

This recipe can easily be halved.

Pâtes Fraîches à l'Oeuf Cassé

—— • ——

HOME-MADE NOODLES WITH POACHED EGGS

—— • ——

250 g / 8 oz cooked Home-made noodles (see opposite)
4 very lightly poached eggs
200 ml / 7 fl oz Chicken stock (page 49)
100 ml / 4 fl oz double cream
100 g / 3½ oz gruyère or parmesan, shaved into slivers
a knob of butter
salt and freshly ground pepper
1 tablespoon snipped chives for garnish

—— • ——

Reduce the chicken stock to a glace: it should be shiny and thick enough to coat the back of a metal spoon. Add the double cream, bring to the boil and season. Keep warm.

Melt a knob of butter in a shallow pan and quickly heat the noodles in it. Add the sauce, mixing it well with the noodles. Divide the noodles between four deep, warm plates and scatter over the cheese shavings. Place a poached egg in the middle, gently nestling it into the pasta. With a sharp knife, cut the yolk so that it runs all over the noodles. Sprinkle over the chives and serve immediately.

Raviolis de Langoustines au Basilic

—— • ——

RAVIOLI OF LANGOUSTINES WITH BASIL

—— • ——

20 raw langoustines
4 tablespoons olive oil
50 g / 2 oz shallots, finely chopped
1 garlic clove, finely chopped
1 tablespoon tomato purée
50 ml / 2 fl oz brandy
200 ml / 7 fl oz whipping cream
150 g / 5 oz Home-made pasta dough (page 196) cut into four 15 cm / 6 in squares
4 basil leaves
1 tomato, blanched, skinned, deseeded, and diced
1 teaspoon finely chopped parsley
salt and freshly ground pepper

—— • ——

Shell the langoustines and crush the shells. Heat 2 tablespoons olive oil in a shallow pan. When hot, add the shells and cook for about 5 minutes, stirring from time to time. Add the shallots and sweat for 3 more minutes. Add the garlic and tomato purée and cook gently for 2 minutes. Add the brandy, stir and let everything steep for 1 minute. Pour in the cream, season and simmer for 10 minutes. Purée the mixture and pass through a fine conical sieve.

Put this sauce into a small pan and reduce over low heat until it coats the back of a spoon. Keep warm. Sprinkle the langoustine tails with salt and pepper.

Bring 3 L / 5 pt salted water to the boil with 2 tablespoons olive oil. Place 5 langoustine tails and a basil leaf on each pasta square and fold the pasta over to make ravioli, pressing well between the palms of your hands. Seal the edges together, using a little water and, make sure there are no holes. Cook in the boiling water for 3 minutes. Drain well and serve on warm plates, pouring the sauce around and scattering on the diced tomato and chopped parsley.

In my new kitchen, near the *pâtissiers'* corner there is room for an extra work-top where I can stretch out the large piece of linen on which I make the filo-like pastry we call *pastis*. This is a traditional, very thin, flaky pastry which is one of the specialities of Gascony. The dough is separated into large balls and then these have to be teased out into fine, fragile sheets, so thin that you can read the print of a newspaper through them. The process is carried out on top of the linen cloth, and it is hard work for the fingers. At La Tante Claire we make this pastry every day, and we are one of the very few remaining restaurants which still do so. Even restaurants in France which specialise in local food have stopped making their own *pastis* because it takes too long and needs too much space. The pastry is essential for the distinctive Gascon pies known as *croustades*, and we nearly always have an apple *croustade* on our dessert menu. It is always a popular dish. The recipe actually takes me back from time to time to the real-life Gascony I knew as a boy, since I buy the special, very fine and not too glutinous *croustade* flour (ordinary flour is no good for this particular pastry) directly from a mill in Fleurance, the market town where my grandmother and I used to go every Tuesday to sell her ducks and geese.

PASTIS

•

ULTRA-FLAKY GASCON PASTRY

•

(Serves 8)
1 kg / 2¼ lb superfine plain flour, plus extra for dusting
4 eggs
a pinch of salt
2 tablespoons oil
400 ml / 14 fl oz tepid water

•

Start making the pastis *several hours before you need it. The given quantities will make enough pastry for 8 people, but you need a large amount of dough to pull it out to the required thinness. Freeze the surplus dough to use in another recipe. Making this pastry is hard work; instead, you can use bought filo pastry.*

Sift the flour into a large mixing bowl and make a well in the centre. Separate the eggs and beat the whites with the salt in an electric mixer until stiff. Still mixing, add the yolks and oil, then very gradually add the tepid water and mix until smooth. Pour this mixture into the well in the flour and, using one hand, gradually draw in the flour with a circular movement and mix until you have a smooth dough. Lightly flour your hand and flip over the dough several times until it no longer sticks to the sides of the bowl.

Lightly oil the work surface, put on the dough and beat it very hard along its length with a rolling pin for about 5 minutes, flipping over the dough 20 or 30 times as you beat, until it no longer sticks to the work surface and has become springy. Lightly oil the work surface again and cut the dough into 4 pieces, rolling each piece into a very smooth ball, and making sure there are no air bubbles, or the dough will break when you stretch it. Rub each ball with oil and wrap in oiled clingfilm. Freeze 2 balls for another use and leave the others to rest at room temperature for 3-6 hours.

When the pastis has rested, spread an old sheet or tablecloth about 1.5 m / 5 ft square over the kitchen table. Sprinkle it lightly with flour and put one ball of dough in the centre. Lightly oil your fingers, put them under the dough and, starting from the middle, carefully pull the dough evenly on all sides into a circular shape until it is so thin that you can read a newspaper through it, and the sides hang over the edges of the table. (Four hands are better than two for this, so try to inveigle someone into helping you pull the pastis. Gently shake the edges of the pastis *so that it undulates. Leave it to dry for 5-10 minutes, but no longer, or it will break. It should feel like smooth parchment.*

Sprinkle some of the melted fat like rain all over the stretched dough, or spray it on with a plant mister. Trim off the thickest part of the pastis from around the edge; you can re-use it, although it will not be as good. Prepare the second ball of dough in the same way to make the top of the croustade.

CROUSTADE DE POMMES CARAMÉLISÉES

•

CARAMELISED APPLES IN CRISP, FLAKY PASTRY

———— • ————

2 balls of *Pastis* pastry (page 198)
6 eating apples
100 g / 3½ oz lard or clarified butter, melted
200 g / 7 oz sugar
50 ml / 2 fl oz armagnac

———— • ————

Leave the pastis to rest at room temperature for 3-6 hours, until soft but not sticky.

While the pastry is resting, peel, core and slice the apples. In a saucepan, cook the apples very lightly in half the melted lard or butter, with 75 g / 3 oz sugar and the armagnac. Drain and leave to cool.

Preheat the oven to 220°C / 425°F / gas 7. Stretch one pastis ball as described in the last recipe, and leave it to dry a little. Then, with a pastry brush or plant mister, sprinkle some of the melted fat like rain all over the stretched pastry. Dust with 40 g / 1½ oz sugar and trim off the thick part of the pastry from the edge.

Butter a 24 cm / 10 in flan tin and dust with 20 g / ¾ oz sugar. Cut three circles out of the pastry, keeping the finest for the top layer. Put one in the flan tin, place another on top and finish with the third pastry circle. Arrange the apples on top.

Clean any pieces of pastry and sugar off the tablecloth, then put on the second ball of pastry and stretch it in

the same way as the first. Cut it into 15 cm / 6 in triangles and crinkle them up into small mounds, like crumpled chiffon scarves. Pile these little mounds on the apples and sprinkle with more melted fat and the remaining sugar. Bake in the hot oven for about 20 minutes, until the top is golden and the sugar has caramelised. Serve warm.

This croustade is also delicious made with pears, cooked quinces or prunes.

———————————

The miller sends bags of flour regularly to La Tante Claire, and, whenever I am in Gascony, I visit him. Flour, however, is not the only commodity I buy on these trips. My centre is normally the old fortified town of Lectoure, with its hill-top cathedral and the honey-coloured eighteenth-century Hotel Bastard, where I usually stay, and from here I go in quest of La Tante Claire's armagnac. From Patrick de Montal at Arton, where his fine old country house nestles peacefully among the Gascon hills and gently sloping fields of vines, I order our supply of *fine blanche*, an excellent white armagnac *eau-de-vie*. From René and Mireille Lassus at the château of Monluc, which overlooks my childhood village of Saint Puy, I get *vin sauvage* and *pousse rapière*, a liqueur which is made from a blend of different armagnacs and flavoured with orange. From Saint Puy I drive south to Tarbes, my birthplace, where I collect a stock of the dried white haricot beans we always use at La Tante Claire. My mother buys me sacks of these in the local market, and I bring them back to London in the car. From Tarbes, if I am on an autumn or winter visit, I often cross the Pyrenees and drive into Spain towards the remote, mountain villages south of Andorra where every year I buy my truffles.

The peasants in these villages know me well by now. They give me a warm welcome but they drive a very hard bargain over the sale of their truffles. In many ways they are similar to peasants anywhere else in the world, but unlike French peasants they are not at all interested in food. Their woods are full of fine truffles, but they sell them all to the French and never seem to eat them themselves. On the farms they have rabbits, pigs and a few chickens, but no other poultry, such as ducks, geese or turkeys. I know nothing about Spanish food in general, but in these small villages, you seem to eat the same sort of stew at every meal. It is rather monotonous, and nobody takes the trouble to encourage your appetite by making the food look interesting or colourful.

You always eat visually, with your eyes, before you put the first forkful of food into your mouth. If it looks attractive, food always seems to taste better than if it is dumped roughly on to your plate, be it the crisp, golden skin of a superbly roasted chicken or the rosy, overlapping slices of a *magret de canard* surrounded by a pool of cep and armagnac sauce. Decoration should always come second to taste and quality, but it is one of their most vital adjuncts. The presentation of restaurant food is now almost universally influenced by the style made fashionable by *nouvelle cuisine*, little clumps of food grouped rather self-consciously together amid splashes of strong colour, though at La Tante Claire I aim at a freer, more robust effect even when thinking along somewhat similar lines. During the *service*, when the kitchen is at its busiest, and when I, in particular, am doing several jobs at the same time, I never lose sight of the important effect on a customer of the visual impact of a dish. At these moments I act as the *aboyeur*, I superintend the work of the cooks, and I also manage to watch each plate as it is collected at the *passe* by a waiter. Sometimes there is a spot of sauce to be wiped away from the border of a plate, or an elderberry has gone astray on a dish of foie gras or an untidy portion of spinach needs coaxing into a better shape. Whatever the problem, it is essential to put it right before the plate arrives in the restaurant.

GALETTE DE FOIE GRAS AUX BAIES DE SUREAU

FRESH FOIE GRAS WITH ELDERBERRY SAUCE

4 good slices of fresh goose or duck foie gras, 1 cm / ½ in thick
2 large potatoes
4 tablespoons vegetable oil
salt

For the sauce:
4 teaspoons wine vinegar
8 teaspoons elderberry syrup
100 ml / 4 fl oz Chicken stock (page 49)
50 g / 2 oz unsalted butter
a few elderberries

Wash and peel the potatoes. Grate them very finely and squeeze to extract as much water as possible. Heat 1 tablespoon oil in a small frying pan, add one-quarter of the potatoes, flatten them with a fish slice, and cook for about 2 minutes on each side, until very crispy and golden. They should look like small pancakes. Make 3 more potato pancakes in this way.

To make the sauce: Put the wine vinegar in a small saucepan and reduce it completely. Add the elderberry syrup and reduce completely, then add the chicken stock and reduce by half. Put in the butter and rotate the pan to incorporate it well. Add the elderberries and set aside.

Cook the foie gras in a lightly greased frying pan for a few minutes on each side. Place the potato pancakes on a serving dish, put the foie gras on top and pour the sauce around.

BALLOTINE DE VOLAILLE AUX CHAMPIGNONS

BALLOTINE OF CHICKEN WITH MUSHROOMS

4 chicken breast fillets
300 g / 11 oz Chicken mousse (page 45)
300 g / 11 oz mushrooms, finely chopped
30 g / 1 oz butter
salt and freshly ground pepper

For the sauce:
150 ml / 5 fl oz Chicken stock (page 49)
20 g / ¾ oz shallots, finely chopped
25 ml / 1 fl oz armagnac or brandy
50 ml / 2 fl oz double cream
a knob of butter

Sweat the chopped mushrooms in the butter until all the moisture has evaporated. Season and leave to cool completely.

Mix the cooled mushrooms with the chicken mousse and refrigerate. With a long, thin, sharp knife, make a cavity in the chicken breasts, taking care not to pierce the surrounding flesh. Fill a piping bag fitted with a wide nozzle with the prepared mousse and pipe an equal quantity of mousse into each cavity. Wrap tightly in clingfilm, making each stuffed breast into a sausage shape. Twist the ends of the clingfilm tightly and fold them underneath. Prepare a steamer, put in the ballotines and steam for 15 minutes.

To make the sauce: Sweat the shallots in butter, deglaze the pan with the armagnac and reduce until no liquid is left. Add the chicken stock and reduce until the sauce coats the back of a spoon. Whisk in the cream, season well and keep warm. Cut each ballotine into 6 slices, arranging them on warm serving plates. Pour the sauce around.

When I am working in the kitchen, I never wear a *toque*, the tall, white hat traditionally associated with the *chef de cuisine*. I make my cooks wear some sort of cap, but I never wear one myself. It is something I find slightly pretentious and at La Tante Claire I avoid pretentiousness as much as I can. In the old days the size of your hat denoted your position in the kitchen hierarchy; cooks wore small caps, the *chefs de partie* medium-sized ones, and the *chef de cuisine* the tallest of all. I had to wear a hat, like everyone else, when I was working for other people, but I never wore one at the Waterside and I shall certainly never wear one at La Tante Claire. I feel the same way over the more recent custom of embroidering chefs' names on their jackets. In my own case Annie insisted on it, but I find it ridiculous and more than unnecessary to have my own name written on me as though I were a packet of cheese. After all, everybody in the restaurant knows who I am!

If customers want to have a talk with me, they are very welcome to come and see me in the kitchen after they have finished their meal. I always enjoy meeting people in that way, though sometimes a customer's visit can be unexpectedly amusing. There is one Frenchman who comes very often to La Tante Claire, and after each dinner never fails to make his appearance in the kitchen, though the reason for his doing so is not to have a friendly chat but to give me what he feels is a much-needed cookery lesson. He makes it very clear that he is the only person in the world who really knows how to cook a steak properly or make a *beurre blanc* or boil a potato or roast a chicken. He alone can do everything I can do, only, of course, he does it rather better. He stays in the kitchen for half an hour, pouring out hints and good advice. He is genuinely sorry for me on account of my knowing so little and having so much to do. Of course, he really understands nothing at all about cooking, but because he is such a good customer, I listen to him and smile politely. He came one evening with four friends, bearing a pound of truffles which he wanted me to cook immediately for him and his party. He seemed to have absolutely no idea of the amount of work this would involve! I nevertheless made a lot of truffle consommé and a big dish of fresh pasta with truffles. There were four truffles left over, even then, and the Frenchman came afterwards to tell me what I had done wrong, and what he himself would have done with the truffles if only he had had the time. It was obvious he knew very little about them, but his attitude was typical of many Frenchmen who make out that they are omniscient experts in all matters relating to food and cooking. The English, by comparison, are much more open. An Englishman will either know nothing at all about food, in which case he will tell you so and be pleased to learn from you, or he will actually be very know-ledgeable about one particular aspect of the subject, and you will find that what he knows, he knows very well indeed. At La Tante Claire we find that the English usually make better customers than the French, who now drink nothing before or after their meal and only have a bottle of cheap wine during it. The English are still old-fashioned enough to have an aperitif before their meal, a good white wine with the fish, a good red wine with the main course, and a liqueur or an *eau-de-vie* with their coffee. I sometimes wonder, in the light of the current campaign against alcohol, how long their enthusiasm will last!

Belgians, too, are good customers. They are *bon viveurs*; they love life, they enjoy eating and drinking and they like to come round and talk to me about their meal. One night, however, the dinner ordered by two Brussels business-men ended with their visiting the kitchen, certainly, but probably not quite in the way they had expected. They had ordered turbot, but when their bill was brought, they com-plained that the fish they had eaten was not really turbot at all, but cod, and that they had been cheated. They came to the kitchen. I told them I never cooked fresh cod at La Tante Claire. They insisted I did. I opened the refrigerator, pointed to the turbot, and told them to show me the cod. They searched for a long time, and, of course, failed to find any, but still insisted I had cheated them. By now I was thoroughly exasperated, so I took two portions of turbot, and made the two men watch as I cooked it. Then I cleared a worktop, laid two places, and ordered them to eat the fish. They ate in silence while all the cooks stopped work and stood in a circle, watching them. When they had finished, I asked them if the fish they had eaten was turbot or cod, and whether it was the same as the fish they had had in the restaurant. They had no other course but to agree, in a rather crestfallen sort of way, that it was, and that it was indeed turbot. Gradually the background to the incident emerged. For years these two men had eaten once a week at a little restaurant in Brussels where they thought the cooking was excellent, and where the chef always served them a fish which was obviously cod but which he told them was turbot. It was the Brussels chef who had cheated them, not I! For years they had been made fools of, and they were now even more furious than before. I often wonder what they said to their favourite chef next time they went to eat at his little restaurant.

Turbot Rôti aux Légumes (recipe p. 204)

TURBOT RÔTI AUX LÉGUMES

— • —

ROAST TURBOT WITH VEGETABLES

— • —

1 × 2 kg / 4½ lb turbot

200 g / 7 oz butter, at room temperature, plus extra
for greasing

75 g / 3 oz carrot, cut into 0.5 cm / ¼ in dice

75 g / 3 oz shallot, finely chopped

75 g / 3 oz leek, finely chopped

100 g / 3½ oz smoked bacon, cut into 0.5 cm / ¼ in
dice

6 parsley stalks

200 ml / 7 fl oz French dry vermouth

400 ml / 14 fl oz Fish stock (page 49)

75 g / 3 oz courgettes, cut into 0.5 cm / ¼ in dice,
blanched in salted boiling water and drained

1 tablespoon chives, finely snipped

salt and freshly ground pepper

350 g / 12 oz Home-made noodles, for serving
(page 196)

——— • ———

Preheat the oven to 180°C / 350°F / gas 4.

*Melt 50 g / 2 oz butter in a large baking tray. Add the
carrot, shallot, leek and bacon and sweat for 3 minutes.
Lay the fish on top with the parsley stalks. Pour over
the vermouth and fish stock, bring to a simmer on the
hob and cover with a piece of lightly buttered foil. Cook
in the preheated oven for 25 minutes, basting the fish
with its stock from time to time during cooking. When
the turbot is cooked, transfer it delicately onto a warm
serving dish.*

*Put the cooking juices and all the vegetables into a
saucepan and bring to the boil. Whisk in the rest of the
butter and the chives and check the seasoning. Pour
the sauce over the fish and serve with lightly buttered
noodles. (Photograph p. 203)*

If the presentation of restaurant food is no
longer as theatrical as it used to be, quite a lot
of theatricality still lingers on in the dining
room. The formal welcome a customer receives
from the head waiter, the ceremony of being
served, discreet personal attentions, and the
ordered array of cutlery and glasses remain an
essential part of the pleasure one takes in eating
at a first class establishment. My own initial
contact with this particular type of theatricality
took place at the Reffye catering college when I
was taught *la salle* by the unforgettable Paul
Dibello. The dining room was only a secondary
subject as far as I was concerned, but Monsieur
Dibello's lessons were a great help to me. He
was an Italian whose family had settled in
France; he must have been in his mid-sixties,
having taken up teaching after his retirement.
His official position in the school was that of
maître d'hôtel, and we students always ad-
dressed him respectfully as '*maître*'. He was
tall, imposing, well-built, and his dark hair,
shining with oil and brushed straight back from
his forehead, gave him the allure of a '30s film
star. When teaching, he wore a long black coat,
a white starched shirt and black tie, a
fawn-coloured waistcoat, striped trousers and
immaculately polished black shoes. In style and
personality he was everyone's idea of the true
Italian; fiery, histrionic, grandiloquent, and
always naturally magnificent. He taught us in
the school restaurant. We stood round him in
our white coats and black trousers, awestruck as
he showed us how to replace a missing fork
with complete and unobtrusive discretion or
reverently lift a bottle of wine as though the act
were part of some sacred ritual. Of all our
teachers Monsieur Dibello was the only one
who was, we were convinced, a genius. He
taught us *la salle* according to classic principles
which reigned in the years before we were
born. He had known the great palace hotels of
the 1920s and 1930s. He had been *maître
d'hôtel* at the Negresco in Nice, the Carlton in
Cannes and at the Régina in Biarritz. He had
served millionaires, South American presid-
ents, English dukes, sovereign princes and
European royalty. Besides speaking French and

Italian, he had a fluent knowledge of English, German and Spanish, and in each language he knew the right form of words to use when greeting distinguished or noble customers or visiting monarchs. *Excellence . . . altesse . . . prince . . . monseigneur . . . majesté.* He would purr the phrases in his mellifluous voice, and show us how even the very slightest inclination of the body could be made to express almost infinite deference, or how the raising of a single eyebrow could bring senior and commis waiters running to obey his orders. At some moments his gestures were almost those of a tragic actor, but at others he could be the complete comedian. If we were overwhelmed by the dignity of his manner when he demonstrated how one should show an imaginary Queen of Spain to her table in the dining room at Biarritz, we could also be reduced to helpless fits of laughter by his cautionary imitations of a short-sighted waiter trying to pour a glass of wine or of a bored commis breaking into a yawn while a customer talked to him.

Most of us at Reffye were the children either of peasants or, at best, of small tradespeople. We had no experience of the remote, glittering world which Monsieur Dibello had inhabited so easily and so illustriously; and we probably never would have. He compelled our admiration because everything about him was unfamiliar. With the cookery teachers it was quite different, since we all knew what the taste of a good meal should be and we could, from our own experience, discuss and argue about the various ways of preparing it. But when the *maître* taught us how to serve food and carry trays, and about the laying of tables or the correct placing and purpose of different knives, forks and glasses or the adroit management of a serving spoon or the folding of a napkin, we found ourselves baffled and amazed by a whole pattern of behaviour which had hitherto been completely unknown to us. It was impossible to argue with Paul Dibello. We could only wonder and learn. It must be remembered too that the waiter's job was very much more complicated in those days than it is now. He had to learn to make and serve all the cold hors d'oeuvre; he had to be a faultless and stylish maker of *crêpes suzette*; but above all he had to be a highly skilled and efficient carver. In many restaurants today, any necessary carving is done in the kitchen, and the waiter's job is mostly to carry plates from the cooks to the customers. Thirty years ago, however, dishes of beef, lamb, poultry, game and the larger fish, such as turbot and salmon, all came into the dining room uncut, and it was the task of the senior waiter first to show the food to the customer, then to carve or fillet it, arrange it decoratively on the plates and hand these to a commis who would finally bring them to the table.

Even in larger restaurants, a good relationship between chef and *maître d'hôtel* was always, and is still, absolutely vital to the smooth running of the establishment. It is really impossible to dissociate the two roles. A chef may be the best cook in the world but if his food is carelessly or impolitely served, customers will not return for more, and similarly the most skilled head waiter will do no better if the dish he places on the table is uneatable. The two men are partners, but there has sometimes been confusion as to which of the two is the senior. At the present moment there is no doubt that it is the chef who is most in the public eye, who is a television personality, who is sought after by the media, but well within living memory, the situation was reversed; and the *maître d'hôtel*, in the manner of Paul Dibello, was the well-known figure who dominated the restaurant scene, whose portrait was painted, and whom diners-out were proud to know and to talk to. In those days this often exacerbated the relationship between kitchen and dining room, especially in the palace hotels and large restaurants, where the kitchen was often below ground and working conditions were bad. The chef and the head waiter could be like rival generals, each in command of his own private army, each fighting the other in an interminable civil war which neither side would ever really win. The chef might command some fifty or sixty cooks; and the brigade in the dining room could be almost as large, a structured hierarchy descending from *maîtres d'hôtel de carré* and wine waiters to carvers, *chefs de rang*, *commis de rang* and *commis de suite*, and ending with the apprentices. At worst nobody had any clear overall picture of what was going on, and the result was that the comfort and well-being of the customer tended to be forgotten. The head waiter would send food back to the kitchen with a complaint; the chef would take his revenge on the head waiter by giving an elaborate *pièce montée* a destructive shake as it was pushed across the *passe* so that some luckless waiter would have to build it all up again before it could be formally presented to the by now very impatient customer.

Over the last twenty years or so, however, the catering world has undergone radical changes, largely because of the rise of the chef-proprietor in charge of his own medium-sized restaurant, much as I am at La Tante Claire. The number of my staff is very small when compared to the old brigades, (there are far fewer of these than there used to be), and working conditions are better and much more pleasant. Cooks and waiters collaborate easily because contact between them is more normal and natural. Another important aspect is that in the case of any small privately-owned restaurant it is vitally important commercially that it should run smoothly and efficiently, as much for the benefit of the staff as for that of the owner. At La Tante Claire, I, as chef, need the co-operation of an outstanding head waiter, and I am very lucky to have someone like Jean-Pierre Durantet to run my dining room. He is a *maître d'hôtel* of the old school who was trained in the same way as Annie and myself and who shares the same professional standards.

From Paul Dibello I learned dining room methods and manners which dated from the age of Escoffier. I have never actually had to apply many of these in my subsequent working career, but the mere fact of having known them has given me an excellent grounding, and provided me with an ideal by which to judge things and people later on. In particular I learned how to appreciate the qualities of a good head waiter. He must have to an outstanding degree all the skills which are essential even for the ordinary waiter: he must have a good memory for faces and for customers' likes and dislikes; and he should have a natural instinct for foreseeing the wants of a customer, even before the customer himself is aware of them. It is this sort of detail which forms the basis of the best restaurant service. The good *maître d'hôtel* must also possess shrewd psychological insight, and he should be ready to react without panic to unexpected incidents, and to have an answer to all sorts of sudden or unexpected questions. He should never be at a loss. Nowhere is his skill better shown than in the way he welcomes a customer and, if necessary, puts him immediately at his ease. Some people like to come and go unnoticed, and would prefer not to be talked to at all; others want to be talked to a great deal; and others are powerful and important figures in their own worlds of industry or business but are unused to eating at a good restaurant, and feel nervous and out of their depth the minute they walk through the door. Everybody is different; and the *maître d'hotel* must be able to sum up a human situation very quickly and adapt to it at once.

When I recall incidents which Jean-Pierre has had to face at La Tante Claire, I remember some which called for his quiet, polite acquiescence, and others which demanded rather more decisive action. A Japanese customer ordered a plate of oysters, but when Jean-Pierre came to remove his empty plate, he noticed that not only had the oysters been eaten but also the decoration round them. 'Yes,' said the customer, 'I liked the oysters, but please convey my very special thanks to the chef for the outstanding quality of his seaweed!' The compliment was duly passed on to me, and I am sure it was quite sincere.

Sometimes people confuse the chocolate sauce I serve with hare with the similar-looking squid ink I pour round scallops. Jean-Pierre once heard an enthusiastic young wife saying to her husband, "Oh yes, darling, it really *is* chocolate with the scallops. What a wonderful combination of flavours!" Here too, it seemed more tactful not to intervene with embarrassing explanations.

COQUILLES ST JACQUES À L'ENCRE DE SEICHE

SCALLOPS WITH THREE SAUCES: SQUID INK, RED PEPPER AND GARLIC

12 very fresh scallops

Squid ink sauce
50 ml / 2 fl oz French dry vermouth
100 ml / 4 fl oz double cream
50 g / 2 oz shallots, chopped
1 small garlic clove, chopped
1 teaspoon squid ink
salt and freshly ground pepper

Red pepper sauce
½ red pepper, thinly sliced
50 ml / 2 fl oz whipping cream

Garlic sauce
2 garlic cloves, chopped
50 ml / 2 fl oz whipping cream

First make the ink sauce: In a small pan, combine the vermouth, double cream, chopped shallots, garlic and squid ink. Reduce by half, season, process in a blender until smooth, then pass through a fine sieve. Keep warm.

For the red pepper sauce: Put the red pepper and cream in a small pan and reduce to 4 tablespoons of sauce. Season. Process in a blender until smooth, then pass through a fine sieve. Keep warm.

Now make the garlic sauce: Put the garlic and cream in a small pan and reduce to about 4 tablespoons of

sauce. Season, process in a blender until smooth, then pass through a fine sieve. Keep warm.

Halve the scallops widthways and season on both sides. Cook in a non-stick pan, briefly on both sides until nicely brown. Keep warm. In the middle of 4 warm plates pour first the ink sauce, then a tablespoon each of the pepper and garlic sauce. Arrange 6 slices of scallops on these sauces.

FILET DE LIÈVRE AU VINAIGRE DE FRAMBOISES ET AU CHOCOLAT AMER

FILLETS OF HARE WITH RASPBERRY VINEGAR AND BITTER CHOCOLATE SAUCE

4 hare fillets, total weight about 600 g / 1¼ lb
2 tablespoons vegetable oil
1 teaspoon finely chopped shallots
25 ml / 1 fl oz raspberry vinegar
500 ml / 18 fl oz red wine
150 ml / 5 fl oz Veal stock (page 49)
50 g / 2 oz bitter chocolate
30 g / 1 oz butter
salt and freshly ground pepper

Heat the oil in a frying pan. When very hot, cook the hare fillets to taste, making sure they are brown all over. Season, transfer to a plate and keep warm. Tip all the fat out of the pan, put in the shallots and sweat until soft. Deglaze with the vinegar and let it reduce completely. Add the red wine and reduce to about 125 ml / 4½ fl oz. Add the veal stock and bitter chocolate. When it has melted, whisk in the butter. Slice the hare fillets and pour the sauce over.

One night we had a party of eight who sat at a big round table in the very centre of the restaurant and could therefore easily be seen from the entrance. Later in the evening a young couple arrived, had a drink at the bar, looked at the menu, and chose their food. When Jean-Pierre came to tell them that their table was ready, the girl walked into the restaurant first and the man followed her. Suddenly, on the very threshold of the dining room, he stopped dead in his tracks, whipped round, and fled like a madman into the cloakroom. After a moment he put his head cautiously out of the door and asked the cashier to send him Jean-Pierre. He was with a girlfriend, he explained, and his wife was one of the people sitting at the big table. Jean-Pierre told him not to worry. He walked over to the girl and suggested that she should come back to the bar immediately, whereupon the couple put on their coats and left La Tante Claire as quickly as they could!

Sometimes we get customers who are frankly dishonest, but I am happy to say it is not very often. Like other restaurants we get bad cheques, and, like them, we are always amazed by the famous or well-known people who proffer them, and who are quite deliberate in their determination not to pay. More difficult for the *maître d'hôtel* to deal with are the people who walk in when the restaurant is full, and pretend that they have booked a table and that you have inefficiently given it to someone else. They make out that they rang the restaurant on such and such a date, that they made the reservation, and that surely you must have it written down somewhere in your book. Of course you cannot find the reservation, you hunt everywhere feeling foolish until at last the penny drops and you realise that the customers are lying.

One thing which surprised me when I first began to run my own restaurant was the discovery that customers can also be thieves. Our first experience of this took place at the Waterside when Annie was *maître d'hôtel*. She was taking an order during Sunday lunch when she happened to glance up and saw, to her amazement, a customer walking slowly out of the dining room with a wine cooler and its stand. He was halfway to the car park before she caught up with him and snatched the object out of his hand. He was quite brazen about it and made every kind of unlikely excuse, but nothing could disguise the attempted theft. At La Tante Claire we had the same sort of trouble with a regular customer who had been coming to us for more than ten years. It is true that he had always been a greedy, aggressive man who tried to get things without paying for them, like extra plates of cakes and biscuits with his coffee, or extra vegetables, or extra food to take away to eat at home. He often looked at the menu, said there was nothing on it he fancied, and demanded that I cook some elaborate dish like a *pithiviers* of sweetbreads with expensive morels, specially for him. Whatever you gave him, he always wanted more. He was odious, but we never thought that he would openly steal. One day Jean-Pierre was showing a customer the way to the cloakroom, when the door of the ladies' lavatory opened and out walked this man. The pockets of his jacket and his trousers were bulging with hand-towels. Jean-Pierre asked him what he was doing there, but though he too made ridiculous excuses, it was quite clear that he was stealing. As it happened, the waiters had been telling me for some time that there seemed to be far fewer towels than there used to be; and Annie had noticed that little silver flower bowls had been disappearing from the ladies' cloakroom, though the flowers which had been in them were always left behind next to the washbasin. I was furious, and made it clear that next time this customer rang for a table he was to be told that there was none available for him. He had had his last meal at La Tante Claire.

PITHIVIERS DE RIS DE VEAU ET CHAMPIGNONS SAUVAGES

———— • ————

PITHIVIERS OF VEAL SWEETBREADS WITH WILD MUSHROOMS

———— • ————

400 g / 14 oz veal sweetbreads, trimmed

250 g / 9 oz chicken breast fillets, skinned and diced

1 egg white

125 ml / 4½ fl oz whipping cream

125 ml / 4½ fl oz double cream

3 tablespoons vegetable oil

3 carrots, diced

1 celery stalk, diced

8 shallots, chopped

2 cloves garlic, chopped

3 tablespoons brandy

150 ml / 5 fl oz port

150 ml / 5 fl oz madeira

300 ml / 10 fl oz Veal stock (page 49)

1 bay leaf

1 sprig of thyme

50 g / 2 oz butter

10 morels or other wild mushrooms, cleaned and halved

250 g / 9 oz Puff pastry (page 42)

1 egg yolk whisked with 1 teaspoon water, for eggwash

salt and freshly ground pepper

100 g / 3½ oz *Chou frisé au lard* (page 85), for serving

———— • ————

Preheat the oven to 190°C / 375°F / gas 5.

First, prepare the chicken mousse with the chicken breasts, egg white and creams, following the instructions on page 45. When the mousse is smooth and homogeneous, refrigerate it.

Heat 2 tablespoons oil in a deep pan. Put in the carrots and cook until they start to brown. Add the celery and cook for about 3 minutes. Add the shallots and cook

until all these vegetables are golden brown. Add the garlic and cook for a few more minutes. Set aside.

In another saucepan, heat 1 tablespoon oil. Season the sweetbreads well and cook them just long enough to give them a nice brown colour. Take them out and deglaze the pan with the brandy, port and madeira. Flame the alcohol, then simmer for a few minutes and add the veal stock, bay leaf and thyme. Put the sweetbreads on the vegetables and pour the sauce over. Cover and cook in the oven for 10 minutes. Raise the oven temperature to 220° / 425°F / gas 7.

Lightly cook the wild mushrooms in half the butter, then leave to cool. Roll out the puff pastry very thinly into 2 circles, one of 19 cm / 7½ in, the other 22 cm / 8½ in in diameter. On the smaller circle spread in this order and in layers the cabbage, then half the mousse, then the sweetbreads. Finally, cover with the rest of the mousse and the large circle of puff pastry. Wet the edges with a little water to seal. Press down firmly with your fingers and make a small incision on the top. Brush with the eggwash. Bake in the preheated oven for about 40 minutes, until browned.

Pass the sauce through a fine conical sieve into a pan. Bring to the boil and whisk in the remaining butter. Serve the pithiviers cut into 4 wedges. Put the portions on individual warm plates and surround them with the sauce. Serve with Chou frisé au lard.

════════════════

As a principal link between customer and chef, the head waiter spends a lot of his time discussing food and explaining recipes. In the past this connection with the kitchen was much more clearly understood than now. In the eighteenth century the *maître d'hôtel* in a large household was senior in rank to the chef; and it was he who, besides looking after the wine and the silver, bought the supplies for the kitchen, told the chef what to cook, and sometimes even drew up the menus. It was an essential qualification for a *maître d'hôtel* to have worked as a cook and to have been in charge of a kitchen. Today, even though a head waiter is not absolutely obliged to have been a cook, it is impossible, in my opinion, to be even a moderately good one if you have not. The ideal *maître d'hôtel* should always be able to cook any of the dishes he recommends to customers.

Jean-Pierre is an excellent example of what I mean. He trained and worked as a cook for several years before he became a head waiter; and just as I can remember my own first big kitchen at the Aubette at Strasbourg, he can remember his life as a commis cook in the kitchen of one of the large palace hotels at the French spa town of Royat. It was a rough place where apprentices were slapped and kicked if they made mistakes, and where the management put salt into the wine and liqueurs used in the kitchen in order to stop the cooks drinking them. Jean-Pierre can advise customers about the menu, and can warn them if he feels they may be unwittingly ordering a similar dish twice. If someone asks for a *pithiviers de ris de veau*, for example, to be followed by a *pieds de cochon*, he will explain that there are sweetbreads in each dish; but his knowledge of cooking, and especially of my own cooking, enables him to describe any of the menu recipes in full detail.

The chef and his *maître d'hôtel* should share the same taste in food. I distrust the idea of 'style', which always makes me think of fashion and appearances, and would always look for the true source of quality and individuality in a chef's work in his sense of taste. This is one of the most essential attributes of any good cook, and it is something he or she is born with, rather as a good musician is born with a natural ear for tones and harmonies. In the kitchen this enables him to know when to leave the inherent flavour of an ingredient unchanged, and when to use it as a base upon which to build another taste which may be altogether different. The more neutral an original taste, the more freedom a chef has to 'invent' a taste with herbs or spices or a sauce. For me the most indeterminate and indefinable of all flavours is that of fish. Is it possible to tell the difference between a sole, a turbot and a skate just by their taste? I doubt it. When we eat them, we differentiate these fish by the texture of their flesh, not by their taste, or by the sauces with which they are served. I regard fish as the ingredient which gives me the greatest freedom, because I can endow it with whatever taste I want simply by means of a sauce. Fish is quick to clean and poach, a sauce is easy to make, and there are many different flavourings and wines you can add to it. When I cook fish, I always feel the excitement of escaping into the unexpected, and perhaps this is why there are always more fish recipes than meat on the Tante Claire menu. I can give salmon a different taste by cooking it with dried, peppered bacon; I combine monkfish with capers and saffron and sea bass with a sweet and sour sauce.

SAUMON RÔTI À LA VENTRÈCHE

ADOUR SALMON WITH PEPPERED BACON

4 salmon fillets, 150 g / 5 oz each
4 tablespoons vegetable oil
8 smoked bacon rashers or peppered bacon, if available
50 ml / 2 fl oz sherry vinegar
100 ml / 4 fl oz madeira
salt and freshly ground pepper

Heat 3 tablespoons vegetable oil in a shallow pan over medium high heat. Season the salmon fillets with salt and pepper. When the oil is very hot, put the fillets in the pan, skin-side down, and cook for about 3 minutes until crisp and golden. Lower the heat and cook the fish slowly on the other side for about 3 minutes. The precise cooking time depends on the thickness of the fillets. As soon as you can slide a larding needle into the flesh without resistance, the fish is ready.

Meanwhile, heat 1 tablespoon oil in a frying pan, over high heat. Put in the bacon rashers and cook until golden and crisp. Keep warm.

Pour away the excess fat from the pan and deglaze with the sherry vinegar. When it has almost evaporated, pour in the madeira and cook until syrupy and thick. Put 2 bacon rashers over each salmon fillets and pour the sauce over. Serve immediately.

MIGNON DE LOTTE AUX CÂPRES, TOMATES ET CÉLÉRI RAVE

ROUNDELS OF MONKFISH WITH CAPERS, TOMATOES AND CELERIAC

600 g / 1¼ lb monkfish, off the bone, cut into
3 cm / 1¼ in rounds
20 g / ¾ oz shallots, finely chopped
100 ml /4 fl oz dry white wine
150 ml / 5 fl oz Fish stock (page 49)
a pinch of saffron
100 g / 3½ oz butter, diced
50 g / 2 oz capers
2 large tomatoes, blanched, skinned, deseeded and
diced
1 tablespoon snipped chives
100 g / 3½ oz celeriac, diced and cooked
salt and freshly ground pepper

Heat 30 g / 1 oz butter in a frying pan. Season the fish and cook it for 2 minutes on each side. Transfer to a dish and keep in a warm place. In the same pan, with the cooking juices, add the shallots, wine and saffron. Reduce almost completely, then add the stock. Reduce by half and whisk in the remaining butter. Check the seasoning. Add the tomatoes, capers and celeriac. Arrange the fish on plates and pour the sauce around. Serve immediately.

FILETS DE BAR À L'AIGRE-DOUX

SEA BASS IN A SWEET AND SOUR SAUCE

4 fillets of sea bass, about 150 g / 5 oz each
30 g / 1 oz sugar
20 ml / ¾ oz vinegar
200 ml / 7 fl oz red wine
50 ml / 2 fl oz port
1 large tomato, blanched, skinned deseeded and
diced
½ courgette, diced, blanched and drained
90 g / 3oz butter, at room temperature
50 ml / 2 fl oz vegetable oil
salt and white pepper

For the sauce: Cook the sugar and vinegar together until thick and golden. Add the red wine and reduce to a little more than half. Whisk in 70 g / 3 oz butter and add the diced tomato and courgette. Season and keep warm.

Heat the oil with the remaining butter in a frying pan. When very hot, add the fish, skin-side down and cook until brown and crispy, turn it over and cook the other side. The cooking time will depend on the thickness of the fillets. Be careful not to overcook them. If necessary lower the heat to allow the fish to cook thoroughly without burning.

Arrange the sea bass on plates and pour the sauce around. Serve at once.

The meat which most resembles fish in terms of taste, or of the lack of it, is that of a chicken, especially the white meat. Ironically this is the part which restaurant customers always prefer, despite the fact that it has the least flavour. It has always seemed to me that the tastiest bits of a chicken are the skin, the gizzard, the wingtips and the parson's nose. When I was a boy, I used to enjoy eating chickens' heads, holding them in my hand and sucking out the brains and the juice, and thought they were delicious. It is unlikely, however, that this would appeal to my customers at La Tante Claire! The meat of a chicken is like fish because it can stand having almost any other taste combined with it. It will take on the flavour of whatever garnish you choose, no matter whether it is crab, curry, mussels, lobster or saffron. Rabbit is the same; it too can be prepared with all sort of other ingredients, but to get the best flavour you must cook it with its bones. Bones always have a lot of taste in them, and even fish cooked with the bones is better than fillets which have been prepared separately.

When it comes to meat, however, taste must be respected at all costs. Here the cook has nothing like the liberty he has with fish or chicken. I adore meat; I am carnivorous by nature, and I would probably always prefer to eat meat rather than fish, even though I find fish fascinating to cook. I would never want to overwhelm the taste of good beef or good lamb with the wrong sauce; and I usually serve meat with a *jus*, which is a light sauce made by taking the natural juice of the meat produced during the roasting, deglazing it with white wine or armagnac, then adding to it a little chicken stock and some shallots. A *jus* will enhance the taste of meat without damaging it. Our customers at La Tante Claire are traditionalists when it comes to meat, as I am myself, and I do not think they would appreciate violent contrasts of taste, however fashionable these might have been a few years ago at the height of the craze for *nouvelle cuisine*. Meat flavours can vary, of course. A good oxtail has much more flavour than a tournedos, although the latter is a finer and nobler cut of meat. Most beef is now roasted in an oven, but an entrecôte grilled over an open fire, especially a fire of vine shoots, will always taste better than one cooked in any other way.

Is it possible to create a completely new taste? I hardly think so. The only way to get a new taste is by discovering an entirely new or unusual ingredient. The turkeys, haricots, maize, potatoes and tomatoes brought to Europe from the New World in the sixteenth century are an obvious example of this, though it took a very long time for most of these novelties to become generally popular. During the years I have been in England, cooks have begun to discover and use unfamiliar herbs, fruit and spices imported from south-east Asia, which have effectively given us some new tastes, and I have been very keen to try them, as when I cook fish with star anise, in my own kitchen. It was easy for me because I have always had a great admiration for Chinese cooking, and I learn from it each time I eat at a good Chinese restaurant.

I work and invent best when I am challenged by some sort of pressure or urgency as when I have to produce something special very quickly and have to improvise. Ideas come to me in the morning when I have to think about what to cook that evening, especially if I know that some exceptional client will be at the restaurant, and I want to give him something original, something he will enjoy. At first each new dish exists only in my imagination; it is unreal, even though I calculate ingredients and quantities, and though I seem to experience the hypothetical taste as clearly and accurately as if the food were already in my mouth. Then I go into the kitchen and make the dish in reality, and in nearly every case the taste corresponds exactly to that which had previously been in my imagination. Whenever possible, I like to meet customers and see them with my own eyes before devising a dish or a menu specially for them. It is good to have an idea of their characters and personalities; you cannot cook the same meal for a fat man as you would for a thin one.

I am never tempted to think of myself as a 'creator' of dishes, even of those which are particularly associated with me, such as my stuffed pig's trotters. If anything I am their arranger, or even re-arranger, nothing more. The feeling goes back to my boyhood reflections when I first heard the story of God's creation of the world. Bang! Wham! Out of absolutely nothing he made absolutely everything, all in the course of a single week. It was incredible! Nobody could ever do that again, I thought, so the only thing men were capable of was to rearrange elements which had already been created. No human being could ever literally create something absolutely new. The problem puzzled me greatly when I was about ten, especially when I heard of so-called 'creative' people or 'creators'; and I am still a little sceptical, even now. At La Tante Claire I thought I had put together a unique *confit* of salmon cooked in duck fat until, one day, I found the same identical dish on the menu of a little restaurant in a village in central France. The chef and I had never previously met or heard of each other, and he had never been to London. Had we thought the dish up independently, or had we both unconsciously copied it from somebody else? Was either of us its creator? Was anybody? One day one of my *pâtissiers* suggested a dessert based on a combination of four sorbets, each of a different colour, and proudly told me that it should be called *palette de l'artiste aux quatre miniatures*. He was convinced that *pâtissiers* and cooks were artists, that they were creators at the same level as painters and composers, and he was very surprised when I disagreed with him completely, and told him that I had never thought of myself as an artist in that sense at all. The word art comes from a Latin word meaning a manual craft. Its meaning was later extended to take in the more refined areas of 'liberal' and 'fine' arts, but the original sense is the one I like best, and the one which does indeed fit the cook. Cooking is a manual trade; and I think of my life as having been that of *un bon ouvrier*, a skilled craftsman who has worked well and built up a good business – nothing more than that.

Another aspect of cooking which has always seemed to me to keep it firmly in its place as a trade and not a fine art is the impermanence of its end-product. The result of hours of labour is briefly admired by a customer, then, in a matter of moments, it disappears for ever. The taste of a sauce may be the triumph of a chef, but there is no way of recording that taste, or of printing it, or of photographing it. Even describing it in words is usually quite difficult. That is why, in my opinion, old menus are little more than so many tombstones commemorating the ephemeral existence of meals which were alive once but which are now irrevocably dead. It is probably why I am rather careless about keeping copies of my own old menus at the Waterside and at La Tante Claire.

overleaf: *Making Pieds de Cochons Farcis aux Morilles (recipe p. 216)*

PIEDS DE COCHON FARCIS AUX MORILLES

STUFFED PIGS' TROTTERS WITH MORELS

4 pigs' back trotters, boned
100 g / 3½ oz carrots, diced
100 g / 3½ oz onions, diced
150 ml / 5 fl oz dry white wine
1 tablespoon port
150 ml / 5 fl oz Veal stock (page 49)
225 g / 8 oz veal sweetbreads, blanched and chopped
75 g / 3 oz butter, plus a knob for the sauce
20 dried morels, soaked until soft and drained
1 small onion, finely chopped
1 chicken breast, skinned and diced
1 egg white
200 ml / 7 fl oz double cream
salt and freshly ground pepper

Preheat the oven to 160°C / 325°F / gas 3.

Place the trotters in a casserole with the diced carrots and onions, the wine, port and veal stock. Cover and braise in the oven for 3 hours.

Meanwhile, fry the sweetbreads in the butter for 5 minutes, add the morels and chopped onion and cook for another 5 minutes. Leave to cool.

Purée the chicken breast with the egg white and cream and season with salt and pepper. Mix with the sweetbread mixture to make the stuffing. Take the trotters out of the casserole and strain the cooking stock, keeping the stock but discarding the vegetables. Open the trotters out flat and lay each one on a piece of foil. Leave to cool.

Fill the cooled trotters with the chicken stuffing and roll tightly in the foil. Chill in the fridge for at least 2 hours. (Photographs pp. 214–5 and p. 218)

SOUPE D'ÉCREVISSES À L'ORANGE

CRAYFISH AND ORANGE SOUP

900 g / 2 lb crayfish
4 kg / 9 lb mussels, scrubbed and debearded
1 garlic clove, chopped
500 ml / 18 fl oz dry white wine
40 g / 1½ oz butter
2 carrots, diced
2 leeks, white part only, diced
2 onions, diced
2 shallots, chopped
2 tomatoes, blanched, skinned, deseeded and diced
blanched zest and juice of 1 large orange
300 ml / ½ pt double cream
1 tablespoon finely chopped flat-leaved parsley
1 tablespoon finely snipped chives
cayenne pepper
salt and freshly ground pepper

Put the mussels and garlic in a large pan and pour the wine over. Cover and cook over high heat until all the mussel shells are open. Strain the cooking juices through a fine sieve and reserve.

Melt 25 g / 1 oz butter in a shallow pan. Add the carrots, leeks, onions and shallots. Cover and cook over gentle heat. When the vegetables are cooked, add the tomatoes, the orange juice and the zest. Set aside. Cook the crayfish for 5 minutes in boiling salted water.

Pull off the tails and claws, shell and set the flesh aside. Crush the shells and put them in the large pan with the strained mussel juices. Simmer gently for 15 minutes without boiling. Pass through a fine sieve into a large pan. Bring to the boil and whisk in the rest of the butter and the cream, little by little. Check the seasoning. Add the mussels, crayfish flesh and the vegetables. Sprinkle with finely chopped parsley, chives and a pinch of cayenne pepper.

When I try to sum up my feelings about La Tante Claire and our achievements there, my final thoughts are inevitably about our customers. Without them we would not exist. By coming to eat at the restaurant they ensure that it flourishes, and they give life and meaning to the work I do in the kitchen. Though in some ways their visits can be almost as ephemeral as the tastes I use my skill to produce, many of them look in regularly and some have become personal friends. They come for different reasons, and their tastes and preferences are always changing. Some customers come because they really enjoy eating; they know a great deal about cooking and about food, and they know that at La Tante Claire they can be sure of eating well. Others come to give their families and friends a special outing; and businessmen come for a prestigious *dîner d'affaires*. The true *gourmands* come singly or in pairs; they want to spend two or three hours concentrating on whatever is on their plate, and to do nothing else; they eat in silence and savour every mouthful. The other types of customer are usually too nervous or too involved in conversation to give any thought at all to what they are eating. The popularity of particular dishes fluctuates. When I first did my *andouillettes de la mer*, it was a great success, but when I brought it back on to the menu recently, after giving it a few months' rest, hardly anyone ordered it. *Raviolis de langoustine* is going very well at the moment, but it may not last! With our English customers lamb is a perpetual favourite, and I can certainly say the

same about *foie gras*. I tried putting cassoulet on the menu, but oddly it was just not right for a restaurant like La Tante Claire. People either ordered it as the single dish of their meal and ate nothing else, or they ignored it altogether.

The long standing favourite of all favourites has been my *pieds de cochon farcis*, an original dish which has done much to make our reputation, and which, in many people's minds, is almost synonymous with La Tante Claire. I have varied the recipe in different ways, and I have even tried taking it off the menu, but each time customers have been upset by its absence and everyone has implored me to put it back!

Customers, and the lively, interesting relationship I have with them, are therefore very much part and parcel of the successful way in which La Tante Claire has developed. People sometimes ask me if there is a recipe for restaurant success, and I always say that I have never heard of one. If one did exist, the main ingredient would be luck, which is really just part of a person's destiny. Annie would probably see our achievement more in terms of committed professionalism, hard work, the creation of a good working relationship with our staff, and the quality of my cooking. All that is the important practical side, but I still have my feelings about the working of destiny.

I have mentioned the luck we had when we opened La Tante Claire, but I think it goes further than that. I was lucky as a boy to have had a mother and a grandmother who were both such fine cooks. I was lucky to like rugby because that brought me to London where I met Annie, and then we were lucky to have the support and encouragement of Albert and Michel Roux. The boy who wanted nothing better than to be a peasant farmer, harvesting the wheat and driving a plough behind a pair of oxen, became instead a cook, a *chef de cuisine* and the owner of La Tante Claire. There was no way then in which he could have foreseen his future life, but now, looking back, it seems as though each step was inevitable, and that nothing which happened could ever have been otherwise. I believe in luck, and I certainly believe in destiny.

Preheat the oven to 220°C / 425°F / gas 7 or prepare a steamer and, when the water is simmering, steam the foil-wrapped trotters until heated through.

Alternatively, put the trotters in a casserole, cover and heat in the oven for 15 minutes.

Put the trotters on a serving dish and remove the foil. Pour the reserved stock into the casserole and reduce by half. Whisk in a knob of butter, pour the sauce over the trotters and serve very hot. (Photographs pp. 214-5 and p. 218)

M. Pierre Koffmann with his family outside La Tante Claire

INDEX

ACKNOWLEDGEMENTS

The authors would like to thank André Daguin for his interest and appreciation. Bernard Ramounéda has been an enthusiastic provider of further memories and anecdotes, especially in connection with the years at Reffye, and he also provided recipes for Croustade d'Agneau Ramounéda, Salade de Boudin and Terrine de Cassoulet. Pierre Koffmann would like to thank Laurence Quiviger for having typed the recipes; and Timothy Shaw is grateful to Thierry and Michèle Varenne for providing him with a quiet working month in the country at an important time. The authors also thank Annie Koffmann and Maryse Shaw for help, encouragement and support.

Recommended Restaurants

ANDRÉ DAGUIN

Hôtel de France, Place de la Libération,

32000 Auch, Gascony, France.

Tel: 62 05 00 44

LE FLORIDA

32410 Castéra-Verduzan,

Gascony, France.

Tel: 62 68 13 22

LE GAVROCHE

43 Upper Brook Street,

London W1Y 1PF, England.

Tel: 071 408 0881

THE WATERSIDE INN

Ferry Road, Bray,

Berkshire SL6 2AT, England.

Tel: 0628 20691

LA TANTE CLAIRE

68 Royal Hospital Road,

London SW3 4HP.

Tel: 071 351 0227